THE POLITICAL ECONOMY OF SPORTS TELEVISION

Drawing from theories of the political economy of communication, this book offers readers a comprehensive, data-rich assessment of contemporary sports television and its evolution.

Providing an in-depth look at the ownership and regulation of sports television in the United States, William M. Kunz analyzes a range of platforms, networks, and sports, with particular focus on the way ownership has become concentrated in five conglomerates: AT&T, CBS, Comcast, Disney, and Fox. The end result of years of media consolidation is that broadcast networks are now married to cable and streaming services under a single conglomerate, which has implications for the cost of contracts and the negotiation of distribution deals. Examining multiple platforms, networks, and sports in an all-inclusive manner, this volume documents the evolution and current state of affairs of sports television.

With historic and current data on rights fees for sports television leagues and events as well as carriage fees and subscription levels for sports-related cable and satellite services, this comparative study offers critical information for students and scholars conducting research on sports television.

William M. Kunz is a Professor in the Division of Culture, Arts & Communication in the School of Interdisciplinary Arts & Sciences at the University of Washington Tacoma. He received his PhD in Communication and Society and MS in Journalism from the University of Oregon. He is the author of *Culture Conglomerates: Consolidation in the Motion Picture and Television Industries* and published various journal articles and book chapters focused on media ownership and regulation. He has also worked in sports television at the network level for over 30 years, most notably with ABC Sports, Turner Sports, and NBC Sports, specializing in international events such as the Olympic Games. He was a producer and writer for ABC's *Wide World of Sports* for a number of years and served as the head of production for the 2000 Winter Goodwill Games in Lake Placid, New York, and 2001 Goodwill Games in Brisbane, Australia. He served in executive roles in industry and academia, including Interim Director of what is now the School of Interdisciplinary Arts & Sciences and Interim Vice Chancellor for Academic Affairs at UW Tacoma.

THE POLITICAL ECONOMY OF SPORTS TELEVISION

William M. Kunz

Routledge
Taylor & Francis Group

NEW YORK AND LONDON

First published 2020
by Routledge
52 Vanderbilt Avenue, New York, NY 10017

and by Routledge
2 Park Square, Milton Park, Abingdon, Oxon, OX14 4RN

Routledge is an imprint of the Taylor & Francis Group, an informa business

Library of Congress Cataloging-in-Publication Data
Names: Kunz, William M., 1961– author.
Title: The political economy of sports television / William M. Kunz.
Description: London ; New York : Routledge, 2020. | Includes
   bibliographical references and index.
Identifiers: LCCN 2019058552 (print) | LCCN 2019058553 (ebook)
Subjects: LCSH: Television broadcasting of sports—Economic
   aspects—United States. | Television broadcasting—Ownership—
   United States. | Television broadcasting of sports—Political
   aspects—United States. | Television broadcasting policy—United States.
Classification: LCC GV742.3 .K86 2020 (print) | LCC GV742.3
   (ebook) | DDC 070.4/49796—dc23
LC record available at https://lccn.loc.gov/2019058552
LC ebook record available at https://lccn.loc.gov/2019058553

ISBN: 978-0-367-35226-4 (hbk)
ISBN: 978-0-367-35224-0 (pbk)
ISBN: 978-0-429-34111-3 (ebk)

Typeset in Bembo
by Apex CoVantage, LLC

To Miyuki, Maya, and Tomo

CONTENTS

TABLES

ACKNOWLEDGMENTS

This research project was many, many years in the making, both literally and figuratively. In a literal sense, the genesis of this book can be traced to a small conference in Portland – What Is Television? – that was hosted by my dissertation adviser, mentor, and friend from the University of Oregon, Dr. Janet Wasko. She encouraged me to present at the conference, and I submitted an abstract that explored some very preliminary research on regional sports networks. That was a point of demarcation, as prior to that conference, I tended to stay away from sports television in my academic research, focusing in some cases on the conglomerates in which I worked but not venturing too close to the sports landscape. After my presentation, I chatted with another mentor, Dr. Eileen Meehan, from Southern Illinois University, and the idea for this book was born. Dalliances in interim administrative positions at the school and campus level placed this project on a back burner for a number of years, but the embers were still burning when I returned to the faculty. I am indebted to Janet and Eileen, two of the leading scholars in the political economy of the media, for their mentorship and encouragement as I worked through this process.

I am also grateful to colleagues at the University of Washington Tacoma (UW Tacoma) for their support of this project. Given the approach taken to this analysis of sports television, consistent information on the economic side of the business was critical. Access to the SNL Kagan database through the S&P Global Market Intelligence platform provided that data, and that would not have been possible without the University of Washington Libraries. On the Tacoma campus, Suzanne Klinger, Head of Reference and Research Services, and Serin Anderson, Collections and Budget Librarian, took the lead in securing the license for that database, while in Seattle, Corey Murata, Director of Collections Analysis and Strategy, helped troubleshoot issues. I am most grateful to them for their support. There are numerous colleagues at UW Tacoma who supported me as I cleared the decks, at least to a degree, over the last few months so I could finish this project. Dr. Randy Nichols, a fellow graduate of the PhD program at Oregon and now a colleague at UW Tacoma, also provided lucid, valuable feedback on the book proposal, introduction, and conclusion, for which I am thankful. At Routledge, I am indebted to Erica Wetter for her enthusiastic support for this project from our first conversation and to Emma Sherriff and Jennifer Vennall for seeing me through the process.

As noted, in many respects, the timeline for this project is much, much longer. My first foray into sports television came in the summer of 1984. I had covered swimming and water polo for the student newspaper, *The Daily Californian*, at the University of California and wanted to see members of the Cal team pursue their Olympic dreams. That led to a research assignment for ABC Sports at the U.S. Olympic Swimming Trials in Indianapolis and then the Olympic Games in Los Angeles. Three and a half decades later, I am still dabbling a bit in television. I have covered some of the greatest events in sports, with the Tour de France and world championships in aquatics, athletics, figure skating, gymnastics, skiing, and speed skating in addition to the Olympic Games, many of those for ABC's *Wide World of Sports*. The events were magnificent and allowed me to see so much of the world, but what made the experience so remarkable was the opportunity to work with the best in the business, both in front of and behind the camera. I never would have continued, or returned to the business so often, if it was not for my colleagues and friends at ABC Sports, Turner Sports, and NBC Sports, and there is a piece of many of them in this book.

Some of the fondest memories of my childhood revolve around sports, starting with Cal football games at Memorial Stadium and San Francisco Giants games at Candlestick Park. The San Francisco 49ers and Golden State Warriors were added to the mix and, for a brief time, the California Golden Seals. The games were always a family affair, with my parents, Thomas and Anne Marie Kunz, and my brothers and sisters. Working in sports made it difficult to continue to be a true fan, a fanatic, but I continue to live vicariously through my dad, siblings, in-laws, nieces, and nephews and marvel at their steadfast devotion to our teams. More than that, I am forever grateful for all of their unyielding support as I followed what could best be called an unusual career path, moving between industry and academia multiple times. Most of all, I am thankful for my wife, Miyuki, and our twins, Maya and Tomo. Miyuki and I made the decision to leave sports television on a full-time basis so we could reclaim a little control over our lives and start a family. Of all the decisions I have made in my life, that was unquestionably the best. This book is dedicated to them.

1

INTRODUCTION

In the preface to *Moneyball*, the 2003 book on which the 2011 film starring Brad Pitt was based, author Michael Lewis argues that many within Major League Baseball (MLB) had concluded that "the game was ceasing to be an athletic competition and becoming a financial one."[1] After spending a year observing the Oakland Athletics front office and general manager Billy Beane, Lewis wrote of a willingness within the A's organization to "rethink baseball" and create "new baseball knowledge" and concluded that "in professional baseball it still matters less on how much money you have than how well you spend it."[2] In 2001, the A's posted the second-best record in the game with 102 wins and the second lowest opening day payroll in baseball, just $33.8 million, compared to $109.8 million for the New York Yankees. That difference in payroll was attributable in large part to local media rights, as the Yankees collected $56.8 million in local television and radio deals compared to just $9.5 million for the A's.[3]

The presence of the small-market A's in the 2018 American League Wild Card Game against the Yankees would suggest that the premise of *Moneyball* still holds true, but the game had changed over the previous 15 years. First, the use of advanced analytics, an area in which Beane and the A's were at the forefront, is now embraced to one degree or another by most MLB teams, so the reliance of so-called sabermetrics is no longer unique. Second, the gap in local television revenue has expanded dramatically, changing the balance sheets to a significant degree. In 2001, the season before Lewis was embedded with the A's, the difference in local media revenue among US-based teams was around $50 million between the highest and the lowest; in 2018, the difference in local television rights alone was over $300 million, between $334 million for the Los Angeles Dodgers and $18 million for both the Miami Marlins and Pittsburgh Pirates in 2018.[4] Such deals have made many MLB owners and players wealthy and made most regional sports networks cash cows, all at the expense of cable, satellite, and telco subscribers which face ever-increasing bills.

The challenges that such deals present are evident from coast to coast, but nowhere more so than Los Angeles. The $8.35-billion deal between the Dodgers and Spectrum SportsNet LA that began in 2014 and extends through 2038 brought the franchise even greater riches, but it also became the opening act of an ongoing melodrama. Regional sports networks, or RSNs, are programming services that hold rights to televise sporting events in a specific geographic region through multichannel video programming distributors (MVPDs) via cable, direct-broadcast-satellite, and telco services. Some regional networks began as premium channels, services that charged a higher price per month to households that wanted that specific content, but the business model has evolved over the last 25 years to one in which RSNs demand carriage on expanded basic programming tiers so that revenue is generated from most television household. In most markets, RSNs rank among the most expensive services on the expanded basic tier, behind only ESPN, but the price of such networks tends to be local issues rather than national ones since there is great variance from market to market. These services are also now significant revenue streams for most teams and collegiate conferences, and oftentimes a point of demarcation between the haves and the have nots, as documented previously with the New York Yankees and Oakland A's.

The proliferation of services in Los Angeles illustrates the potential impact of RSNs on local markets. In April 2012, there were two Fox Sports regional networks in Los Angeles: Fox Sports West and Prime Ticket. Those two services held the rights to six professional teams in the major professional sports: the Dodgers and Angels in baseball, the Lakers and Clippers in basketball, and the Kings and Ducks in hockey. The combined fee for the two Fox services, moreover, was about $5 per month. When the Dodgers signed the deal with Time Warner Cable to create SportsNet LA in January 2013, it came just three months after the launch of another new service, TWC SportsNet, to feature the Los Angeles Lakers. The debut of that service was a relative success, as TWC SportsNet was in an average of 2.4 million households in the Los Angeles-designated market area in 2013, its first full calendar year. That was within shouting distance of Fox Sports West and Prime Ticket, both of which were in 3.2 million households, on average, in the same year. The entry into the market for SportsNet LA in February 2014, however, was far more turbulent. Time Warner Cable could feed the service to the estimated 1.3 million subscribers it had in Los Angeles at that time, but most other operators balked at the per month carriage fee, including DirecTV, Dish, AT&T, and Verizon, and SportsNet LA averaged just 1.5 million households per month in 2014. As the service observed its fifth anniversary in 2019, Charter Communications was its new parent corporation and its name was Spectrum SportsNet LA, but it was still in an estimated 1.5 million households in the Los Angeles-designated market area with 3.64 million multichannel video subscribers. The options were rather limited for Charter, for while it could add SportsNet LA to the systems it controlled in Los Angeles, the cable MSO held few bargaining chips in negotiations with other MVPDs through ownership of other programming services or local televisions stations. And in the 2010s, such leverage meant everything in these negotiations.

The fate of SportsNet LA is a microcosm of issues and debates that were prominent in the sports television marketplace at the end of the 2010s. First, the Dodgers represent the migration of sports from free over-the-air broadcast stations to pay television platforms. The launch of SportsNet LA eliminated the broadcast of Dodgers games on local broadcast stations for the first time since the team moved to Los Angeles in 1959, although the last six games of the 2014 regular season were carried on local stations as the carriage impasse continued, with a handful of games on broadcast stations in most seasons since then. Second, the ongoing stalemate represents the battle over the inclusion of sports programming in large bundles. Time Warner Cable, and now Charter, sought carriage for SportsNet LA on expanded basic or similar services rather than on a sports tier or on an à la carte basis. The resistance to that approach was evident in a "promise" DirecTV made to its subscribers, which stated "anyone with no interest in sports should not be forced to pay a huge premium for something they don't care to watch."[5] Third, the connection between SportsNet LA and Time Warner Cable contributes to ongoing debates over horizontal and vertical integration and media conglomeration. The merger between Charter Communications and Time Warner Cable was announced in May 2015, and just two weeks after that deal was struck, Charter, which did not carry SportsNet LA in 2014, launched the network on its Los Angeles area systems on Spectrum TV Select, its most widely distributed subscriber tier. Those three topics are recurring themes in the analysis that follows.

The dawn of the new decades provides an important point to consider such questions. First, the AT&T merger with WarnerMedia was completed in 2018 and the Disney acquisition of 21st Century Fox assets and the creation of Fox Corp. closed in 2019, which included the mandated divestment of the Fox regional sports networks that was part of the Department of Justice approval of the sale. While there will no doubt be other deals in the offing, most national sports television assets now reside in five media conglomerates – AT&T Inc., CBS Corp., Comcast Corp., Fox Corp., and Walt Disney Co. – so it is appropriate to evaluate the path to concentration and conglomeration. Second, while there will likewise be some minor properties open for bidding over the next year or so, most major television contracts are locked up until at least 2021, including Major League Baseball (2021/ESPN and Turner), National Football League (2021 ESPN and 2023/CBS, FOX, and NBC), National Hockey League (2022/NBCUniversal), and National Basketball Association (2025/ESPN and Turner). The rights for one of the most valuable international "football" properties was also locked up into 2022, with the contract between the Premier League and NBC Sports extending through the 2021–22 season. To be certain, there are deals that are locked in place for much longer. At one point in time, Fox Sports and Telemundo deals for the FIFA World Cup were set to expire after the 2022 tournament, but that deal was quietly extended in 2015, without open bidding, through 2026, in part to avoid a lawsuit for moving the 2022 World Cup to the winter because of the sweltering summer heat in Qatar.[6] The Fox contract with Major League Baseball was set to expire in 2021, but that was extended through 2028 in November 2018. Moreover, NBCUniversal has the Olympic Games, and the team of CBS and Turner has the NCAA March Madness basketball tournament through 2032. That said, there remains an important moment to consider the evolution of the marketplace before a new series of deals are negotiated.

The great unknown in those negotiations is whether there will be a true migration of sports properties to direct-to-consumer streaming services. In the early 2010s, Brett Hutchins and David Rowe argued that the "case presented leads to the conclusion that the 'digital revolution' is so far proving less than revolutionary in the context of sports."[7] They concluded that "major sporting events are becoming more so because of human, financial, and media resource advantages." There is no question that there was a significant increase in sports content available on direct-to-consumer services in the United States over the last decade, most notable with the launch of ESPN+, B/R Live, and DAZN in 2018. Those services, for the most part, have thus far focused on supplemental content as well as secondary rights in the U.S. market, such as European football. When marquee content is carried on such services, it is in sports with a pay-per-view tradition, such as boxing and mixed martial arts. It remains to be seen when, and if, major events will migrate to such services.

Sports Television and Critical Political Economy

The drama that followed the launch of SportsNet LA touches on the cornerstones of the critical political economy of the media, the most important of which are the allocation of resources and shifting interactions between government and industry. On July 25, 2014, U.S. Representative Tom Cárdenas and seven other Los Angeles area representatives called on Federal Communications Commission (FCC) Chairman Tom Wheeler to mediate the negotiations between Time Warner Cable and television service providers. A few days later, one of the signatories on the letter to Wheeler, Brad Sherman, and five other representatives sent a letter to Robert Marcus, CEO and chairman of Time Warner Cable, and Michael White, CEO, president, and chairman of DirecTV, calling on the parties to enter binding arbitration. Wheeler entered the fray before the end of the month, sending a letter to Marcus and Time Warner Cable stating that he was "troubled by the negative impact that your apparent actions are having on consumers and the overall video marketplace" and promising to "intervene as appropriate" to bring relief to consumers.[8] The letter from Wheeler came as the Commission and Department of Justice were reviewing a proposed merger between Comcast Corp. and Time Warner Cable, a bid that was announced in February 2014 but ended in April 2015 in the face of opposition from the federal government. That proposed combination was abandoned when the FCC said it would require hearings before an administrative law judge to weigh the impact of the deal on the broadband market. At the end of 2014, Comcast had 22 million high-speed Internet customers, while Time Warner Cable had another 11.7 million, so the concentration of ownership was within the purview of the Commission and Antitrust Division of the Department of Justice, all the more so when combined with the "significant programming interests" within Comcast.[9] There were no such issues with SportsNet LA, so despite repeated calls for action from members of the House of Representatives and others, the government was powerless to end the dispute between the programming service and multichannel service providers.

The questions that are central to this case and the broader discussion of sports television in the United States are the same that are at the foundation of the critical political economy of the media. Dallas Smythe outlined two basic questions in his seminal work that are fundamental to these topics: "(1) Who gets what scarce goods and service, when, how and where? . . . (2) Who takes what actions in order to provide what scarce goods and services, when, how and where?"[10] This aligns with the framework that Vincent Mosco advanced decades later.[11] He argues that critical political economy is the study of "social relations, particularly power relations, that mutually constitute the production, distribution and consumption of resources."[12] Within Mosco's framework, power is "both a resource to achieve goals and an instrument of control within social hierarchies." Peter Golding and Graham Murdoch describe the foundation of this approach as the examination of the "balance between capitalist enterprise and public intervention" and outline four "historical processes" that are critical to understanding changes in such balances.[13] Golding and Murdoch focus on the "growth of the media; extension of corporate reach; commodification; and the changing role of state and government intervention."[14]

The historical processes Golding and Murdoch outlined appear time and again in the analysis of sports television, as do the themes that Janet Wasko advanced in her overview of the political economic approach to the media.[15] Wasko argues that political economic research has focused on the "evolution of mass communications/media as commodities that are produced and distributed by profit-seeking organizations in capitalist industries."[16] That analysis of "media as business" revolves around a collection of key concepts: commodification/commercialization, diversification/synergy, and horizontal/vertical integration and concentration. She also states that this approach "incorporates historical analysis, for it is essential to document change as well as continuity."[17] Once again, these trends are evident throughout this analysis and the historical component of this study is quite important, including the influence of shifts in technology.

These concepts are critical to this analysis and need to be unpacked. In its most basic form, commodification refers to the process of transforming use value into exchange value, from value that derives from the satisfaction of a human want or need into value based on what it derives in the market. The classic opening of ABC's *Wide World of Sports* trumpeted the "thrill of victory and the agony of defeat . . . the human drama of athletic competition," and the long-running anthology show highlighted the human dimension of sports. The success of that approach related to the use value of television and the emotions stirred in viewers as athletes pursued victory or defeat. There was a time when the cost of acquiring the rights for the cavalcade of sports and events that appeared on *Wide World* were minimal and the production costs were manageable, both of which were offset by the advertising revenue that ABC could generate on Saturday afternoon from 4:30 pm to 6:00 pm Eastern and Pacific. That is the calculation of the exchange value in sports television, and when ABC could no longer generate a profit, or even break even, on *Wide World of Sports* in the face of a fragmented marketplace and raising costs for both rights and production, the show was cancelled. The dichotomy between use value and exchange value is also evident with SportsNet LA, between the desire of Dodgers fans to watch their team on television and the desire of Charter to extract a carriage fee from every multichannel video subscriber in Los Angeles that was high enough to offset the deal it inherited from Time Warner Cable.

Diversification takes various forms in media industries, with a basic distinction between market diversification and product diversification, with a further differentiation in the latter between industrial diversification and related or concentric diversification. The most prominent form of market diversification is geographic, with the search for non-primary markets to generate additional revenue. Such geographic diversification is clear in the string of ESPN networks around the world, with more than 20 networks reaching over 60 countries and territories across all seven continents as of 2019. Those same concepts are also evident in the sale of out-of-market rights to local baseball, basketball, football, and hockey telecasts in the United States. Product diversification is a tried-and-true approach to spurring growth and reducing risk. There was a time when industrial diversification, the expansion into unrelated business sectors, was prominent, with the General Electric acquisition of NBC in 1986 being a clear example. Related or concentric diversification, which is based on a strong core business with diversification into areas close to that core that leverage those strengths, has become far more common with media conglomerates. Most of those involved in television were focused on a relatively small range of businesses. The current home of NBC is a prime example, with almost all assets within Comcast related to the production, distribution, and transmission of media content.

The corporate connection between Comcast and NBC are also seen in the definitions of horizontal and vertical integration, which focus on production, distribution, and exhibition/transmission or what David Croteau and William Hoynes translated to products, platforms, and pipes.[18] With horizontal integration, firms acquire additional units at the same level of production, distribution, or exhibition/transmission, which enables them to consolidate and extend control within a given sector and maximize economies of scale. Comcast began with a single 1,200 subscriber cable system in Tupelo, Mississippi, in 1963, but through acquisitions, large and small, it had 30.3 million customers at the start of 2019, with 500,000 or more in 21 different local hubs, including 16 of the top 25 markets in the United States. With vertical integration, firms acquire additional units at different levels of production, distribution, and exhibition/transmission, which reduces vulnerability to fluctuations in the supply and cost of essential materials and services. The integration of the Comcast cable systems with the NBCUniversal films and television programs and distribution platforms, a so-called vertical combination, raised red flags within the FCC and Department of Justice when it was announced in 2009, but the merger was approved, with conditions, in January 2011. Similar concerns led to a lawsuit from the federal government to block the combination of AT&T Inc. and Time Warner Inc., a suit that the courts rejected in 2018.

The processes of integration, horizontal and vertical, and diversification, both product and geographic, lead to concentration in media markets. While Ben Bagdikian's famous measure of the marketplace was titled *The Media Monopoly*, that was something as a misnomer, since a true monopoly would feature exclusive control over a commodity or service in a designated market by a single company. While one can argue that media markets are highly concentrated, they do not conform to that strict definition. The more accurate descriptor is oligopoly, a market structure in which there are small groups of sellers of a product or service, so few that the actions of any one of them will have a measurable impact on its competitors. With oligopolies, because there are so few sellers, each is aware of the actions of the others and there is a high risk of collusion. One of the conditions of the Comcast/NBCUniversal merger was that the conglomerate had to relinquish its management rights in Hulu, which NBCUniversal co-owned at the time with Disney, News Corp., and Time Warner. Those conglomerates owned four of the six major motion picture studios and three of the four major broadcast networks, so in one area they were supposed to be competitors but in another they were business partners. And that is just one example of many collaboration and joint ventures within that group.

The measures of concentration connect with another important concept. The fragmentation of the television marketplace, and media markets, which has accompanied the development of cable, satellite, and telco systems, has fueled claims that the prominence of television has diminished, and, in turn, questions related to ownership have been become unimportant. That argument has been the justification for the broad deregulation of media industries that has occurred over the last two decades. Former FCC commissioner and chairman Michael

Powell advanced the main elements of that position in a speech to the Media Institute in April 1998:

> With scarcity and the uniqueness of broadcasting such demonstrably faulty premises for broadcast regulation, one is left with the undeniable conclusion that the government has been engaged for too long in willful denial in order to subvert the Constitution so that it can impose its speech preferences on the public ... the time has come to move toward a single standard of First Amendment analysis that recognizes the reality of the media marketplace and respects the intelligence of American consumers.[19]

While it is impossible to refute the claim that the sheer number of outlets has increased, it is far easier to question whether such abundance has resulted in a true diversification of cultural products. Graham Murdock argues that "diversity is not multiplicity. It is possible to greatly increase the number of channels and the number of goods in circulation without significantly extending diversity. More does not necessarily mean different."[20] This is where the concentration of ownership becomes critical, and a cornerstone of this analysis. The potential for a 500-channel on MVPDs fueled the argument that diversification will be a by-product of multiplication, but one must question such assertions. There is a critical distinction that must be made between an abundance of outlets, what is often called numerical diversity, and the presence of a full range of voices in the marketplace of ideas, what is often called source diversity. There is little question that the penetration of cable, direct-broadcast-satellite, and telco systems has increased the number of television channels available in most American households, oftentimes to a dramatic degree. Mere numerical abundance, however, does not guarantee the diversification of voices.

The rapid expansion of the television marketplace is the common justification for changes in policies and regulations enacted by Congress and/or implement by the FCC in the United States. Critics of regulation, such as Powell, claim that the growth of cable, satellite, and telco services has nullified the central tenet of the scarcity rationale, the legal argument that finite broadcast spectrum allows for some limitations of the First Amendment rights of broadcast licensees. While the transformation of television in the United States since the mid-1970s is impossible to refute, it is also critical to understand other factors that fueled such change. There are clear connections, for example, between the extent and nature of state intervention in television and the rise of neoliberalism, an ideological framework that promotes laissez-faire economics and free market capitalism, including privatization and deregulation. Those ideas are prominent in debates over various ownerships rules in the United States as well as the assault on public service broadcasters around the world.

It is natural to frame such discussions around the characteristics that make television unique, but it might be more insightful to consider them within broader regulatory regimes. Such regimes are patterns of political intervention throughout history that have structured government-business relations. Ellis Hawley argues that "ideas and ideology have been important determinants in shaping national regulatory policy and mechanisms for supplementing it" and that without the "ideological dimension it is difficult to explain the mechanisms that emerged or what happened later."[21] Richard Harris and Sydney Milkis outline three characteristics of such regulatory regimes: "a constellation of (1) new ideas justifying government control over business activity, (2) new institutions that structure regulatory politics, and (3) a new set of policies impinging on business."[22] Such frameworks align quite well with the political economic approach.

Congress and the FCC relaxed or eliminated various rules in the 1980s, the decade in which cable television emerged as a robust content provider. Mark S. Fowler, the chairman of the Commission from 1981 to 1987, was among those who argued that cable and satellite systems had rendered the scarcity rationale obsolete. Fowler, however, can also be viewed as a disciple of the laissez-faire ideologies of the Reagan administration and neoliberalism, as he arrived at the Commission with a deep and abiding commitment to deregulation. The need to view Fowler through the wider prism is perhaps most evident with one of his most famous claims, that a television is "just another appliance. It's a toaster with pictures."[23] From such a vantage point, the television marketplace could be regulated in the same manner as the markets for other products, with the government focused on the safe operation of television sets. In turn, there need be no concerns over the concentration of ownership of television stations, networks, and services or the kind of content carried on those outlets.

The Role of the State in Sports and Sports Television

The connection between sports and politics in undeniable and the moving images transmitted around the world to televisions, computers, tablets, and smartphones assumes a critical role in such discussions. Much has been written about the Rugby World Cup in South Africa in 1995 and the impact of the live television coverage of an integrated team defeating New Zealand in overtime and Nelson Mandela presenting the trophy to Francois Pienaar.[24] The South African captain was a white Afrikaner, raised to believe Mandela was a "terrorist" who must remain behind bars, which made his interactions with the man who spent his life fighting to overthrow Apartheid all the more powerful.[25] That was an organic moment, but televised events such as the Olympic Games are oftentimes used to make political statements and/or announce an arrival, or return, to the world stage. Politics were part of the Olympic tapestry long before the 1968 Olympic Games in Mexico City, but the images of U.S. Olympians Tommie Smith and John Carlos raising black-gloved fists and bowing their heads on the medal podium of the 200 meters during the national anthem to protest the treatment of African Americans added gravitas to that moment. The Olympic Games were the platform for another statement four decades later when it was estimated that over two billion people, almost one third of the world's population, watched the Opening Ceremony for the 2008 Games in Beijing. That spectacle was of immense importance to the Chinese government, described as an event that "challenged Western domination of global events and placed China in the international spotlight reflecting its growing global importance."[26] There are countless other examples, global and local, including the protests against police brutality that Colin Kaepernick initiated during the national anthem prior to NFL games in 2016, which coincided with the presidential campaign in the United States, but suffice it to say there is a political dimension to every mega event on the world stage, as well as many national events, and television gives power to such messages.

The televised intersection of politics and sports generates the most attention, but the behind-the-scenes bartering between representatives of the government and those of media conglomerates is often more consequential. In the United States, Congressional concerns over the rising cost of cable bills dates to the late 1980s, a short time after the Cable Communication Policy Act of 1984 eliminated most local regulation of basic cable rates. Those rates alone increased 19.7% in 1987, the first full year after the implementation of the act. ESPN was one of the services that benefited from deregulation, and the bundling of the sports network with others in a basic tier has long drawn the ire of Congress, leading to debates over à la carte models, some of which mandated multichannel service providers to offer networks on an individual basis. In 2013, Senator John McCain authored such legislation for a second time, citing the rising cost of basic cable rates from an average of $22.25 a month in 1995 to $57.46 per month in 2011.[27] The Television Consumer Freedom Act of 2013 was introduced and referred to the Committee on Commerce, Science and Transportation, never to be acted upon. One of the loudest voices in the battle against McCain was none other than Michael Powell, the chief lobbyist for the cable industry. A decade earlier, Powell assumed a different role in the dance between government and industry as the chairman of the FCC between 2001 and 2005.

The Powell chairmanship was an interesting time at the Commission. As discussed earlier, Powell was a staunch advocate of a marketplace approach to regulation, and he announced wholesale relaxation of ownership rules in 2003 and then watched as first Congress and then the U.S. Court of Appeals rewrote or remanded those changes. In 2004, the House Committee on Energy and Commerce requested that the FCC perform a study that examined the merits and drawbacks of à la carte pricing for cable and satellite services. The Commission issued an "Initial Report" six months later, concluding that requiring multichannel service providers to offer program services on an à la carte basis would increase costs for most households and reduce program diversity.[28] Less than three months later, in February 2005, the Commission released a "Further Report" that reached a contradictory conclusion, stating that à la carte pricing would likely lower monthly bills for 40% of cable households and 100% of satellite households that received digital service.[29] The change was attributed to methodological issues, but far more critical was a transfer of power within the FCC during the Republican administration of President George W. Bush, as Kevin Martin replaced Powell as Commission chair at the start of 2005. Martin later testified to Congress that the initial report "relied on problematic assumptions and presented incorrect and at times biased analysis."[30]

It was in that climate that McCain introduced the Consumers Having Options in Cable Entertainment Act, better known as the CHOICE Act, in June 2006. While the basic tenets of the revised FCC report supported the legislation, the industry had spent considerable time, and resources, lobbying against such rules. Disney did not hold the rights to the Super Bowl in 2005, but it was not without weapons. With Jacksonville serving as the host of the game, Disney invited advertisers and other guests to Walt Disney World in Orlando, and among that group was the chairman of the House committee that requested the initial à la carte report, Republican Joe Barton. Disney spent over $6,000 hosting Barton and his wife that weekend, and within a few weeks, Disney and ESPN employees donated $7,500 to Barton's political action committee.[31] Barton and his committee assumed an important gatekeeping function for any à la carte legislation, and Disney was dead-set on doing everything in its power to stop such rule writing. The Media Services division was the most successful within Disney, with ESPN the most lucrative in that group. In the fiscal year ending October 1, 2005, the Media Networks segment accounted for 41.3% of total revenue and 59.1% of operating income within Disney, with an increase in carriage fees for ESPN singled out as the biggest cause.[32] McCain's à la carte proposal died in the Senate Commerce Committee in June 2006 by a 20–2 vote. Afterward, McCain said of Disney's lobbying effort, "They beat me like a drum."[33]

There were times when McCain's proposal might have been successful, when the balance between capitalist enterprise and public intervention was quite different. In the 1950s, the FCC created the so-called "Rule of Sevens" that limited corporations to ownership of just seven local broadcast stations in each of three formats: television, AM radio, and FM radio. In the process, the Commission advanced a clear articulation of its goals: "The purpose of the multiple ownership rules is to promote diversification of ownership in order to maximize diversification of program and service viewpoint as well as prevent any undue concentration of economic power contrary to the public interest."[34] In the 1970s, the Commission introduced the Financial Interest and Syndication Rules, which were designed to limit the participation of the big three broadcast networks – ABC, CBS, and NBC – in primetime program production, both in terms of first-run program ownership and off-network syndication. The rationale was similar, with the FCC arguing that "the public interest requires limitation on network control and an increase in the opportunity for development of truly independent sources of prime time programming" and "diversity of program ideas."[35] The relaxation of the 7–7–7 rule starting in the 1980s triggered waves of consolidation, with the expiration of the final elements of the fyn-sin rules in 1995 opening the door for the combination of broadcast networks and motion picture studios under the same corporate umbrella. These changes in regulation were part of a much broader embrace of market forces and a repudiation of New Deal principles that the federal government was needed to address socioeconomic problems that took root during the Reagan administration.

The passage of the Telecommunications Act of 1996 further fueled the consolidation and conglomeration of media properties. Some would argue that technological innovation made such change inevitable, but it is better understood as differences in the balance between capitalist enterprise and public intervention. The back and forth over à la carte points to the need to consider when and where the state intervenes in the marketplace, and where it does not, and how this varies from place to place. Some have argued, for example, that Congress has been over-zealous in its extension of copyright terms over the last half-century, while it has done nothing more than hold hearings to address antitrust concerns related to professional sports leagues. While the rights of producers are protected, those of viewers are not. Most of the discussion of the legislation and litigation that impacts on sports television is integrated into the chapters that follow, but it is valuable to explore broader issues that touch on numerous areas of sports television.

Antitrust Exemptions

There are countless areas in which government and sports are intertwined in the United States, and the long-standing antitrust exemption for Major League Baseball is a clear example. The National League was formed in 1876, with the American League established in 1901. The American League wanted to compete on equal footing with the National League and tried to lure players away from the senior circuit with higher salaries. Rather than compete with the new league, the National League chose to combine forces, signing the National Agreement for the Governance of Professional Base Ball Clubs in 1903. That accord brought peace to professional baseball, but it accomplished that on the backs of the players, sustaining and expanding a reserve clause that bound them to teams even after their contracts expired. What is remarkable is that the merger was executed in an era of trust-busting that followed passage of the Sherman Antitrust Act in 1890, which empowered the federal government to combat anticompetitive practices, including monopolies, and preserve competition.

The reserve clause, a clause in contracts that stated that a team retained the rights to a player even upon the expiration of that contract, became a focal point for court battles for decades as did the almost incestuous relationship between the state and the game. In 1914, the Federal League tried to follow the path the American League cut in the previous decade, offering higher salaries as an enticement to players to jump leagues. When those efforts failed, the league filed suit against the reserve clause in U.S. District Court in Illinois in 1915, where

Kenesaw Mountain Landis was the presiding judge in the case. Landis was noted for an earlier decision against Standard Oil, which gave him the reputation as a trust-buster, but in this instance his concern was for the sport of baseball. That was most evident during the hearings when he stated, "I think you gentlemen here all understand that a blow at this thing called baseball – both sides understand this perfectly – will be regarded by this court as a blow at a national institution."[36] He heard arguments in January 1915 but never issued a ruling, sitting on the case for over a year until the two sides reached a settlement, with the Federal League being absorbed into the two established leagues. When the case was dismissed, Landis admitted that he "resolved to do nothing" since the decision he would have been compelled to make "would have been if not destructive, vitally injurious to the subject matter of the litigation. That is the plain truth."[37]

The owners of the Baltimore Terrapins of the Federal League did not sign the settlement and later filed their own suit in federal court against the American League, National League, and National Commission, the three-person body that included the heads of both leagues that administered baseball. The Baltimore club received a judgment in its favor and was awarded damages under the Sherman Act, but that decision was reversed by the Court of Appeals and affirmed by the Supreme Court in *Federal Baseball Club of Baltimore v. National League* in 1922.[38] The Supreme Court ruled that baseball, although it involved teams that crossed state lines for games in front of paying fans, did not involve interstate commerce and, as such, did not violate the Sherman Antitrust Act, a ruling that is the basis for its antitrust exemption. Judge Oliver Wendell Holmes argued that such travel was "incident, not the essential thing" and argued that the "business is giving exhibitions" which are "purely state affairs" and that the "personal effort" of the players was "not a subject of commerce."[39] The Supreme Court issued its ruling in May 1922, two months after Kenesaw Mountain Landis resigned from his judicial appointment and two years after he was named the first commissioner of baseball, ushering in a period in which the game was ruled by a sitting federal judge.

Landis never ruled in favor of Major League Baseball, but the decision not to address the reserve clause in 1915 established a clear pattern. In 1953, in *Toolson v. New York Yankees*, the Supreme Courts once again ruled in favor of baseball. George Earl Toolson was a pitcher in the Yankee's organization who reached the AAA level in the 1940s. He argued that he could pitch in the major leagues with another organization but could not pursue such options because of the reserve clause. In affirming lower court decisions that cited the 1922 decision, the Supreme Court shifted the burden, stating, "Congress has had the ruling under consideration but has not seen fit to bring such business under these laws by legislation. . . . [I]f there are evils in this field which now warrant application to it of the antitrust laws, it should be by legislation."[40] In short, the court determined that Congress had "no intention of including the business of baseball within the scope of the federal antitrust laws."[41] In this moment, the court decided to remain in the dugout and see how the game played out.

One of the lawyers for MLB in the Toolson case was Bowie Kuhn, the future commissioner and the named defendant in *Flood v. Kuhn*, a Supreme Court decision in 1972 that upheld the antitrust exemption. Curt Flood was a member of the St. Louis Cardinals but was traded to the Philadelphia Phillies after the 1969 season.[42] Flood attempted to overturn the reserve clause under whose provisions he was traded against his will. In the Supreme Court ruling, Judge Harry Blackmun dismissed Flood's suit, arguing that while the antitrust exemption might be the product of a different era, the Court did not see enough reason to overturn it. What was most remarkable about that decision is that Blackmun began with a soliloquy about the game of baseball, which included a list of "many names, celebrated for one reason or another." In his dissent of *Flood v. Kuhn*, Justice William O. Douglass wrote that an "industry so dependent on radio and television as is baseball and gleaning vast interest revenues . . . would be hard put to say in the Federal Baseball Club case that baseball was only a local exhibition, not trade or commerce."

The antitrust exemption that organized baseball holds remains a judicial anomaly, one reserved for the national pastime. That does not mean that other professional leagues do not make similar claims and benefit from similar privileges. In late 1995 and early 1996, NFL Commissioner Paul Tagliabue testified before the U.S. Senate Committee on the Judiciary multiple times and requested a limited antitrust exemption to allow the NFL to block teams from moving without approval of the league. Those hearings came less than a year after the Los Angeles Rams announced a move to St. Louis and the Los Angeles Raiders returned to Oakland and as the league negotiated with Art Modell on the relocation of his franchise from Cleveland to Baltimore. Tagliabue's appearance also came more than a decade after the Court of Appeals for the Ninth Circuit affirmed lower court decisions barring the NFL from preventing a Raiders move from Oakland to Los Angeles.[43] Two decades later, the Rams were back in Los Angeles, along with the Chargers, and the Raiders were scheduled to move to Las Vegas. The NFL, on the other hand, generated billions in television revenue each year, thanks to the Sports Broadcasting Act of 1961, which granted the league a limited antitrust exemption. That act will be discussed in detail in Chapter 3.

Copyright

There are other areas in which the government has interceded in the sports marketplace, with some acts of state intervention less transparent than others. The Sonny Bono Copyright Term Extension Act was much discussed when it passed Congress and was signed into law by President Bill Clinton in October 1998. Much of the debate centered on the length of the extension, which added 20 years to the existing statute, making it life of the author plus 70 years or 95 years after publication for works of corporate authorship. The Copyright Clause in the Constitution gave Congress the power to "promote the progress of

Science and useful Arts" through the granting to inventors and authors "exclusive right to their respective writing and discoveries" for "limited" times. The initial term for copyright in 1790 was 14 years, with the option of renewal for an additional 14 years, and an argument in the unsuccessful court challenge to the 1998 extension, *Eldred v. Ashcroft*, was that Congress had exceeded its power based on the "limited times" provision. The time frame was important, as the extension meant that initial Disney films such as *Steamboat Willie*, released in 1928, remained outside of the public domain. The Walt Disney Co. was so prominent in the lobbying for the extension, in fact, that while the act was named after Sonny Bono, the singer-songwriter who was a member of Congress when he died in January 1998, some called copyright extension the Mickey Mouse Protection Act.[44]

The promotion and protection of corporate interests was a recurring theme in debates over copyright, although it was not framed in Congress in those terms. Far less visible were the rights extended to sports leagues and teams. Prior to passage of the Copyright Act of 1976, a series of sports and broadcast executives appeared before Congressional committees, including NFL Commissioner Pete Rozelle, MLB Commissioner Kuhn and NBA Commissioner J. Walter Kennedy. A decade earlier, Rozelle had testified about an earlier attempt to revise copyright law, arguing, "We must have copyright protections if we are to reestablish our right to sell and to broadcast our programs in accordance with our proper ownership rights."[45] The bill under consideration at that time, in the assessment of the Copyright Office, would extend protection to scripted and pre-recorded programs, which presented an obstacle for sports leagues, Rozelle argued, since "their programs are – and must necessarily continue to be – unscripted and not prerecorded. Sports programs must be presented simultaneously with the action on the playing field if fan interest is to be maintained. There is no escape form this."[46] In time, Congress found a solution for that dilemma.

The Copyright Act of 1976 makes little mention of sports in the legislation, with a lone mention covering royalties for sports programming, but the protections Rozelle and his peers desired were in place. The 1976 act outlined seven categories of "authorship" that included literary works, musical works, dramatic works, sound recordings and other areas. One category was for "motion pictures and other audiovisual works."[47] Sporting events were included under "other audiovisual works" so long as the "work consisting of sounds, images, or both, that are being transmitted, is 'fixed' for purposes of this title if a fixation of the work is being made simultaneously with its transmission."[48] In other words, copyright was extended to sporting events so long as a recording was made by "any method now known or later developed" simultaneous to its live transmission. That section of the act, without mention of sports, extended the same protections to live televised sporting events that were available for scripted and pre-recorded programs. The Digital Millennium Copyright Act of 1998, moreover, brought those property rights into the digital age.

Anti-Siphoning

The state apparatus in the United States, including the White House, Congress, and federal courts, has long focused on the extension and expansion of the rights of copyright holders, with the major media conglomerates being the main beneficiaries. Those same institutions, on the other hand, have shown little interest in another debate over rights that has evolved in Europe and elsewhere, namely the rights of viewers. David Rowe argues that television is a "vital component of any current conception of sport" and that "television sport is a key component of any consideration of right pertaining to contemporary cultural citizenship."[49] That thesis raises questions about access and equity for sports on television and what Rowe calls "viewing" rights. Outside the United States, public service broadcasters were once the natural home for events of national importance, but the rise of commercial broadcasters altered that relationship in many settings. Even with that shift, such events were still available on free-to-air terrestrial television services and could be accessed regardless of wealth. The migration of events to pay-television platforms has altered that relationship in the United States and around the world and become an important area of analysis.

There was a time when there was concern for the migration of sports programming in the United States. In 1975, the FCC imposed anti-siphoning regulations that stated that a cable channel could not devote more than 90% of its time to film and sports. Films that were less than three years old could not be shown on such channels, and annual sporting events that had aired on broadcast outlets in the previous five years could not be "siphoned off" to cable. Home Box Office, which debuted as a national service in 1975, was the focus of such debates, and the legal case that followed, but sports television was also on the docket. As discussed in more detail in Chapter 5, the "new" Madison Square Garden opened for business in New York in February 1968, and during the 1968–69 season some home games of the NBA Knicks and NHL Rangers were transmitted to cable households via Sterling Manhattan Cable Television, which would later start HBO. In time, the U.S. Court of Appeals for the DC Circuit ruled that anti-siphoning rules were a violation of the First Amendment in *Home Box Office v. Federal Communications Commission*.[50] This was predicated on an argument that cable bandwidth was not a scarce resource and not subject to more limited First Amendment protection prominent in broadcast regulation. The court concluded that the degree of limitation was "grossly overboard." There has been little formal discussion of anti-siphoning rules in the four decades that followed.

The laissez faire attitude toward this topic in the United States stands in contrast to that is other modern democracies. The identification of protected events in the United Kingdom, known as the "crown jewels" of televised sports, can be traced to lists developed by then Home Secretary Kenneth Baker in 1991, although the list of events of "national interest" did not have legal footing until passage of the Broadcasting Act 1996. Australia introduced an anti-siphoning scheme as part of the Broadcasting Services Act of 1992 and maintains a list of events that should be available "free to the general public" based on their national and cultural signifi- cance. One of the topics addressed in the Television Without Frontiers Directive in Europe was the desire to preserve the broadcasting of events deemed to be of major importance for society. As part of the Audiovisual Media Services Directive, adopted in 2010, member states were allowed to compile lists of events that were of "major importance to society" and, as such, should remain on free-to-air televi- sion as to not "deprive a substantial proportion of the public" of following such events. The creation and maintenance of lists of protected events was triggered by the awarding of the television rights for the 2002 and 2006 FIFA World Cup to German media giant KirchGroup in 1996, covering worldwide rights except for the United States. Sporis/Kirch sold the rights to national or regional television platforms, but the move away from a consortium of public service broadcasters that held the rights to the 1998 World Cup caused consternation across Europe.

Given the impetus for the protection of certain events, it is not surprising that the men's World Cup figures prominently on such lists. Most include the semifinals and finals as well as the matches of a given national team, although the United Kingdom included the entire tournament. In 2013, the Court of Justice of the European Union rejected an appeal from FIFA and UEFA, the world and European governing bodies, over the listing of the final stage of the World Cup in the case of Belgium and the final stage of the World Cup and European Cham- pionship in the case of the United Kingdom. The court acknowledged that the designation imposed limitations on certain rights, but ruled "such obstacles are justified by protecting the right to information and ensuring wide public access to television coverage of those events."[51] It is interesting to consider the discussion of rights in that ruling in relation to that in *Home Box Office v. Federal Communica- tions Commission*.

The Road Ahead

The focal point for this political economic analysis is sports television in the United States at the dawn of a new decade, with two notable caveats. First, the political economic approach, at its roots, is historical, believing that it is "essential to document change as well as continuity."[52] To understand the marketplace in the 2010s, one must document the evolution of sports television, and media con- glomerates, since the 1970s, not to mention regulations that were put in places even earlier than that. Second, while such studies are often set in a single national setting to address the uniqueness of a given market, the political economic approach frames such discussions within the global expansion of media industries. The nature of globalization is different with sports television, with the sale of exclusive rights to sports properties in a specific territory or territories creating some limitations. That does not mean, however, that the international dimensions are not important. As discussed earlier, ESPN operates networks around the world that carry its name, with long-term investments in others, and Disney expanded its portfolio with the addition of Fox Sports International and Star Sports in its acquisition of assets from 21st Century Fox in 2019.

There are various parallels between sports television in the United States and markets around the world, but there are also aspects that make it unique. That supports a more singular focus in this analysis. First, the public service sector is underdeveloped in the United States, and commercial broadcasters were long the driving force behind sports television. That is unlike most settings around the world, where public service broadcasters assumed prominent roles and continue to do so in many settings. The 2020 Olympic Games in Tokyo, for example, will be broadcast in the U.K., Canada, and Japan on the BBC, CBC, and NHK, respectively. Elsewhere in Europe, where the International Olympic Committee sold the rights to Discovery, Inc., the U.S.-based conglomerate that owns Eurosport, that contract mandates a minimum number of hours on free-to-air television in each nation, and many of those outlets are public broadcasters. That makes it harder to compare the United States to other markets in the analysis of sports television. Second, the financial stakes are also quite different. In 2016, Comcast paid the International Olympic Committee $1.22 billion for the rights to the Olympic Games in Rio de Janeiro, almost twice the amount collected from all of Europe ($649 million) and 42.5% of the worldwide total ($2.868 billion). There is also a need to focus on the leagues and conferences based in the United States, the National Football League, National Basketball Association, and Major League Baseball, in particular.

The comprehensive analysis of the sports television market in the United States requires a multi-dimensional approach, one that includes both examinations across market sectors and within market sectors. The first question will be the focus of Chapter 2, which examines the conglomeration of sports television platforms and properties since the 1980s. There are striking similarities between the sports television outlets connected to the four major broadcast networks, ABC, CBS, FOX, and NBC, but the road to conglomeration was quite different, and it is hard to understand the current state of the respective sports groups without that history. With that foundation in place, the chapters that follow will examine four different market sectors: national multi-sport networks; national single-sport, league, and conference networks; regional sports networks; and streaming and out-of-market services. The analysis across these sectors of sports television presents a more complete picture of the marketplace and documents the dominance of five major media conglomerates.

Notes

1. Michael Lewis, *Moneyball* (New York: W.W. Norton & Company, 2003), XI.
2. *Moneyball*, XIII.
3. Roger D. Blair, *Sports Economics* (Cambridge: Cambridge University Press, 2011), 22.

4. S&P Global Market Intelligence, "MLB sports rights database," SNL Kagan database. Accessed September 3, 2018.
5. DirecTV, "DirecTV Programming Disputes – Updates & Facts," 2015. Directvpromise. com.
6. Richard Sandomir, "Why FIFA Made Deal With Fox for 2026 Cup," *The New York Times*, February 27, 2015, B15.
7. Brett Hutchins and David Rowe, *Sport Beyond Television: The Internet, Digital Media and the Rise of Networked Media Sport* (New York: Routledge, 2012), 47.
8. Quoted in Ted Johnson, "FCC Chairman Threatens to Intervene to Resolve Dodgers TV Dispute," *Variety*, July 29, 2014.
9. Tom Wheeler, "Statement from FCC Chairman Tom Wheeler on the Comcast-Time Warner Cable Merger," *Federal Communications Commission*, April 24, 2015.
10. Dallas Smythe, "On the Political Economy of Communication," *Journalism Quarterly* 37, no. 4 (1960): 564.
11. Vincent Mosco, *The Political Economy of Communication*, 2nd ed. (Thousand Oaks: Sage, 2009).
12. *The Political Economy of Communication*, 24.
13. Peter Golding and Graham Murdoch, "Culture, Communication and Political Economy," in *Mass Media & Society*, 3rd ed., ed. James Curran and Michael Gurevitch (New York: Oxford University Press, 2000), 72–74.
14. "Culture, Communication and Political Economy," 74.
15. Janet Wasko, "The Study of the Political Economy of the Media in the Twenty-First Century," *International Journal of Media & Cultural Politics* 10, no. 3 (2014): 259–271.
16. "The Study of the Political Economy," 261.
17. "The Study of the Political Economy," 263.
18. David Croteau and William Hoyes, *Media/Society: Technology, Industries, Content and Users*, 6th ed. (Thousand Oaks: Sage, 2018).
19. Michael K. Powell, "Willful Denial and First Amendment Jurisprudence," Speech to the Media Institute, April 22, 1998.
20. Graham Murdock, "Large Corporations and the Control of the Communications Industries," in *Culture, Society and the Media*, ed. Michael Gurevitch, Tony Bennett, James Curran, and Janet Woollacott (London: Methuen, 1982), 120.
21. Ellis W. Hawley, "Three Facets of Hooverian Associationalism: Lumber, Aviation and Movies, 1921–1930," in *Regulation in Perspective*, ed. Thomas K. McGraw (Cambridge, MA: Harvard University Press, 1981).
22. Richard A. Harris and Sydney M. Milkis, *The Politics of Regulatory Change*, 2nd ed. (New York: Oxford University Press, 1996), 25.
23. Mark Fowler, "Interview with Mark S. Fowler," *Reason*, November 1, 1981.
24. See Marta Evans, "Mandela and the Televised Birth of the Rainbow Nation," *National Identities* 12, no. 3 (September 2010): 309–326; Lynette Steenveld and Larry Strelitz, "The 1995 Rugby World Cup and the Politics of Nation-Building in South Africa," *Media, Culture & Society* 20 (1998): 609–629.
25. Quoted in David Smith, "Francois Pienaar: 'When the Whistle Blew, South Africa Changes Forever'," *The Guardian*, December 8, 2013, para 5.
26. Chwen Chwen Chen, Cinzia Colapinto, and Qing Luo, "The 2008 Beijing Olympics Opening Ceremony: Visual Insights into China's Soft Power," *Visual Studies* 27, no. 2 (2012): 195.
27. Todd Shields and Alex Sherman, "Cable Bills Focus of Congress for A La Carte Prices," *Bloomberg*, May 14, 2013.
28. Charles B. Goldfarb, "The FCC's 'A La Carte' Reports," Congressional Research Services (CRS) Reports for Congress, March 30, 2006.
29. "The FCC's 'A La Carte' Reports."

30. Quoted in Arshad Mohammed, "Cable by the Channel Favored; FCC Chairman Aims to Limit Indecency," *The Washington Post,* November 30, 2005, D1.
31. Richard Sandomir, James Andres Miller, and Steve Eder, "To Protect Its Empire, ESPN Stays on Offense," *The New York Times,* August 26, 2013.
32. The Walt Disney Co., *2005 Form 10-K,* December 2005.
33. Quoted in "To Protect Its Empire."
34. Federal Communications Commission, *Amendments of Section 3.35, 3.240 and 3.636 of the Rules and Regulations Relating to Multiple Ownership of AM, FM and Television Broadcasting Stations,* 18 FCC 288 (1953).
35. Federal Communications Commission, *Amendment of Part 73 of the Commission's Rules and Regulations with Respect to Competition and Responsibility in Network Television Broadcasting, Report and Order,* 23 FCC 2d 382 (1970).
36. Quoted in Stuart Banner, *The Baseball Trust: A History of Baseball's Antitrust Exemption* (New York: Oxford University Press, 2013), 58.
37. Quoted in, *The Baseball Trust,* 61.
38. Federal Base Ball Club of Baltimore, Inc. v. National League of Professional Base Ball Clubs, et al., 259 US 200 (1922).
39. 269 US @ 200 (1922).at 209.
40. Toolson v. New York Yankees, Inc., 346 US 356 (1953) at 357.
41. 346 US 356 (1953) at 357.
42. Flood v. Kuhn, 407 US 258 (1972).
43. Los Angeles Memorial Coliseum Commission v. National Football League. United States Court of Appeals for the Ninth Circuit, 726 F2d 1381 (1984).
44. Lawrence Lessig, "Copyright's First Amendment," *UCLA Law Review* 48, no. 5 (2001): 1065.
45. Copyright Law Revision, "Hearings Before the Subcommittee No. 3 of the Committee of the Judiciary, House of Representatives," 89th Congress, 1st Session on H.R. 4347, September 1, 1965, 1825.
46. Copyright Law Revision, 1825.
47. Copyright Act of 1976, Pub. L. 94–553. 90 STAT. 2541 (1976). 17 USC §102.
48. Copyright Act of 1976, §101.
49. David Rowe, "Watching Brief: Cultural Citizenship and Viewing Rights," *Sports in Society* 7, no. 3 (2004): 398.
50. Home Box Office, Inc. v. Federal Communications Commission. United State Court of Appeals for the District of Columbia Circuit, 567 F. 2d 9 (1977).
51. Union of European Football Associations (UEFA) and Federation Internationale de Football Associations (FIFA) v. European Commission, Cases C-201/11 P, C-204/11P and C-205/11 P (Court of Justice of the European Union, 2013).
52. "The Study of the Political Economy," 263.

Further Reading

Golding, Peter, and Graham Murdoch. "Culture, Communication and Political Economy." In *Mass Media & Society,* 3rd ed., edited by James Curran and Michael Gurevitch, 70–92. New York: Oxford University Press, 2000.

Murdock, Graham. "Large Corporations and the Control of the Communications Industries." In *Culture, Society and the Media,* edited by Michael Gurevitch, Tony Bennett, James Curran, and Janet Woollacott, 118–150. London: Methuen, 1982.

Rowe, David. "Watching Brief: Cultural Citizenship and Viewing Rights." *Sports in Society* 7, no. 3 (2004): 385–402.

Smith, Paul, Tom Evens, and Petros Iosifidis. "The Regulation of Television Sports Broadcasting: A Comparative Analysis." *Media, Culture & Society* 37, no. 5 (2015): 720–736.

Smythe, Dallas. "On the Political Economy of Communication." *Journalism Quarterly* 37, no. 4 (1960): 563–572.

Wasko, Janet. "The Study of the Political Economy of the Media in the Twenty-First Century." *International Journal of Media & Cultural Politics* 10, no. 3 (2014): 259–271.

Chapter Bibliography

Banner, Stuart. *The Baseball Trust: A History of Baseball's Antitrust Exemption.* New York: Oxford University Press, 2013.

Blair, Roger D. *Sports Economics.* Cambridge: Cambridge University Press, 2011.

Chen, Chwen C., Cinzia Colapinto, and Qing Luo. "The 2008 Beijing Olympics Opening Ceremony: Visual Insights Into China's Soft Power." *Visual Studies* 27, no. 2 (2012): 188–195.

Copyright Act of 1976, Pub. L. 94–553. 90 STAT. 2541 (1976). 17 USC, §102.

Copyright Law Revision. "Hearings Before the Subcommittee No. 3 of the Committee of the Judiciary, House of Representatives." 89th Congress, 1st Session on H.R. 4347, September 1, 1965

Croteau, David, and William Hoyes. *Media/Society: Technology, Industries, Content and Users,* 6th ed. Thousand Oaks: Sage, 2018.

DirecTV. "DirecTV Programming Disputes – Updates & Facts." (2015). www.Directvpromise.com.

Evans, Marta. "Mandela and the Televised Birth of the Rainbow Nation." *National Identities* 12, no. 3 (2010): 309–326.

Federal Base Ball Club of Baltimore, Inc. v. National League of Professional Base Ball Clubs, et al. 259 US 200 (1922).

Federal Communications Commission. *Amendments of Section 3.35, 3.240 and 3.636 of the Rules and Regulations Relating to Multiple Ownership of AM, FM and Television Broadcasting Stations,* 18 FCC 288 (1953).

———. *Amendment of Part 73 of the Commission's Rules and Regulations with Respect to Competition and Responsibility in Network Television Broadcasting, Report and Order,* 23 FCC 2d 382 (1970).

Flood v. Kuhn, 407 US 258 (1972).

Fowler, Mark. "Interview with Mark S. Fowler." *Reason,* November, 1981.

Goldfarb, Charles B. "The FCC's 'A La Carte' Reports." Congressional Research Services (CRS) Reports for Congress, March 30, 2006.

Golding, Peter, and Graham Murdoch. "Culture, Communication and Political Economy." In *Mass Media & Society,* 3rd ed., edited by James Curran and Michael Gurevitch, 70–92. New York: Oxford University Press, 2000.

Harris, Richard A., and Sydney M. Milkis. *The Politics of Regulatory Change,* 2nd ed. New York: Oxford University Press, 1996.

Hawley, Ellis W. "Three Facets of Hooverian Associationalism: Lumber, Aviation and Movies, 1921–1930." In *Regulation in Perspective: Historical Essays,* edited by Thomas K. McGraw, 95–123. Cambridge, MA: Harvard University Press, 1981.

Home Box Office, Inc. v. Federal Communications Commission. United State Court of Appeals for the District of Columbia Circuit, 567 F. 2d 9 (D.C. Cir. 1977)

Hutchins, Brett, and David Rowe. *Sport Beyond Television: The Internet, Digital Media and the Rise of Networked Media Sport.* New York: Routledge, 2012.

Johnson, Ted. "FCC Chairman Threatens to Intervene to Resolve Dodgers TV Dispute." *Variety,* July 29, 2014.

Kagan. "MLB Sports Rights Database." S&P Global Market Intelligence. Accessed September 3, 2018.

Lessig, Lawrence. "Copyright's First Amendment." *UCLA Law Review* 48, no. 5 (2001): 1057–1074.

Lewis, Michael. *Moneyball*. New York: W.W. Norton & Company, 2003.

Los Angeles Memorial Coliseum Commission v. National Football League. United States Court of Appeals for the Ninth Circuit, 726 F.2d 1381 (9th Cir. 1984).

Mohammed, Arshad. "Cable by the Channel Favored; FCC Chairman Aims to Limit Indecency." *The Washington Post*, November 30, 2005, D1.

Mosco, Vincent. *The Political Economy of Communication*, 2nd ed. Thousand Oaks: Sage, 2009.

Murdock, Graham. "Large Corporations and the Control of the Communications Industries." In *Culture, Society and the Media*, edited by Michael Gurevitch, Tony Bennett, James Curran, and Janet Woollacott, 114–182. London: Methuen, 1982.

Powell, Michael K. "Willful Denial and First Amendment Jurisprudence." *Speech to the Media Institute*, April 22, 1998.

Rowe, David. "Watching Brief: Cultural Citizenship and Viewing Rights." *Sports in Society* 7, no. 3 (2004): 385–402.

Sandomir, Richard. "Why FIFA Made Deal With Fox for 2026 Cup." *The New York Times*, February 27, 2015, B15.

Sandomir, Richard, James A. Miller, and Steve Eder. "To Protect Its Empire, ESPN Stays on Offense." *The New York Times*, August 26, 2013.

Shields, Todd, and Alex Sherman. "Cable Bills Focus of Congress for A La Carte Prices." *Bloomberg*, May 14, 2013.

Smith, David. "Francois Pienaar: 'When the Whistle Blew, South Africa Changes Forever'." *The Guardian*, December 8, 2013. https://www.theguardian.com/world/2013/dec/08/nelson-mandela-francois-pienaar-rugby-world-cup

Smith, Paul, Tom Evens, and Petros Iosifidis. "The Regulation of Television Sports Broadcasting: A Comparative Analysis." *Media, Culture & Society* 37, no. 5 (2015): 720–736.

Smythe, Dallas. "On the Political Economy of Communication." *Journalism Quarterly* 37, no. 4 (1960): 563–572.

Steenveld, Lynette, and Larry Strelitz. "The 1995 Rugby World Cup and the Politics of Nation-Building in South Africa." *Media, Culture & Society* 20 (1998): 609–629.

Toolson v. New York Yankees, Inc., 346 US 356 (1953).

Union of European Football Associations (UEFA) and Federation Internationale de Football Associations (FIFA) v, European Commission, Cases C-201/11 P, C-204/11P and C-205/11 P (Court of Justice of the European Union, 2013).

Walt Disney Co., The, 2005 Annual Report, Form 10-K. December 7, 2005.

Wasko, Janet. "The Study of the Political Economy of the Media in the Twenty-First Century." *International Journal of Media & Cultural Politics* 10, no. 3 (2014): 259–271.

Wheeler, Tom. "Statement from FCC Chairman Tom Wheeler on the Comcast-Time Warner Cable Merger." *Federal Communications Commission*, April 24, 2015. www.fcc.gov.

2

CONGLOMERATION OF SPORTS TELEVISION NETWORKS AND SERVICES

The impact of conglomeration on sports television is most evident in the rise and fall of ABC Sports. In the mid-1970s, the ABC network, long an also-ran behind CBS and NBC, ascended to the top of the Nielsen primetime ratings with sports as a centerpiece, providing both high ratings and a platform for promotion of other network shows. The 1976–77 season was the first ever at number one in the Nielsen ratings for ABC, and a foundation for that success was laid in the summer with the Olympic Games from Montreal and through the fall with ABC's *Monday Night Football*. The three decades that followed were not as kind to ABC Sports, with the ten-year anniversaries of Montreal telling much of the story. In 1986, Capital Cities Communications merged with ABC Inc. and ushered in an era of cost-cutting at the network that spread across all divisions. In 1996, The Walt Disney Co. completed its acquisition of Capital Cities/ABC and two months later announced that long-time ESPN president Steve Bornstein would take the controls of ABC Sports as well, the first step in the folding of the network sports division into the cable giant. In 2006, the final remnants of the sports division were disbanded, and programming on the ABC network was branded as *ESPN on ABC*. The sports television division that created *Wide World of Sports* and *Monday Night Football* was no more.

There is not one consistent pattern of conglomeration among the major sports television groups. There are cases where a cable network such as ESPN rose to dominance over a broadcast cousin such as ABC, and there are cases where a broadcast division such as Fox Sports launched subordinate cable services such as Fox Sports 1 and Fox Sports 2. There are also combinations born out of mergers and acquisitions, such as the marriage of NBC Sports and NBC Sports Network, which evolved from Outdoor Life Channel into Versus before Comcast acquired NBC and merged two sports operations into one. While there are clear differences, however, there are also similarities as the groups within Comcast, Disney, Fox, and ViacomCBS all combine broadcast networks with national sports programming services built around a single integrated operation for production and distribution. The collection of platforms and properties within AT&T Inc. are different, since it does not include a big four broadcast network, but the importance of sports within WarnerMedia News & Sports and DirecTV at different points in time is difficult to overstate.

Roots of Conglomeration

The transformation of broadcast sports divisions from unique, stand-alone units into platforms within vast conglomerates mirrors the changes that occurred in the networks themselves. From the time ABC debuted as a third network in the mid-1950s until FOX launched as a fourth in the mid-1980s, the networks were the standard-bearers of the corporations that housed them: ABC and ABC Inc., CBS and CBS Corp., and NBC and RCA Corp. Those conglomerates followed different paths, with ABC Inc. focused more on broadcasting, television, and radio, while RCA Corp. became far more diversified, venturing into rental cars (Hertz) and frozen foods (Banquet) among other non-media-related pursuits. CBS fell between those two, with most of its ventures in concentric or related diversification, with Columbia Records the most prominent example, although it also owned the New York Yankees from 1965 to 1972. There was an important similarity, however, as each network was connected to its long-standing leaders, William Paley and CBS, David Sarnoff and NBC, and Leonard Goldenson and ABC, much as their sports units were identified by their on-air talent and signature properties.

The relative steadiness that marked sports television between the mid-1960s and mid-1980s was most evident on weekend afternoons in the autumn. CBS inked a national television contract with the National Football League prior to the 1962 season, while NBC signed a similar deal with the American Football League prior to the 1965 season. Those links would last for over three decades, long after the two leagues merged operations in 1970. There was also rare permanence in the announce booth. Pat Summerall joined CBS Sports in 1962 and ascended to the lead national crew in 1968, when CBS stopped assigning announce crews to specific teams. Summerall moved from analyst to play-by-play in 1971, and he remained on the lead team for over a quarter century, until CBS lost the National Football Conference package following the 1993 season. While NBC could not match that stability, it was not far behind, with Curt Gowdy in the lead role from 1965 through 1977 before handing off to Dick Enberg, who held down the lead play-by-play role for the two decades that followed. On many of those autumn weekends, viewers could also rely on college football games on ABC, often with Keith Jackson behind the microphone, and then follow-up with ABC's *Monday Night Football* with Frank Gifford, Howard Cosell, and Don Meredith.

That all began to change in the mid-1980s, and the rewriting of federal regulations assumed a critical role. In 1985, the Federal Communications Commission finalized new regulations that increased the number of television licenses a single corporation could own, raising the limit from 7 to 12. That opened the door for the aforementioned $3.5 billion merger of Capital Cities Communications Inc. and ABC Inc., which closed in January 1986 and combined the seven television stations Capital Cities owned with the five that ABC owned.[1] That June, the federal government gave final approval of the $6.28 billion agreement for General Electric Co. to acquire RCA Corp., which paired one of the largest defense contractors with the NBC broadcast network. That September, Laurence Tisch and Loews Corp. gained effective control of CBS with a 24.9% share of the corporation, with Tisch becoming the chief executive officer.[2] And, finally, in October 1986, 20th Century Fox launched the FOX television network.

Federal largesse assumed an important role in the birth and subsequent growth of FOX. When Rupert Murdoch and News Corp., an Australia-based corporation, agreed to purchase the Metromedia station group for $2 billion in 1985 to create a foundation for the FOX network, Murdoch announced his plans to file for U.S. citizenship in order to skirt foreign ownership rules.[3] In time, the FCC approved the transfer of the licenses based, in part, on the argument that News Corp. would control just 24% of the voting power in Twentieth Holdings Corp., the direct parent of Fox Inc., with Murdoch controlling the rest.[4] A decade later, when the renewal of the license for WNYW-TV in New York was challenged, Fox stated that News Corp. contributed over 99% of the capital invested in Twentieth Holdings Corp. and held virtually all the economic interest.[5] The Commission ruled that News Corp. was in violation of the foreign ownership rule in May 1995 but allowed the corporation to either bring its ownership structure into compliance or argue that such an ownership structure served the public interest. That summer, the Commission waived its ownership rules, concluding that it was "consistent with the public interest" to allow Fox to "retain its present level of alien equity."[6] That was not the lone waiver that News Corp. received, as Fox was also granted a waiver of the Financial Interest and Syndication Rules (fin/syn) in 1990 when it passed the threshold of 15 hours per week in primetime programming and a waiver of the newspaper/broadcast cross-ownership rules in 1993 so News Corp. could own both WNYW-TV and the *New York Post*.

The waiver of the fin/syn rules allowed News Corp. to hold a financial interest in programs on the FOX primetime schedule, many of which were produced through 20th Century Fox Television. In 1995, the Commission allowed the final remnants of those rules to expire, which set in motion a series of mergers and acquisitions that forever changed the state of sports television. In 1996, as discussed above, Disney completed its acquisition of Capital Cities/ABC Inc. for $19 billion, creating the largest entertainment conglomerate in the world at that time. In 2000, Viacom and CBS merged in what was then billed as the largest media transaction ever, with an enterprise value of $80 billion. And in 2004,

NBC and Universal merged to create NBCUniversal, with General Electric Co. owning 80% of the combined unit. Far more significant for the sports division of NBC was the Comcast acquisition of NBCUniversal in 2011, which married NBC Sports with a cable and satellite service dedicated to sports, what is now known as NBC Sports Network.

Walt Disney Co.: ABC and ESPN

There was a time when sports telecasts on ABC ended with an emphatic boast: "Recognized around the world as the leader in sports television." There was even a time when that claim held some merit. Between the 1964 Olympic Winter Games in Innsbruck and the 1988 Olympic Winter Games in Calgary, ABC Sports held the U.S. rights to all but two installments of the Games: the 1972 Winter Olympics in Sapporo and the 1980 Summer Olympics in Moscow, both of which belonged to NBC. During that same era, ABC introduced the American audience to an eclectic mix of sports and stars from near and far through *Wide World of Sports*, which debuted in 1961. As discussed earlier, it was also sports that helped transform ABC from a distant third to a leader in primetime television, with the ratings and promotional platforms it generated through the Olympic Games and one of the most transformative sports properties ever, ABC's *Monday Night Football*. While one can support the claim of ABC as a worldwide leader in sports television, one can also argue that no network sports division was impacted more by conglomeration than ABC.

The transformation of ABC Sports began with the Capital Cities Communications acquisition of ABC Inc., a deal announced in March 1985 and completed in January 1986. Capital Cities owned seven local television stations as well as a collection of newspapers and other publishing interests when the purchase was announced, but it was one-fourth the size of ABC and was not well known in the public. Within media industries, however, Capital Cities had a long-standing reputation for cost-cutting and budget discipline and that was soon the fate of ABC. Before the first month of Capital Cities' control ended, Roone Arledge, the architect of ABC Sports, was removed from day-to-day operations of the division. Arledge was emblematic of the free-spending "limousine mentality" that Capital Cities chairman Thomas Murphy and other executives saw at ABC.[7] While Arledge remained in control of ABC News, a series of changes occurred within ABC Sports over the 12 months that followed, including the departures of his long-term lieutenant, Senior Vice President Jim Spence, and numerous changes both in front of and behind the cameras.

The Capital Cities acquisition of ABC came at a turning point for sports television. In February 1986, a cover of *Sports Illustrated* featured the logos of the three broadcast networks over a television emblazoned with an ominous message: "WHY TV SPORTS ARE IN BIG TROUBLE."[8] ABC Sports was a focal point of the *Sports Illustrated* article after running a "staggering $30 to $50 million in the red" in 1985.[9] Much of that loss was pegged to the rights fee to ABC's *Monday Night Football*, but it was also attributed to the "glut" of sports on television and shifts in the television marketplace that made non-sports programming more attractive, and more affordable, to advertisers. Dennis Swanson, who oversaw ABC's owned and operated station after leading the turnaround of WLS-TV in Chicago, was the successor to Arledge and brought a Capital Cities ethos to the operation of the sports division. While the imprint of the former Marine captain was undeniable, the times had also clearly changed. One network sports executive was quoted at the time as saying, "For years TV sports has been run like the Pentagon – everything was cost overruns. From now on it's going to be run like a business."[10]

The bottom-line focus at ABC Sports came at the exact time when ESPN was beginning to soar. ABC Inc. was an early investor in the cable service, agreeing in 1982 to supply programming to ESPN in exchange for an option to acquire up to 49% of the company.[11] ABC Sports owned the rights to countless events in which it did not air all of the available content, and ESPN became a willing recipient of the leftovers. In 1981, for example, ABC broadcast 3.5 hours of the British Open Golf Championships, all on Saturday and Sunday. In 1982, ABC duplicated that schedule, but ESPN added 11 hours of coverage on Thursday and Friday. ABC Inc. exercised its option and obtained 15% of ESPN from Getty Oil in January 1984 for around $30 million and then acquired the other 85% months later for $202 million after Texaco completed its purchase of Getty, which included the 13% owned by the network founder, Bill Rasmussen.[12] Later that summer, ABC sold a 20% interest in ESPN to Nabisco Brands Inc. for $60 million in cash.[13] In 1990, Nabisco sold its share of ESPN to Hearst Corporation for $165 to $175 million.[14] Hearst retained that interest in ESPN three decades later.

The divergent paths of ABC and ESPN were most evident in 1985. ESPN lost $100 million in its first six years of existence but registered a pre-tax profit of $1 million in 1985. That stood in sharp contrast to the $30 to $50 million loss for ABC Sports that same year. ESPN recorded a profit of $13 million in 1986 and had a positive cash flow of over $100 million before the end of the decade. Over that same period, ABC Sports struggled with rights deals signed before the merger with Capital Cities. The sports division suffered a loss estimated at $65 million at the 1988 Olympic Winter Games in Calgary after bidding $309 million for the rights in 1984.[15] And over a six-year period, 1984 through 1989, ABC Sports lost over $100 million on its contract with Major League Baseball signed in 1983. There was soon little doubt as to which was the favored sports unit within Capital Cities/ABC.

Access to programming was just one of the benefits ESPN received from its corporate connections to ABC. The Cable Television Consumer Protection and Competition Act of 1992 required cable operators to receive retransmission consent from local broadcast stations for the use of their signals. ESPN was in a unique position in such negotiations, since both of its corporate parents, Capital Cities/

ABC and Hearst, owned large local station groups when "express authority" was first required. And it was the expansion of the ESPN enterprise that became the focus for ABC and Hearst. In October 1993, ESPN launched a companion network, ESPN2, in just under 10 million households. With a graffiti inspired logo and studio hosts wearing leather jackets and print shirts rather than suits and ties, "The Deuce" was designed to appeal to a younger, hipper audience. Behind the scenes, however, ESPN2 was very much a business proposition and its corporate parents used the ABC and Hearst station groups as leverage in negotiations for household penetration and carriage fees. ESPN2 was the fastest growing basic cable network between the end of 1993 and the end of 1996, with an increase of 32.2 million households, and surpassed 50 million households in 1997.[16]

There was an ever-increasing presence of ESPN on ABC through the first half of the 1990s, most notable when John Saunders became the host of ABC's college football studio show in 1992 and *Wide World of Sports* in 1993. That subtle influence changed forever in February 1996 when Disney completed its $19 billion acquisition of Capital Cities/ABC. When the deal was first announced, Disney Chairman Michael Eisner was clear about the perceived value of ESPN:

> We know that when we lay Mickey Mouse or Goofy on top of products, we get pretty creative stuff. ESPN has the potential to be that kind of brand. ABC has never had our resources, and we haven't had ESPN. Put the two together and who knows what we get.[17]

As discussed earlier, Eisner soon after expanded the portfolio of Steve Bornstein, with the ESPN executive becoming the president of ABC Sports as well in April 1996. It was not long after that Bob Iger, then the president of ABC Inc., said that Disney was "moving slowly towards moving [ESPN and ABC Sports] together," stating further that "it's an idea I'm thoroughly intrigued with."[18] The goal was to see "if we can take the value of the ESPN brand and use it on ABC, while using ABC's massive distribution system to help ESPN."[19]

That was in 1998, and it was in that time period that the fate of ABC Sports started to take form, which was most evident when Disney acquired the broadcast and cable rights to the National Hockey League for $600 million over five years. The deal was structured around a fee that averaged $50 million per year for the broadcast rights on ABC and $70 million per year for the cable rights on ESPN and ESPN2.[20] Fox had the right to match the offer as the broadcast rights holder but requested an extra week to negotiate in August 1998, claiming it did not have the required information about the Disney deal. The NHL Board of Governors rejected that request and awarded the rights to Disney. That deal proved to be unusual, as ESPN paid the entire rights fee and bought time on ABC for the games that it broadcast. In that case, ABC was little more than a distribution platform that allowed ESPN to fend off an expected bid from Fox to obtain all NHL rights, both broadcast and cable. ESPN signed a similar deal with the

National Basketball Association that started with the 2002–03 season. Newspaper headlines heralded a "Jump to ABC, ESPN," but the bulk of the games shown on Disney outlets, both in the regular season and playoffs, were carried on ESPN or ESPN2.[21] Under the new contract, ABC was slated to broadcast just 10 to 15 regular season games and the NBC Finals.

The integration of ABC was just one example of the expansion of the ESPN brand, which extended to radio, magazines, local and regional websites, and even restaurants. The core business, however, remained the cable programming services. The evolution of ESPN2 after 1993 became a tried-and-true formula for the creation of new services and the acquisition of existing services. ESPN2 was conceived as a hip alternative to ESPN, but it became little more than a mirror of its older sibling as Disney acquired and created more and more content. In 1996, ESPN Inc. launched ESPNews, featuring news, highlights, and press conferences, content that was in house for *SportsCenter* and other programs. In 1997, it acquired Classic Sports Network for $175 million and rebranded the service as ESPN Classic, relaunching in 1998. And in 2005, it created ESNPU, which debuted in under 10 million households but expanded to over 60 million within four years.

The birth of ESPNU reveals a great deal about the Disney approach. In 2004, the antitrust division of the U.S. Department of Justice opened an inquiry into how ESPN acquired and distributed college football and basketball programming.[22] At that time, ESPN held television rights to regular season basketball and/or football games with five of the six major conferences: Atlantic Coast (ACC), Big East, Big Ten, Big 12, and Southeast Conference, with the Pacific-10 the one outlier. One of the questions before the Justice Department was whether ESPN was "warehousing" content, televising a small portion of the games it controlled and then limiting the conferences from making deals with other networks. No action was taken against ESPN, but with the launch of ESPNU, football and basketball games that did not fit on the schedules of ESPN and ESPN2, not to mention ABC, found a home under the ESPN umbrella.

The importance of collegiate athletics to the creation and subsequent expansion of ESPN is undeniable, and it also represented a rare area of growth in the 2010s. In 2011, ESPN joined forces with the University of Texas to launch the Longhorn Network, dedicated to the athletic exploits of a single university. More significant was the debut of the SEC Network in 2014. The Southeastern Conference expanded from 12 to 14 teams in 2012 with the addition of Texas A&M and Missouri, but more important than the mere number of teams was the expansion of the geographic footprint of the conference to cover 11 states, including Texas. The SEC Network launched in August 2014 and was in over 60 million households by the end of that year, although it later dipped below that threshold.[23] In 2018, Kagan estimated its average per household fee at $0.78 per month and its annual affiliate revenue at over $560 million.[24] ESPN owned the SEC Network outright, although it did share profits with the conference members.

That same model was replicated in 2016 when ESPN and the Atlantic Coach Conference announced the creation of the ACC Network. Once again, expansion had stretched the footprint of that conference with the addition of Louisville, Pittsburgh, and Syracuse, reaching nine states in football, increasing to 10 states with the inclusion of Notre Dame in basketball. And while the linear network did not launch until August 2019, it began delivering online content through ACC Network Extra in 2016.

Collegiate content was also an example of the movement of programming from one network to another in the mid-2010s, revealing the true impact of conglomeration. The Disney collection of outlets is detailed in Table 2.1. Thanksgiving Weekend in 2018 provided a vivid example. On that Saturday alone, the ESPN networks televised a total of 17 games on linear networks, including four each on ESPN and ESPNU and three each on ABC, ESPN2, and SEC Network. That same day, it streamed another 18 games, which included the eight first rounds games of the NCAA Football Championships Subdivision (FCS) Playoffs on ESPN3. More significant, perhaps, were the eight games on direct-to-consumer subscription services, with six games on ESPN+ and two games on

TABLE 2.1 Walt Disney Co. television and streaming properties as of December 31, 2019

	Properties with Ownership Interest
Broadcast Network(s)	ABC Television Network and 8 ABC-affiliated local stations (100%), including 6 in Top 10 markets (New York, Los Angeles, Chicago, Philadelphia, Houston, and San Francisco)
National Sports Networks	ESPN, ESPN2, ESPNU, ESPNEWS, and ESPN Deportes (all 80%) and SEC Network and ACC Network (both 80%)
Regional Sports Networks	Longhorn Network (80%)
Other National Networks	Disney Channel, Disney Junior, and Disney XD (all 100%); Freeform (100%); A&E, History, Lifetime, Lifetime Movie Channel, and FYI (all 50%); FX, FXX, and FXM (100%); National Geographic Channel and Nat Geo Wild (73%)
Streaming Services	ESPN+ and ESPN3 (both 80%), Disney+ (100%), and Hulu (67%)
Non-U.S. Sports Platforms	ESPN International, Fox Sports International, and Star Sports
Sports-Related Websites	ESPN.com and ESPNDeportes.com, FiveThirtyEight. com, TheUndefeated.com, ESPNCricinfo. com, ESPNBoston.com, ESPNChicago.com, ESPNDallas.com, ESPNLosAngeles.com, and ESPNNewYork.com

Source: Walt Disney Co. annual report for the 2019 fiscal year and corporate websites.

ACC Network Extra. While football was the feast on Saturday, basketball was the focus on Thursday, Friday, and Sunday. On those three days, the ESPN networks telecast 31 men's college basketball across its linear networks.

The reach of ESPN, and in turn Disney, in sports and television is undeniable, but some of the headlines that ESPN fueled in the later stages of the 2010s were not positive ones. In April 2017, John Skipper, president of ESPN Inc. and co-chairman of Disney Media Networks, announced the layoffs of 100 anchors, reporters, and analysts. The following November, he announced 150 more, this time from behind the cameras. Those two announcements came on the heels of 300 layoffs in 2015. The impetus for those cuts was twofold, with the increasing cost of rights for key packages, including the NFL and NBA, coming at the same time as significant declines in households' penetration that resulted from cord cutting. Skipper stepped down in December 2017 citing substance abuse after a cocaine extortion attempt.[25] Disney reached into its consumer products and interactive media division to find his successor, James Pitaro. Prior to working for Disney, Pitaro was an executive at Yahoo!, and his background in digital media proved valuable when Disney launched its subscription streaming service ESPN+ in April 2018, the month after he became co-chair of Disney Media Networks.

There was a point in time when it appeared that Pitaro would have even more terrain to oversee. The $71.3 billion agreement reached in June 2018 for Disney to acquire entertainment assets from 21st Century Fox also included the latter's ownership interest in 22 regional sports networks (RSNs), including 80% of YES Network. The valuation of those networks accounted for just over $20 billion of the total price Disney agreed to pay for the Fox entertainment units and libraries. When the original deal was announced the previous December, Iger, then chairman and chief executive officer of Disney, said about the combination of ESPN and the Fox regional networks, "We love it because it's the local complement to the national footprint that is ESPN."[26] A headline in AdAge, meanwhile, proclaimed that the addition would be a "Game-Changer for ESPN."[27]

While Iger loved the local and national combination the deal represented, the Department of Justice did not. In its review of the merger, the government focused on the designated market areas (DMA) in which the Fox regional networks operated. The Justice Department argued that the acquisition would

a. substantially lessen competition in the licensing of cable sports programming in each of the DMA Markets; b. eliminate actual and potential competition among Disney and Fox in the licensing of cable sports programming in each of the DMA Markets; and c. cause prices for cable programming in each of the DMA Markets to increase.[28]

As a condition of its approval, the Justice Department required Disney to sell the RSNs within 90 days of the close of the merger. In time, Disney sold the 21 Fox

RSNs outright to Sinclair Broadcast Group for $10.6 billion and sold the 80% interest in YES Network back to the Yankees for $3.5 billion.

Comcast Corp.: NBC, NBC Sports Network, and Golf Channel

The evolution of NBC Sports in the era of conglomeration was altogether different from that of ABC Sports. Like ABC, the ownership of NBC changed hands in 1986, bringing with it a much tighter focus on the bottom line. The General Electric acquisition of RCA Corp. and, in turn, NBC for $6.28 billion in 1986 came at a time of transition and tumult in the sports television industry. As discussed earlier, advertising revenues were stagnant, rights fees were escalating, and packages were jumping from network to network in the mid-1980s. In the decade that followed, properties long associated with NBC went to other networks, including the Major League Baseball *Game of the Week*, a network exclusive from 1966 to 1989, and the American Football Conference portion of the NFL contract, which stretched from 1970 to 1997, not counting the five years prior to that when the American Football League was on NBC. What was different about NBC Sports is that the division experienced stability in executive leadership for over 20 years following the appointment of Dick Ebersol as president of NBC Sports in April 1989.

Ebersol was best known as the executive who teamed with Lorne Michaels to launch *Saturday Night Live* in 1975 while he was the head of late night programming at NBC. It was his roots in television, however, that proved to be more significant for NBC Sports. In 1967, Ebersol temporarily dropped out of Yale University to become an Olympic researcher at ABC Sports for the Games of Mexico City in 1968, working with Roone Arledge. NBC broadcast the 1988 Olympic Games from Seoul prior to his return to the network and even acquired the rights to the 1992 Olympic Games in Barcelona for $401 million before his return, but Ebersol's passion for the Olympic movement, coupled with the resources of General Electric, defined his tenure at NBC. In 1993, NBC outbid ABC and CBS to claim the rights for the 1996 Olympic Games in Atlanta for $465 million. In August 1995, NBC claimed the rights to the 2000 Olympic Games in Sydney and 2002 Olympic Winter Games in Salt Lake City for a combined $1.25 billion, and then four months later, it made a preemptive bid of $2.3 billion for the 2004 and 2008 Summer Olympics and 2006 Winter Olympics before the sites of those games were even known. Then, in 2003, NBC outbid ESPN/ABC and Fox with a $2.0 billion commitment for the 2010 Winter Games and 2012 Summer Games.

The rising cost of the rights for the Olympic Games is part of the story, but the coverage on NBC also tells the tale of conglomeration. In 1992, NBC teamed with Cablevision Systems Corp. to offer three pay-per-view channels from the Games of Barcelona to supplement network coverage. The ill-fated Olympic Triplecast lost around $100 million, and four years later, NBC broadcast a grand total of 171 hours, all on NBC, for Atlanta. That does not mean that the 1996 Games did not impact NBC cable assets. In 1994, NBC launched a new cable programming service, America's Talking, and used retransmission consent for the NBC-owned and operated stations to secure carriage agreements. When NBC launched MSNBC in a joint venture with Microsoft in 1996, it replaced America's Talking on cable systems. Some operators balked at the switch, arguing that the format for the new service did not conform to that described in existing contracts, rendering those agreements null and void. Thomas Rogers, the president of NBC Cable, declared that cable operators that did not allow the transfer of America's Talking outlets to MSNBC could not retransmit the NBC network during the 1996 Olympic Games from Atlanta. Rogers stated, "As a quid pro quo in the event that an operator dropped the channel, we have every right to drop their NBC television network programming. Why anyone would want to get into that fight, we don't know."[29] The threat worked, and MSNBC launched on schedule on July 15, 1996, four days prior to the Opening Ceremony in Atlanta.

The cable platforms NBC used for each Olympic Games expanded as its corporate cousins grew. For the 2000 Olympic Games in Sydney, NBC utilized the two cable news channels that General Electric owned at that time, CNBC and MSNBC. The merger of NBC and Universal that created NBCUniversal was finalized in May 2004 and three months later USA Network made its Olympic debut from the Games of Athens. Those same Olympics included Bravo and Telemundo, properties that General Electric acquired in 2002. Oxygen joined the NBC lineup with the 2008 Olympic Games in Beijing after NBCUniversal acquired the network in 2007. NBC Sports Network became the featured cable outlet for the London Games after the completion of the Comcast acquisition of NBCUniversal in January 2011. And in 2016, Golf Channel was added to the collection when golf made its Olympic return in Rio de Janeiro. The total hours for the NBC Sports Group, counting streaming, increased from 171 in 1996 to 442 in 2000 to 1,210 in 2004 to more than 3,500 in 2008, more than 5,500 in 2012, and more than 6,500 in 2016.

Ebersol did not remain as chairman of the NBC Sports Group for long after the merger was complete, stepping down in May 2011, but his influence remained. A month later, NBCUniversal bid $4.38 billion for the 2016 and 2020 Summer Games and 2014 and 2018 Winter Games, and in 2014 it locked up the rights for 2022 through 2032 for $7.75 billion.[30] More significant, Ebersol protégés assumed leadership roles across the Comcast sports properties. Sam Flood, who started his career at NBC as an Olympic researcher for the 1988 Olympic Games in Seoul, became executive producer of NBC Sports in 2010 and added that same title for NBC Sports Network in 2011. In 2012, Molly Solomon, who started her career at NBC as an Olympic researcher for the 1992 Olympic Games in Barcelona, became the executive producer of Golf Channel, which became part of NBCUniversal following the merger with Comcast. And in 2019, when Jim Bell stepped down as president of NBC Olympics after three decades at NBCUniversal that included executive roles in sports, news, and late-night, Solomon was named as his replacement, adding the Olympic Games to her duties at Golf Channel.

The integration of Comcast and NBC was most evident in April 2011 when NBC Sports Group claimed the broadcast and cable rights to the National Hockey League for $2.0 billion over ten seasons, starting in 2011–12. NBC and Versus had televised the NHL for the previous six seasons but would soon do so under one corporate umbrella and one brand, as Versus became NBC Sports Network in January 2012. That integration became even easier in March 2013 when NBC Sports moved its operations into a single complex in Stamford, Connecticut, bringing NBC Sports, NBC Sports Network, NBC Regional Sports Networks, and NBCSports.com under one roof as NBC Sports Group. While Golf Channel remained in its original home in Orlando, Florida, the flow of talent from NBC to Golf Channel and vice versa, not to mention production personnel, made clear that it was also part of NBCUniversal.

TABLE 2.2 Comcast Corp. television and streaming properties as of December 31, 2019

	Properties with Ownership Interest
Broadcast Network(s)	NBC Television Network and 11 NBC-affiliated local stations (100%), Telemundo network and 30 Telemundo-affiliated local stations (100%)
National Sports Networks	Golf Channel and NBC Sports Network (both 100%), NHL Network (15.6%), and Olympic Channel
Regional Sports Networks	9: NBCS Bay Area, NBCS Boston, NBCS California, NBCS Chicago, NBCS Northwest, NBCS Philadelphia, NBCS Philadelphia and NBCS Washington (all 100%), and SportsNet New York (8%)
Other National Networks	USA Network, SyFy, E!, MSNBC, CNBC, Bravo, Oxygen, Universal Kids, CNBC World (all 100%)
Streaming Services	NBC Sports Gold (100%) and Hulu and iNDEMAND (both 33%)
Non-U.S. Sports Platforms	Sky Sports
Sports-Related Websites	NBCSports.com, TelemundoDeportes.com, NBCOlympics.com, GolfChannel.com, GolfNow.com, and Rotoworld.com; Regional: NBCSportsPhiladelphia.com, NBCSportsChicago.com, NBCSportsWashington.com, NBCSportsBayArea.com, NBCSportsBoston.com, and NBCSportsNorthwest.com

Source: Comcast Corp. annual report for the 2019 fiscal year and corporate websites.

The NBC Sports Group domestic portfolio remained more or less in place from the Comcast merger in 2011 through the end of the decade, with the launch of the Olympic Channel in partnership with the International Olympic Committee and United States Olympic Committee in 2017 one addition. Those properties are listed in Table 2.2. Comcast Corp. was not idle in this period, however. In June 2018, the day after a federal judge approved the merger of AT&T Inc. and Time Warner Inc., Comcast bid $65 billion to acquire the entertainment assets that 21st Century Fox had agreed to sell to Disney in December 2017. That offer forced Disney to increase its offer from one valued at $52.8 billion to one valued at $71.3. While that battle was being waged, Comcast and Disney were also bidding for Sky PLC, the European satellite service in which Fox held a 39.14 percent interest. In September 2018, Comcast emerged from a blind bidding process for Sky as the winner, and it took control in November 2018. Sports was the foundation of BSkyB when it acquired Premier League rights in the early 1990s, and the first sign of the new corporate coupling came in January 2019 when NBC Sports Network simulcast Sky's "Transfer Deadline Day" telecast in the United States.

ViacomCBS Inc.: CBS and CBS Sports Network

The route toward conglomeration followed a different path within ViacomCBS. When Congress passed the 1992 Cable Act and introduced retransmission consent to negotiations for broadcast carriage agreements, CBS did not possess the same corporate connections to cable services as other broadcast networks. CBS was a driving force behind the Cable Act, and Chairman Laurence Tisch, who gained control of CBS in 1986, was looking for cold hard cash in exchange for retransmission. Predictions attributed to Tisch pinning the value of such consent agreements at around $1 billion a year for local stations were a point of contention in Congressional hearings. When the Cable Act passed and such direct payments were not forthcoming, however, CBS was on the outside looking in without cable networks to tie to broadcast consent agreements. The $5.4 billion sale of CBS to Westinghouse Electric in 1995 expanded its broadcast portfolio, combining the seven CBS-owned and operated stations with five Group W stations as well as those held by a joint venture the two corporations created the previous year. That combination gave the owned and operated group 15 local television stations, in excess of the national ownership limit of 12, but the FCC granted a waiver of that rule so the deal could be completed. The new CBS Corp. became the largest broadcaster in the United States, on both television and radio, but it did not venture into cable services until 1997 when it acquired The Nashville Network and Country Music Television from Gaylord Entertainment.

The CBS foray into the Olympic Games in 1992 represents the prominent role sports assumed under Tisch, although the resulting financial losses contributed to its decline and subsequent sale to Westinghouse. The 1987–88 primetime season was a disaster for CBS, the first time the Tiffany Network ever finished third in the primetime ratings. Tisch and CBS Sports president Neal Pilson responded with the acquisition of sports properties that could air in primetime but could also provide a platform for promotion, trying to replicate the rise of ABC in the 1970s. The first deal came in May 1988 when CBS won the rights to the 1992 Olympic Winter Games in Albertville for $243 million, well beyond a $175 million bid from NBC. At the time, Tisch said, "I think this is one of the building blocks in the resurgence of CBS."[31] The second deal was a bigger shock, as in December 1988, CBS bid $1.1 billion for exclusive network rights to Major League Baseball for four years starting in 1990, a deal which included just 16 regular season games but both League Championship Series and the World Series.

While those were the most noteworthy deals, CBS also committed $1 billion in November 1989 to expand its rights to the NCAA Men's Basketball Tournament for seven years and another $1 billion in March 1990 to the NFL to retain the rights to the NFC package for four years. When one adds in $300 million pledged in November 1989 for the rights to the Lillehammer Olympics, CBS spent over $3.6 billion on sports rights in less than two years. When the Albertville deal was signed, Tisch rebuffed claims that the network overpaid for the rights, stating, "At the worst, I see it as a break-even for CBS."[32] And while it reported that it covered its costs in Albertville, three months before the Games began, CBS announced its largest ever quarterly loss, $169.1 million, with a $322 million pre-tax write-off in anticipation of future losses from sports programming.[33] Combined with a previous pre-tax write-off of $282 million specific to its baseball deal, CBS wrote off a total of $604 million on its sports contracts.

The fate of those deals paved the way for the loss of the rights to professional baseball and football and the sale of CBS to Westinghouse in 1995. It also ushered out a cadre of executives, including CBS Inc. president Howard Stringer and Pilson. In December 1996, Sean McManus, the son of long-time ABC Sports host Jim McKay, became the president of the sports division with the stated goal of bringing the NFL back to CBS, a goal that was accomplished 13 months later. More than two decades later, McManus remained at the helm of the sports division; CBS remained at least part of the corporate moniker; and the network still featured the NFL, the NCAA Men's Basketball Tournament, and some of the marquee professional golf tournaments, including The Masters and PGA Championships. Those visible signs of continuity belie some of the turmoil it endured, however. Viacom Inc., the parent corporation of Paramount Pictures as well as MTV, Nickelodeon, and Showtime, acquired CBS Corp. in 2000, but Sumner Redstone, who wielded control through National Amusements, split the corporation in two in January 2006, bringing back the CBS Corp. name.

While McManus and CBS were determined to rebuild CBS Sports, it was far less aggressive in the realm of cable sports networks. In January 2006, CBS Corp. completed the acquisition of CSTV (College Sports Television) for $325 million. CSTV launched in April 2003 but had just 12 million subscribers at the end of

2005 when CBS took control of the network.[34] CSTV co-founder Brian Bedol continued to run the network until January 2008 when it was integrated into the CBS organization, with then executive producer Tony Pettiti adding operational control of CSTV to his duties with CBS Sports. Two months later, in March 2008, it was rebranded as CBS College Sports Network. Finally, in April 2011, the "college" was dropped from its name as it was rebranded as CBS Sports Network. While the connection between CBS and CBS Sports Network mirrored that of ABC and ESPN, the former was far less powerful. At the end of 2011, CBS Sports Network was in fewer than 45 million households, whereas ESPN and ESPN2 had close to 100 million subscribers.[35] CBS Sports Network was in just over 50 million households at the end of 2018 and averaged just 14 cents per household per month in carriage fees. The properties within ViacomCBS are detailed in Table 2.3.

Without a prominent cable service to collaborate with, CBS has often looked out from under its corporate umbrella to find partners for big deals to share the costs and the risk. For the Olympic Winter Games in Albertville, Lillehammer, and Nagano in the 1990s, it sold cable rights to Turner Broadcasting. That connection between CBS and Turner was born in a different era, when Tisch oversaw CBS and Ted Turner controlled the corporation that bore his name. That relationship was reborn in 2010 in a much different environment, when CBS Corp.

TABLE 2.3 ViacomCBS Inc. television and streaming properties as of December 31, 2019

	Properties with Ownership Interest
Broadcast Network(s)	CBS Television Network (100%) and CW Network (50%) and 29 local broadcast stations, including 15 CBS-affiliate stations (100%)
National Sports Networks	CBS Sports Network (100%)
Regional Sports Networks	None
Other National Networks	Showtime, MovieChannel, and Flix (all 100%) and Smithsonian Channel, a joint venture between Showtime Networks and the Smithsonian Institute, in which Showtime holds a majority interest, were part of CBS Corp. Viacom Inc. owned the MTV, Nickelodeon, and VH1 families of networks as well as BET, CMT, Comedy Central, Logo TV, Paramount Network, and TVLand
Streaming Services	CBS Sports HQ, CBS All Access, CBSN, Showtime Anytime, and Pluto TV
Non-U.S. Sports Platforms	Network Ten (Australia), Channel 5 (Great Britain)
Sports-Related Websites	CBSSports.com, Max Preps, 247Sport, Scout, and Boxing Scene

Source: Viacom Inc. annual report for the 2019 fiscal year, CBS Corp. annual report for the 2019 fiscal year, and corporate websites.

and Time Warner Inc. joined forces in a 14-year, $10.8 billion deal for rights to the NCAA Basketball Tournament starting in 2011. While CBS contributed the broadcast platform to the deal, Turner supplied three of its cable outlets, TNT, TBS, and truTV. The lack of a strong in-house partner is also evident with the major championships in golf. While corporate cousins NBC and Golf Channel shared the rights to the British Open and Fox and FS1 did likewise with the U.S. Open, CBS had much different partnerships with the Masters Tournament and PGA Championship. CBS has broadcast the Masters since 1956 and the PGA since 1991, but ESPN claimed the rights to the first two rounds to the Masters starting in 2008 and did likewise with the PGA starting in 2020, taking over for Turner Sports after 19 years. CBS was well known for its coverage of Southeast Conference football in the fall, but it also shared those rights with ESPN while CBS Sports Network focused on the Group of Five conferences, which stand a notch below the so-called Power 5. These include rights to Conference USA and Mountain West Conference and sublicensing agreements with ESPN for games in the American Athletic Conference and Mid-American Conference.

As noted earlier, CBS and Viacom were split in two in January 2006, a move that was designed to untether the new media properties within Viacom from the old media properties within CBS. Such forecasts proved to be misguided, as CBS prospered while Viacom struggled. That was just part of the drama. There were various attempts to bring the two back together, but those were unsuccessful. That turbulent process included a lawsuit brought by CBS Corp. to strip the Redstone family of its control of the corporation and claims of sexual harassment and abuse that led to the dismissal of CBS chairman Les Moonves in September 2018. That removed a barrier to unification, and the boards of the two Redstone-controlled companies voted to reunite in August 2019 in a victory for Shari Redstone, who became the chairwoman of ViacomCBS Inc. The new corporate structure did not offer clear synergies for CBS Sports, since there were not sports assets on the Viacom side of the house, and there was some degree of trepidation, since Moonves was long an advocate for sports programming as a cornerstone for CBS. Executives of the sports division visited league partners following the departure of Moonves to assure them sports remained central to the network's strategy, but it remained to be seen how the ViacomCBS merger would impact on sports properties.[36]

Fox Corp.: FOX, Fox Sports 1, Fox Sports 2, and Big Ten Network

It would be difficult to overstate the importance of sports programming to the Fox brand, both in the ascent of the network and in the future of Fox Corp. It is easy to trace the start of that rise to December 1993, when Fox captured the rights to the highest profile professional team sports property, the National Football Conference half of the NFL contract, for $395 million per year for four years. The impact of that deal on sports television will be analyzed further in the next chapter, but it is also critical to understand how it fueled the rise of the FOX network and altered the local television landscape in numerous major markets. When the NFL deal was announced, most FOX affiliates were on weaker, lower-rated UHF stations, although News Corp. did own a handful of more powerful VHF stations, including owned-and-operated stations in New York (WNYW), Los Angeles (KTTV), and Washington, DC (WTTG) that were part of the Metromedia acquisition in 1986 that launched the FOX network. The relative power of the affiliate group changed, however, before the NFL season arrived.

Signing the NFL contract was a defining moment for Rupert Murdoch and made the bigger headlines, but the second act was just as significant. In May 1994, News Corp. announced a $500-million investment in New World Communication. That deal gave News Corp. a 20% interest in New World, but far more significant was the fact that it secured a change in affiliate status for 12 local stations: eight CBS affiliates, three ABC affiliates, and one NBC affiliate. The stations affiliated with CBS were the most significant of this group, since it included powerful VHF stations in five markets with NFC teams: Dallas (KDFW), Detroit (WJBK), Atlanta (WAGA), Phoenix (KSAZ), and Tampa (WTVT), as well as Milwaukee (WITI), a large market for the Green Bay fan base, and Cleveland (WJW), home of the AFC Browns. The deal landed a sixth NFC market station, with KTVI in St. Louis switching from ABC to FOX. There would be other affiliate swaps and News Corp. would acquire New World outright in 1997, but there is little question that the events of May 1994, called a "sweeping realignment of the television industry" in *The New York Times* and a "drive toward big network parity" in *The Washington Post*, changed the game.[37]

The $1.58 billion that News Corp. committed to the NFL in December 1993 proved to be just the start of a buying spree for the newest of the four major broadcast networks. That was all part of what Fox chairman Chase Carey called an "event-driven programming" strategy to build the network.[38] Nine months after obtaining the NFC contract, Fox acquired the broadcast rights to the National Hockey League for five seasons. The deal with the NHL was quite different from that with the NFL, as the guaranteed cost was just $155 million over five years. The contract was a significant one for the NHL, however, as the 1994–95 seasons marked the first time in two decades that regular season games aired on a national broadcast network. The price tag was much higher a little more than a year later when Fox added rights to Major League Baseball, committing $575 million in November 1995 for a five-year deal that included the World Series in 1996, 1998, and 2000, a collection of other playoff games, the All-Star Game in 1997 and 1999, and a Saturday afternoon *Game of the Week*. In less than 24 short months, Fox Sports acquired rights to the National Football League, Major League Baseball, and the National Hockey League, and the fledgling fourth network was suddenly a force in the sports marketplace.

The $575 million that Fox committed to baseball in 1995 was the largest piece of a $1.7-billion, five-year deal with Major League Baseball that also included NBC and ESPN. A minor part of that deal also involved Fox, as the FX network obtained the rights to air two mid-week games starting with the 1997 season. At that time, FX was part of Fox/Liberty Networks, a joint venture between News Corp. and the Liberty Media unit of Tele-Communications, Inc., that also included the regional sports networks that carried the Fox name. That connection between broadcast and cable became clearer when Fox first claimed rights to NASCAR starting with the Daytona 500 in February 2001. News Corp. bought the first half of the NASCAR schedule for $1.2 billion over six seasons, which included rights to what were then known as the Winston Cup and Busch Grand National Series. That was a great deal of content, and News Corp. programmed NASCAR on both FX and Fox Sports Net in addition to FOX. It soon extended that integration to another cable network, completing the acquisition of Speedvision in May 2001. Fox/Liberty Networks had acquired a minority interests in Speedvision and Outdoor Life in 1998, but that did not provide control, and News Corp. sold its financial interest in Golf Channel and Outdoor Life to Comcast in 2001 and acquired the other two-thirds of Speedvision it did not own.[39] News Corp. moved Speedvision to Charlotte, the heart of NASCAR country, and soon after rebranded the network as SPEED.

In October 2012, Fox locked up NASCAR rights through 2022, committing $300 million a year over eight years, a total of $2.4 billion, starting with the 2015 season. Ten months later, in August 2013, it added races and years to that deal, signing a new $3.8-billion contract for 16 Sprint Cup races, 14 Nationwide Series races, and the Camping World Truck series through 2024.[40] While that deal linked Fox and NASCAR for the decade to come, the conglomerate moved forward without a 24-hour auto racing network. In the middle of the month that Fox Sports inked the new deal, SPEED morphed into Fox Sports 1 (FS1), and Fuel TV, which focused on extreme sports, including skateboarding, snowboarding, and motocross, became Fox Sports 2 (FS2). The programming on FS1 was more diverse than that on SPEED, but in the eyes of the Fox Sports Media Group co-president Eric Shanks, it was more about the Fox attitude:

> Fans know when they see the Fox Sports shield that they are going to get something that is probably a little bit different, done a different way, with on-air talent you really want to sit down and have a beer with, and you're going to have a little bit of fun.[41]

While the rebranding might have changed the attitude, it also came with an increase in revenue, as the carriage fees Fox Sports Group received from cable operators increased from an average of around 24 cents per month in 2013 to 48 cents per month in 2015 to 64 cents per month in 2017.

The consolidation and common branding of FOX, FS1, and FS2 followed the patterns set at other sports television conglomerates, but the Fox Sports Media Group was a little different in one area: regional sports networks. While the NBC Sports Group also included regional networks, which were part of Comcast before the merger, that collection of RSNs was at a much smaller scale than at Fox Sports. After acquiring a majority interest in YES Network in January 2014, Fox Sports Net Inc. owned and operated a total of 22 regional sports networks when sub-feeds are included, reaching approximately 61 million subscribers as of 2017.[42] Just as significant as the number of networks that Fox Sports owned was the number of professional sports teams with which it was linked. At that time, it held local television rights to 44 of the 81 teams in Major League Baseball, National Basketball Association, and National Hockey League.[43] While Fox Sports held national rights to Major League Baseball, it did not do likewise with the NBA and NHL, and there were not clear synergies between the national and regional services.

The Fox Corp. that welcomed the 2020s was altogether different from its predecessors, the result of the $71.3-billion deal that sent most of the Fox entertainment assets to Disney. Those properties are listed in Table 2.4. Gone was 20th Century Fox, the film studio that Murdoch acquired in 1985 as his first foray into the film and television market in the United States. That included 20th Century Fox Television, the production unit that produced *The Simpsons* and many of the primetime shows featured on the FOX network. Gone were the Fox regional sports networks, a collection of services that News Corp. cobbled together through a series of transaction and branded with the Fox Sports shield. Gone too were the final remnants of the satellite systems Murdoch once controlled that gave him access to Europe and Asia, Sky and Star, respectively, with Sky in the hands of Comcast and Star in the hands of Disney. That included two sports brands, Sky

TABLE 2.4 Fox Corp. television and streaming properties as of December 31, 2019

	Properties with Ownership Interest
Broadcast Network(s)	FOX Television Network and 28 local broadcast stations (100%), including 17 FOX-affiliated stations with 9 of those in Top 10 markets
National Sports Networks	Fox Sports 1 (FS1), Fox Sports 2 (FS2), and Fox Soccer Plus (all 100%), and Big Ten Network (51%)
Regional Sports Networks	None
Other National Networks	Fox News Channel, Fox Business Channel
Streaming Services	Fox Sports GO
Non-U.S. Sports Platforms	Fox Sports Racing
Sports-Related Websites	FoxSports.com

Source: Fox Corp. annual report for the 2019 fiscal year and corporate websites.

Sports and Star Sports, with the international channels that carried the Fox name also gone. What remained were the news and sports assets that were part of 21st Century Fox, including Fox Sports Media Group, which provided the sports programming for FOX and operated FS1, FS2, and BTN (Big Ten Network). Those properties are detailed in Table 2.4. With the "new" Fox Corp. focused on live news and sports, the latter was never more important.

AT&T Inc.: WarnerMedia Sports and DirecTV

AT&T Inc. carries one of the oldest brands in the business world, one that dates to the formation of American Telephone and Telegraph Co. in 1885, but it is a relative newcomer to sports television. The modern-day AT&T was built on the remains of Southwestern Bell Corp., one of the seven Baby Bells that were created on January 1, 1984, when AT&T Corp. gave up ownership of the local operating companies in a consent decree to resolve anti-trust action with the Department of Justice. Southwestern Bell changed its name to SBC Communications in 1995 and then to AT&T Inc. in 2005 when it acquired what remained of AT&T Corp. for $16 billion. While the focus of AT&T remained on telephony until the mid-2010s, the expansion of the corporation was evident at the home of the San Francisco Giants, which opened as Pacific Bell Park in 2000, was renamed SBC Park in 2004 following the merger with Pacific Telesis, and then became AT&T Park in time for the 2006 season.

The AT&T foray in the sports television resulted from deals that focused on other assets, but sports rights assumed a prominent role in those investments. In 2015, it completed the acquisition of DirecTV for $49 billion. That deal focused on the 20 million video subscribers DirecTV contributed to the merger, but it also included three regional sports networks – ROOT Sports Pittsburgh, Rocky Mountains, and Southwest – and a minority interest in ROOT Sports Northwest, as well as investments in the Tennis Channel, MLB Network, and NHL Network. The vertical integration of programming and distribution was a prominent concern in the FCC review of the merger, with a focus on sports programming.[44] That integration existed within DirecTV, but it was expanded with the link between that programming and the AT&T U-verse broadband video service. The Commission resisted claims from rival distributors that the combination would "disadvantage rival MVPDs by withholding or artificially raising costs for these programming assets" and did not impose conditions on the merger, including an arbitration condition that was part of the *Liberty Media-DIRECTV Order* that had expired.[45]

Far more prominent in the merger between AT&T and DirecTV was *NFL Sunday Ticket*, which allows subscribers to view out-of-market NFL games. While other such services, including MLB Extra Innings, NBA League Pass, and NHL Center Ice, are available through most cable, satellite, and telco providers, DirecTV had exclusive rights to *NFL Sunday Ticket*. When the AT&T acquisition of DirecTV was announced in May 2014, *Sunday Ticket* was approaching the end of a $4-billion deal that covered the 2011 through 2014 seasons and was in negotiations with the NFL. At that time, approximately one in ten subscribers to DirecTV also purchased the *Sunday Ticket* package, which started at $240 per season.[46] The NFL package was seen as being so critical to DirecTV that the $49-billion agreement allowed AT&T to "terminate the merger agreement in the unlikely event DirecTV and the NFL do not renew this contract."[47] DirecTV completed a new eight-year, $12-billion deal with the NFL in the fall of 2014, and the AT&T acquisition of DirecTV from Liberty Media was finalized in May 2015.

One of the stated reasons the FCC did not impose conditions on the transfer of control of DirecTV was that the AT&T broadband TV service, U-verse, was not available in Denver, Houston, Pittsburgh, or Seattle, the cities in which DirecTV operated regional sports networks, so it did not increase vertical connections.[48] That was not the case in October 2016 when AT&T announced the $85.4-billion acquisition of Time Warner Inc., since the integration of DirecTV and the rebranded U-verse (AT&T Internet) distribution platforms with the programming services under HBO and Turner Broadcasting raised myriad vertical issues. While Time Warner did not own either a broadcast network with prominent sports rights or a programming service that focused solely on sports, the rights to sports programming, most notably the *NBA on TNT* and NCAA Final Four on TBS, became a focal point in the government review of the merger and the subsequent attempt to block it in federal court based the argument that it would "substantially lessen competition and harm consumers."[49]

The complaint filed in the U.S. District Court cited a Time Warner report to its board of directors that stated, "[T]hese sports rights provide us with the base of must-watch content that should enable us to achieve our targeted rate increases."[50] Anti-trust cases hinge in part on the definition of the relevant market, and in June 2018, U.S. District Court Judge Richard J. Leon began his opinion with the following summary: "If there ever were an antitrust case where the parties had a dramatically different assessment of the current state of the relevant market and a fundamentally different vision of its future development, this was the one."[51] The court ruled that the government had failed to meet its burden to prove that the merger would substantially lessen competition and denied injunctive relief, with the U.S. Court of Appeals for the DC Circuit affirming that decision in February 2019.[52]

The AT&T and Time Warner merger was completed in June 2018 after the initial victory in federal court, with Chairman Randall Stephenson heralding the combination of the "content and creative talent at Warner Bros., HBO and Turner" with "AT&T's strengths in direct-to-consumer distribution."[53] The AT&T television and streaming properties at the start of the 2020s are detailed in Table 2.5. The three content units functioned more or less as private fiefdoms within Time Warner, a testament to their divergent origins. That changed under AT&T, with a

TABLE 2.5 AT&T Inc. television and streaming properties as of December 31, 2019

	Properties with Ownership Interest
Broadcast Network(s)	CW (50%)
National Sports Networks	Operates NBA TV and *NFL Sunday Ticket* without ownership interest
Regional Sports Networks	AT&T SportsNet Pittsburgh, AT&T SportsNet Rocky Mountains, and AT&T SportsNet Southwest (100%) and ROOT Sports Northwest (29%)
Other National Networks	TNT, TBS, truTV, CNN, HLN, TCM, Cartoon Network, and Boomerang (all Turner Broadcasting), HBO, and Cinemax services (all Home Box Office)
Sports Streaming Services	Bleacher Report Live and HBO PPV; operates NCAA March Madness Live
Non-U.S. Sports Platforms	None
Sports-Related Websites	BleacherReport.com (100%); operates NBA.com, NCAA.com, PGA.com, and PGATour.com through Turner Sports Interactive

Source: AT&T Inc. annual report for the 2019 fiscal year and corporate website.

new organizational model for WarnerMedia announced in March 2019 after the federal government lost its challenge in the Court of Appeals. That restructuring included the creation of WarnerMedia News & Sports, combining CNN Worldwide with Turner Sports, Bleacher Report, and the AT&T Regional Networks. Jeff Zucker, the president of CNN Worldwide, became the head of the new unit. While much of his experience was in news, including a tenure as executive producer of *Today* at NBC, he broke into network television as a researcher for the 1988 Olympic Games and oversaw sports at a high level as the president and chief executive of NBCUniversal. As part of that restructuring, the units within Turner Broadcasting were broken up and the Turner name was no more, outside of representing the first letter of TBS and TNT.

Summary

The road to conglomeration and, in turn, concentration in the ownership of sports television outlets in the United States shows no single path, but there are clear patterns to the collections that are in place. In the cases of Comcast, Disney, Fox, and ViacomCBS, broadcast networks are paired in each case with cable programming services devoted to sports content. The relative strength of these services varies, from the Disney-owned ESPN on one end of the spectrum to the ViacomCBS-owned CBS Sports Network on the other, but in all cases the outlets are under common management with at least some content flowing from one platform to another under a common corporate umbrella. AT&T is something of an outlier, since it controls just 50% of the CW network and that platform has not ventured into sports programming. The combination of DirecTV and WarnerMedia could create a powerful force as sports media markets evolve over the next decade. Sinclair Broadcast Group is the other conglomerate that now functions on the fringe of this group, combining ownership of the Tennis Channel and the Fox regional sports networks with one of the large local television station groups in the United States as well as other assets. However, without ownership of a national broadcasting network, Sinclair is a different kind of conglomerate.

Notes

1. David A. Wise, "Capital Cities Communications to Buy ABC for $3.5 Billion," *The Washington Post*, March 19, 1985, A1.
2. David A. Wise, "FCC Questions Whether CBS Had Changed Its Ownership," *The Washington Post*, September 18, 1986, E1.
3. Reginald Stuart, "For TV Deal, Murdoch Will Seek Citizenship," *The New York Times*, May 4, 1985, 35.
4. Federal Communications Commission, "Applications of Metromedia Radio & Television, Inc. to News America Television, Memorandum Opinion and Order," 102 FCC 2d 1334, November 27, 1985.
5. Federal Communications Commission, "Application of Fox Television Stations, Inc. for Renewal of License of Station WNYW-TV, New York, New York," Memorandum Opinion and Order, 10 FCC Rcd 4961 (1995).
6. Federal Communications Commission, "In re-Application of Fox Television Stations, Inc. for Renewal of License of Station WNYW-TV, New York, New York, Second Memorandum Opinion and Order," 11 FCC Rcd 5714 (1995).
7. Ken Auletta, "The Network Takeovers: Why ABC Survived Best," *The New York Times*, July 28, 1991, A20.
8. William Taaffe, "TV to Sports: The Bucks Stop Here," *Sports Illustrated*, February 24, 1986, 20.
9. "TV to Sports: The Bucks Stop Here," 20.
10. Quoted in "TV to Sports: The Bucks Stop Here," 25.
11. "ABC Unit to Buy Stake in ESPN," *The New York Times*, January 4, 1984, D4.
12. N.R. Kleinfield, "ABC to Acquire ESPN as Texaco Sells It 72%," *The New York Times*, May 1, 1984, D1.
13. Phillip H. Wiggins, "Nabisco Buying 20% of ESPN," *The New York Times*, September 12, 1984, D1.
14. Geraldine Fabrikant, "Hearst to Bay 20% of ESPN From RJR," *The New York Times*, November 9, 1990, D17.
15. Jim Spence, "View of Sport: Are Olympic TV Rights Worth the Price?" *The New York Times*, November 20, 1988, S11.
16. Paul Kagan Associates, Inc., "Marketing New Media," February 17, 1997; Kagan, "Network Economics: EPSN2," S&P Global Market Intelligence. Accessed November 13, 2016.
17. Quoted in Bill Carter and Richard Sandomir, "The Trophy in Eisner's Big Deal," *The New York Times*, August 6, 1995, 3.1.
18. Quoted in Bruce Orwall, "Disney's ABC Unit Weighs Deeper Ties for ESPN and ABC Sports Operations," *Wall Street Journal*, February 26, 1998, B2.
19. Quoted in "Disney's ABC Unit Weighs Deeper Ties."

20. Leonard Shapiro, "New NHL TV Deal Is Set to Be Announced; ABC/ESPN's $600 Million Deal Supplants Fox," *The Washington Post*, August 22, 1998, C3.
21. Leonard Shapiro, "NBA to Jump to ABC, ESPN," *The Washington Post*, December 15, 2001, D1.
22. Richard Sandomir, "Antitrust Inquiry Focuses on ESPN's Practices," *The New York Times*, June 27, 2004, SP9.
23. "Network Economics: SEC Network." Accessed August 31, 2019.
24. "Network Economics: SEC Network."
25. James Andrew Miller, "John Skipper Details His ESPN Exit and a Cocaine Extortion Plot," *The Hollywood Reporter*, March 15, 2018.
26. Bob Iger, "Question and Answer Session," *The Walt Disney Co.*, December 14, 2017.
27. Anthony Crupi, "Fox Regional Sports Networks Would Be a Game-Changer for ESPN," *AdAge*, December 5, 2017.
28. United States of America v. The Walt Disney Company and Twenty-First Century Fox, Inc., Complaint, 18 Civ. 5800 (S.D.N.Y. 2018).
29. Quoted in Ray Richmond, "NBC Plays Hardball in News Carriage Game," *Daily Variety*, June 4, 1996.
30. Richard Sandomir, "NBC Wins US Television Rights to Four More Olympics," *The New York Times*, June 7, 2011, B13; Richard Sandomir, "NBC Extends Olympic Deal Into Unknown," *The New York Times*, May 7, 2014, A1.
31. Quoted in John McManus, "'Tiffany Network' Slam Dunks NCAA Deal," *AdWeek*, November 27, 1989.
32. Quoted in Richard Tedesco, "CBS Bullish on Olympic Move," *Electronic Media*, May 30, 1988.
33. Geraldine Fabrikant, "Sports Write-Offs Give CBS Record Loss," *The New York Times*, November 2, 1991, D17.
34. CBS Corporation, 2005 Annual Report, Form 10-K, March 16, 2006.
35. CBS Corporation, 2011 Annual Report, Form 10-K, March 2, 2012; The Walt Disney Co., 2011 Annual Report, Form 10-K, November 23, 2011.
36. John Ourand, "CBS Confirms Its Commitment to Sports Following Departure of Moonves," *Sports Business Journal*, September 24, 2018.
37. Bill Carter, "Fox Will Sign Up 12 New Stations; Takes 8 From CBS," *The New York Times*, May 24, 1994, A1; John Carmody, "Fox Nabs 12 Affiliates From Rivals; Deal Boosts Network in Major Markets; CBS Is Hit Hardest," *The Washington Post*, May 24, 1994, A1.
38. Quoted in John Dempsey, "Fox's Hockey Deal Leaves Affils Chilly," *Variety*, September 19, 1994.
39. Peter Lauria, "Fox Gets Full Control of Speedvision," *Daily Deal*, May 22, 2001.
40. Tripp Mickle and John Ourand, "Fox Sports Adds Races, Years to NASCAR Deal," *Sports Business Journal*, August 5, 2013.
41. Quoted in Alex Ben Block, "Fox Sports 1 Execs Reveal Strategy to Take on ESPN," *HollywoodReporter.com*, July 22, 2013.
42. 21st Century Fox, Inc., 2017 Annual Report, Form 10-K, August 2017.
43. 21st Century Fox, Inc., 2012 Annual Report, Form 10-K, August 19, 2013.
44. Federal Communications Commission, AT&T Inc. and DIRECTV, Memorandum Opinion and Order, July 24, 2015.
45. AT&T Inc. and DIRECTV, 62–63.
46. Shalini Ramachandran, Kevin Clark, and Thomas Gyrta, "NFL Is Pivotal to DirecTV Takeover – AT&T Can Walk Away From $49 Billion Acquisition If Rights to 'Sunday Ticket' Games Are Lost," *The Wall Street Journal*, 20 May 2014, B1.
47. AT&T Inc., "Top Q&A for AT&T," Prospectuses and communications, business combinations, Rule 425, Filed by the AT&T Inc. with the Securities and Exchange Commission, May 19, 2014.

48. AT&T Inc. and DIRECTV.
49. United States of America v AT&T Inc., DirecTV Group Holdings, LLC and Time Warner Inc., Complaint, United States Court of Appeals for the District of Columbia, November 11, 2017.
50. United States v. AT&T, DirecTV and Time Warner.
51. United States v. AT&T, Inc., No. 17–2511 (D.C.C. June 12, 2018);
52. United States v. AT&T, Inc., No. 18–5214 (D.C. Cir. 2019).
53. AT&T Inc., "AT&T Completes Acquisition of Time Warner Inc." Press release, June 15, 2018.

Further Reading

Curtis, Bryan. "The Great NFL Heist: How Fox Paid for and Changed Football Forever." *Ringer.com*, December 13, 2018.

Deutschman, Alan. "Sly as Fox." *The New York Times Magazine*, October 18, 1998, 68–73.

Garrett, Alan G., and Philip R. Hochberg. "Sports Broadcasting and the Law." *Indiana Law Journal* 59, no. 3 (1984): 155–193.

Kimmelman, Gene, Mark Cooper, and Magda Herrera. "The Failure of Competition Under the 1996 Telecommunications Act." *Federal Communications Law Review* 58, no. 3 (2006): 511–518.

Ruane, Kathleen Ann. "Legal Challenge to the FCC's Media Ownership Rules: An Overview of *Promethius Radio v. FCC* and Recent Regulation Developments." *Journal of Current Issues in Media and Telecommunications* 3, no. 3 (2017): 203–213.

Ruane, Kathleen Ann, and Brian T. Yeh. "Selected Laws Governing the Broadcast of Professional Sports Events." CRS Reports to Congress, Congressional Research Service (2013).

Chapter Bibliography

21st Century Fox, Inc. 2012 Annual Report, Form 10-K. August 19, 2013.
———. 2017 Annual Report, Form 10-K. August 2017.
"ABC Unit to Buy Stake in ESPN." *The New York Times*, January 4, 1984, D4.
AT&T Inc. "Top Q&A for AT&T." Prospectuses and communications, business combinations, Rule 425, May 19, 2014.
———. "AT&T Completes Acquisition of Time Warner Inc." Press release, June 15, 2018.
———. AT&T Inc. 2018 Annual Report, Form 10-K. February 20, 2019.
Auletta, Ken. "The Network Takeovers: Why ABC Survived Best." *The New York Times*, July 28, 1991, A20.
Block, Alex. "Fox Sports 1 Execs Reveal Strategy to Take on ESPN." *HollywoodReporter.com*, July 22, 2013.
Carmody, John. "Fox Nabs 12 Affiliates From Rivals; Deal Boosts Network In Major Markets; CBS Is Hit Hardest." *The Washington Post*, May 24, 1994, A1.
Carter, Bill. "Fox Will Sign Up 12 New Stations; Takes 8 From CBS." *The New York Times*, May 24, 1994, A1.
Carter, Bill, and Richard Sandomir. "The Trophy in Eisner's Big Deal." *The New York Times*, August 6, 1995, 3.1.
CBS Corp. 2005 Annual Report, Form 10-K. March 16, 2006.
———. 2011 Annual Report, Form 10-K. March 2, 2012.

———. 2018 Annual Report, Form 10-K. February 15, 2019.

Comcast Corp. 2018 Annual Report, Form 10-K. January 31, 2019.

Crupi, Anthony. "Fox Regional Sports Networks Would Be a Game-Changer for ESPN." *AdAge*, December 5, 2017.

Dempsey, John. "Fox's Hockey Deal Leaves Affils Chilly." *Variety*, September 19, 1994.

Fabrikant, Geraldine. "Hearst to Bay 20% of ESPN from RJR." *The New York Times*, November 9, 1990, D17.

———. "Sports Write-Offs Give CBS Record Loss." *The New York Times*, November 2, 1991, 1.37.

Federal Communications Commission. "Applications of Metromedia Radio & Television, Inc.to News America Television, Memorandum Opinion and Order." 102 FCC 2d 1334, November 27, 1985.

———. "Application of Fox Television Stations, Inc. for Renewal of License of Station WNYW-TV, New York, New York, Memorandum Opinion and Order." 10 FCC Rcd 4961, 1995.

———. "Application of Fox Television Stations, Inc. for Renewal of License of Station WNYW-TV, New York, New York, Second Memorandum Opinion and Order." 11 FCC Rcd 5714, 1995.

———. AT&T Inc. and DIRECTV, Memorandum Opinion and Order, July 24, 2015.

Fox Corp. 2019 Annual Report, Form 10-K. August 9, 2019.

Iger, Bob. "Question and Answer Session." The Walt Disney Co., December 14, 2017.

Kagan. "Network Economics: EPSN2." S&P Global Market Intelligence. Accessed November 13, 2016.

———. "Network Economics: SEC Network." S&P Global Market Intelligence. Accessed August 31, 2019.

Kleinfield, N.R. "ABC to Acquire ESPN as Texaco Sells It 72%." *The New York Times*, May 1, 1984, D1.

Lauria, Peter. "Fox Gets Full Control of Speedvision." *Daily Deal*, May 22, 2001.

McManus, John. "'Tiffany Network' Slam Dunks NCAA Deal." *AdWeek*, November 27, 1989.

Mickle, Tripp, and John Ourand. "Fox Sports adds Races, Years to NASCAR Deal." *Sports Business Journal*, August 5, 2013.

Miller, James Andrew. "John Skipper Details His ESPN Exit and a Cocaine Extortion Plot." *The Hollywood Reporter*, March 15, 2018.

Orwall, Bruce. "Disney's ABC Unit Weighs Deeper Ties for ESPN and ABC Sports Operations." *Wall Street Journal*, February 26, 1998, B2.

Ourand, John. "CBS Confirms Its Commitment to Sports Following Departure of Moonves." *Sports Business Journal*, September 24, 2018.

Paul Kagan Associates, Inc. "Marketing New Media." February 17, 1997.

Ramachandran, Shalini, Kevin Clark, and Thomas Gyrta. "NFL Is Pivotal to DirecTV Takeover – AT&T Can Walk Away From $49 Billion Acquisition if Rights to 'Sunday Ticket' Games Are Lost." *The Wall Street Journal*, May 20, 2014, B1.

Richmond, Ray. "NBC Plays Hardball in News Carriage Game." *Daily Variety*, June 4, 2996.

Sandomir, Richard. "Antitrust Inquiry Focuses on ESPN's Practices." *The New York Times*, June 27, 2004, SP9.

———. "NBC Wins US Television Rights to Four More Olympics." *The New York Times*, June 7, 2011, B13.

———. "NBC Extends Olympic Deal into Unknown." *The New York Times*, May 7, 2014, A1.

Shapiro, Leonard. "New NHL TV Deal Is Set to Be Announced; ABC/ESPN's $600 Million Deal Supplants Fox." *The Washington Post*, August 22, 1998, C3.

———. "NBA to Jump to ABC, ESPN." *The Washington Post*, December 15, 2001, D1.

Spence, Jim. "View of Sport: Are Olympic TV Rights Worth the Price?" *The New York Times*, November 20, 1988, S11.

Stuart, Reginald. "For TV Deal, Murdoch Will Seek Citizenship." *The New York Times*, May 4, 1985, 35.

Taaffe, William. "TV to Sports: The Bucks Stop Here." *Sports Illustrated* 64, no. 8 (1986): 20–25.

Tedesco, Richard. "CBS Bullish on Olympic Move." *Electronic Media*, May 30, 1988.

United States v. AT&T Inc., DirecTV Group Holdings, LLC and Time Warner Inc., Complaint. US Court of Appeals for the District of Columbia, November 11, 2017.

———. No. 17–2511 (D.C.C. June 12, 2018).

———. No. 18–5214 (D.C. Cir. 2019).

United States v. The Walt Disney Company and Twenty-First Century Fox, Inc., Complaint, 18 Civ. 5800 (S.D.N.Y. 2018).

Viacom, Inc. 2019 Annual Report, Form 10-K. November 14, 2019.

Walt Disney Co., The. 2011 Annual Report, Form 10-K. November 23, 2011.

———. 2019 Annual Report, Form 10-K. November 20, 2019.

Wiggins, Phillip H. "Nabisco Buying 20% of ESPN." *The New York Times*, September 12, 1984.

Wise, David A. "Capital Cities Communications to Buy ABC for $3.5 Billion." *The Washington Post*, March 19, 1985, A1.

———. "FCC Questions Whether CBS Had Changed Its Ownership." *The Washington Post*, September 18, 1986, E1.

3

NATIONAL MULTI-SPORT NETWORKS

It was a masterstroke that announced the arrival of a new contender in the battle for prominence in network television and launched the transformation of the broadcast marketplace across the United States. On December 17, 1993, the National Football League accepted a preemptive bid from Rupert Murdoch for one of the crown jewels of sports television. For $1.58 billion over four years, the upstart FOX network, with its highest rated primetime show, *Married . . . With Children*, struggling to place in the top 50 on a week-to-week basis, acquired the rights to the National Football Conference.[1] In that moment, the conference of NFL royalty, including the New York Giants, Chicago Bears, and Green Bay Packers, ended a relationship with CBS Sports that dated back to the 1950s, trading the so-called Tiffany network for one fronted by Al Bundy. Ten days earlier, FOX executives made their pitch to the NFL television committee, trying to convince the league that the fledgling network was worthy of its marquee package. FOX opened the presentation with a video entitled "Revolution" and the changes to the television landscape that flowed from that deal proved worthy of the title.[2]

While the *NFL on FOX* fueled a four-way battle among the broadcast networks in the 1990s, a deal signed 15 years later confirmed the arrival of a new day in sports television, and this time Fox was on the other end of the stick. In November 2008, ESPN acquired the rights to the Bowl Championship Series (BCS), including the Fiesta Bowl, Orange Bowl, and Sugar Bowl, for $500 million over four years starting in 2011. The Walt Disney Co. also held rights to the Rose Bowl, a deal that included a clause that allowed for the migration of the game from ABC to ESPN if the BCS signed a contract with a cable network instead of an over-the-air broadcaster.[3] And in 2011, after the previous 59 games were broadcast on NBC or ABC, the Rose Bowl did move to ESPN with the start of the new BCS contract. What was significant about the deal was that the Disney bid was $100 million more than the best that News Corp. could muster to retain the rights. That agreement, moreover, came during what some have called the "Great Recession," which lasted from December 2007 to June 2009. In a statement after Fox elected not to match the ESPN offer, the network said,

> Even with today's vast economic uncertainties, Fox Sports made a very competitive bid to keep broadcasting the BCS games in every home in America, one that included a substantial rights fee increase, and certainly as much as any over-the-air network could reasonably risk.[4]

The last line revealed the sea change that the deal represented. The impact of the Great Recession on broadcast television, national and local, was severe, with Nielsen estimating the year-over-year decline in network advertising revenue at 3.5% in 2008 and another 9.9% in 2009. Fox paid an estimated $320 million over four years under the previous deal and was reported to have offered an increase to $400 million over the next four years but opted to go no further with a business model based on one revenue stream in the midst of a recession.[5] While the retransmission fees broadcasters receive from cable and satellite operators pursuant to the 1992 Cable Act now generate significant revenue, that was not the case in 2008. What made the difference was that ESPN did have a robust second revenue stream in addition to advertising: carriage fees it received through cable and satellite operators for approximately 98 million subscribers nationwide. The average fee per month per household for ESPN alone topped four dollars in 2009 and total affiliate revenue surpassed $5 billion for the first time in 2010. The carriage fees, with built-in annual increases, were part of agreements with cable, satellite, and telco operators, so there was less impact from economic ebbs and flows that impact on advertising.

ESPN claimed that "College Football Lives Here" in its promotional campaigns even before it acquired the BCS package, and it telecast more games than anyone, but the move of the four biggest bowl games and the championship from broadcast to cable was altogether different. That deal enriched the BCS and the major football conferences, but it also deprived millions of television households of the biggest games of the year. ESPN was in over 99 million households in 2011 when the major bowl games and championship moved to the pay platform, but Nielsen pegged the total number of TV households in the United States at 115.9 million in the 2010–11 season, so more than 16 million households could not access the games.[6] That was the focal point of critics when the deal was struck. Leonard Shapiro wrote in *The Washington Post* that the "voracious cable television wolf know as ESPN made another big, bad move" in "pouncing on the rights for the Bowl Championships Series" and reminded his readers that "even if most of us have become so used to ESPN's all-encompassing reach we sometimes forget we're shelling out money every month to our cable operators for the right to watch." The National Association of Broadcasters turned its attention to educating

Congress on the impact of such a deal, with its spokesperson, Dennis Wharton, asking, "The question is whether college presidents and athletic directors at publicly funded institutions should be complicit in disenfranchising 20 perfect of citizenry from access to the most popular college football games."[7]

The migration of sports programming from free-to-air broadcast networks to pay television platforms exemplified in the contract the BCS and ESPN signed in 2008 was a recurring theme in the decade that followed. The unwillingness of Congress or the Federal Communications Commission to implement regulations that stopped the bundling of programming services, a so-called à la carte model, enabled ESPN and other services to continue to raise their fees while mandating carriage on the most widely distributed tiers. That does not mean that ESPN and others were immune to changes in the marketplace, with cord cutting and skinny bundles hitting its bottom line hard. The average revenue per average subscriber for ESPN doubled between 2010 and 2018, surpassing $7 per subscriber per month in the latter. Over the same period, however, the total number of subscribers declined, from an average of 99.4 million to an average of 86.4 million in 2018. That slowed the growth of affiliate revenue for the network at a time when it was locked into expensive long-term contracts for professional football, basketball, and baseball, among others, including the BCS.

There was a second change in the marketplace that frames this analysis. As mentioned earlier, when News Corp. opted to walk away from the BCS after four years, the absence of a second revenue stream to counteract the carriage fees that ESPN could command was a critical factor. That too changed in the decade that followed. The 1992 Cable Act required multichannel video programming distributors to receive permission from broadcast television stations to retransmit their signals but did not state how broadcasters should be compensated for retransmission consent. In the 1990s, ABC, FOX, NBC, and others used their prominent station group to leverage in kind compensation, increased distribution, and/or revenue for programming services, including ESPN2, FX, and MSNBC, respectively, but that changed over time. In the 2010s, the focus shifted to cash compensation and those numbers became significant over the course of the decade. Kagan estimates that total broadcast retransmission fees increased from around $500 million in 2008 to $10.57 billion in 2018.[8] The vast majority of those fees went to stations connected to ABC, CBS, FOX, and NBC, with over 80% of the fees paid to owned-and-operated stations and affiliates combined in 2018. What is also significant is that in the same year those four networks received $3.070 billion in reverse retransmission, the network share of retrains fees paid to non-owned and operated affiliates.[9] The value of those deals was evident with the FOX network, which reported $1.708 billion in revenue from affiliate fees in its television segment for the fiscal year ending in 2019, a 24% increase over 2018.[10] Kagan, moreover, estimated that over $750 million of the total affiliate revenue FOX received in the 2019 calendar year would be in the form of reverse retrains fees from stations it did not own.

The analysis of sports television makes one thing clear: content is king and the programming that is most valuable in the United States is the rights to the professional leagues and collegiate conferences. To be certain, there are stand-alone events that bring prestige to the networks that carry them, such as the NCAA Men's Basketball Tournament and the Olympic Games. There are also packages outside of team sports that provide the bulk that networks desire, such as the PGA Tour on CBS. In the end, however, it is the numbers in the team sports that are most valuable, whether those are from the primetime slot for *Sunday Night Football* on NBC, the highest-rated series on television, or from the NBA packages with Disney and AT&T, with as many as 151 regular season plus playoff games on ABC/ESPN and 109 regular season plus playoff games on TNT. The examination of national multi-sport networks also makes clear that the separation of free-to-air broadcast networks from cable programming services is a false dichotomy. That is most evident with the rise of ESPN, but it is also clear with rights packages for properties such as NASCAR, where the races are split between Fox Corp. networks, FOX and FS1, and Comcast networks, NBC and NBCSN. These trends dictate an integrated approach to the analysis of sports networks.

The League of Leagues

The National Football League is the natural starting point for the analysis of network television and professional sports leagues. While baseball, basketball, and hockey might surpass football in terms of the number of available games, there is no disputing that football is the king of sports television in the United States. The preeminence of the league in television terms is evident in the sum of the annual fees collected from various rights holders, including multiple broadcast networks, ESPN and DirecTV in 2018, and in the total audience it generates for the Super Bowl, which accounted for 19 of the 20 highest ranked broadcasts through 2019, with the final episode of *M*A*S*H* in 1983 the lone interloper. The NFL also stands as something of an outlier, however. First, while the revenue from regional sports networks has created disparities between large and small market teams in the other professional leagues, the NFL generates almost all its television revenue from national packages, with pre-season games the only rights under the control of individual teams. Second, while Sunday remains the heart of the NFL week, the league was the first to create other marquee windows with the creation of *Monday Night Football* on ABC in 1970. Third, while baseball, basketball, and hockey migrated from broadcast to cable, the NFL remains a cornerstone of broadcast television, with *Monday Night Football* on ESPN and the *Thursday Night Football* games exclusively on NFL Network the exceptions, although even those games are broadcast in local markets.

There is another reason to start the discussion with the NFL, for without the power and prominence of the league, the structure of sports television in the United States might be altogether different. In the 1950s, when television was first establishing its roots, teams retained their media rights and negotiated their own television and radio deals with broadcasters. The league, however, exerted central control over those agreements, conferring on the commissioner "unlimited power" to "prevent any and all clubs from televising ... any or all of its game or their games" with a clear focus on protecting the local market for all teams.[11] The federal government argued that this was a violation of the Sherman Act, the foundation for anti-trust regulation in the United States that passed Congress in 1890, which states that "Every contract, combination ... or conspiracy, in restraint of trade or commerce among several States ... is declared to be illegal." In a decision handed down in the U.S. District Court for the Eastern District of Pennsylvania in 1953, Judge Allan K. Grim issued a split decision, blocking the NFL from enforcing parts of its television restrictions, while allowing the league to continue to prohibit teams from television games within 75 miles of another league city on the day that the home club of the other city was playing at home. That provision was designed to protect home attendance at games. While acknowledging that this rule was a "clear case of allocating territories among competitors," Judge Grim also stated that such an allocation was "not always illegal" and acknowledged that "professional football is a unique type of business," concluding that it was "both wise and essential that rules be passed to help the weaker clubs in their competition with the stronger ones and to keep the League in fairly even balance."[12]

The landscape changed forever more in April 1961 when NFL teams pooled their television rights and signed a two-year deal with CBS, which gave it exclusive rights to all league games. That agreement was for $4.65 million, a sum that was to be shared equally among the 14 teams in the league. The government went to court to block the deal, and while that contract was consistent with the balancing argument advanced in the 1953 decision, it did restrict the areas in which the games could be telecasts and Judge Grim prohibited the contract from going into effect.[13] That decision was handed down on July 20, 1961, but in a clear affirmation of the power of the NFL, the league had a solution to its dilemma in a little over two months as it took its cause to friends in Washington, DC, rather than fighting it further in the courts. On September 30, 1961, Congress passed the so-called Sports Broadcasting Act of 1961, which amended antitrust law and stated that professional football, baseball, basketball, and hockey teams could sign a "joint agreement" that "sells or transfers all or any part of the rights of such league's member clubs in the sponsored telecasting of the games of football, baseball, basketball, or hockey."[14] There was also a degree of social engineering in the act, as Congress stipulated that the release from antitrust enforcement did not extend to any agreement that allowed for the "telecasting of all or a substantial part of any professional football game" on Friday after 6:00 pm or on any Saturday from the second Saturday in September through the second Saturday in December. With that provision, Congress protected high school and college football from competition from the NFL.

That was not the last time that the NFL needed Congress to protect the pooling of television rights, and the mixing of sports and politics was a constant in such tales. In the mid-1960s, the proposed merger between the NFL and upstart American Football League came before Congress. The AFL launched in 1960 with eight franchises, and while some of those added a second team in major markets such as New York, the league also brought professional football to new cities, including Boston, Buffalo, Denver, Houston, and Oakland, with San Diego and Kansas City added to that list in 1961 and 1963, respectively. The fear that some of those franchises would fail with continued competition between the two leagues was palpable in hearings. NFL Commissioner Pete Rozelle argued in hearings before the House antitrust subcommittee that the merger was of "considerable public interest" since without such a combination "franchise moves and/ or failures will occur as a matter of course within a few years."[15] In time, Congress amended the Sports Broadcasting Act to include language that exempted "member clubs of two professional football leagues" from antitrust scrutiny in regard to pooled television rights so long as the merger "increases rather than decreases the number of professional football clubs so operating."[16]

In order to curry favor and secure votes, the two leagues agreed to expand, adding franchises in Atlanta and New Orleans in the NFL and Miami and Cincinnati in the AFL before the merger was completed in 1970. The addition of the New Orleans franchise was front and center, with House Majority Whip Hale Boggs (D., Louisiana) stating in the House hearing that "New Orleans is the prime candidate for a franchise in the merger plans. The New Orleans area is ready for a professional football team. It is what New Orleans and Louisiana wants. It is what the South wants."[17] That franchise also wielded power on the Senate side, as Russell Long (D., Louisiana) joined others to attach the merger bill as an amendment to a larger investment credit bill. The NFL-AFL merger was consummated, and the combined league was set to make billions in television revenue.

The long-term impact of the Sports Broadcasting Act on professional football is hard to overstate. In 1966, after the proposed merger between the NFL and AFL was first announced, the NFL received $22 million from CBS for exclusive rights to its games as part of a new three-year contract, while the AFC received $6.4 million from NBC in the second year of a five-year contract.[18] When the leagues merged four years later in 1970 and the National Football Conference and American Football Conference were born, the NFC and AFC were still aligned with CBS and NBC, respectively, with ABC's *Monday Night Football* debuting that same year. While the connections for CBS and NBC might have remained the same, the financial side of the equation changed to a dramatic degree, with the television rights fees from the three networks increasing 800% between 1970 and 1986.[19] The NFL received an average of approximately $46.5 million per season from 1970 through 1973, $67 million per season from 1974 through 1977, $161.5 million per season from 1978 through 1981, and $420 million per season from 1982 through 1986.[20] ABC, CBS, and NBC retained the same rights from

1987 through 1993, with the league adding a Sunday night package over that span. ESPN acquired the rights to eight games over the second half of the season from 1987 through 1989 with TNT and ESPN then splitting the entire season from 1990 through 1993. From 1990 through 1993, the league generated an estimated $900 million per season from its broadcast and cable partners.

The deal with News Corp. that moved the NFC from CBS to FOX in 1994 placed more money in NFL coffers, but it also set in motion an escalation in the fight for major deals in the years that followed. The departure of the NFC resulted in the exodus of some of the biggest names in CBS Sports. While the move of Pat Summerall and John Madden from CBS to FOX in 1994 was the most noticed, just as important was the departure of those behind the cameras, including Ed Goren, who became the executive producer at Fox Sports and brought a collection of CBS producers and directors with him. Far more deleterious for the network was the loss of the NFL as a promotional platform for its primetime programming as well as a lead-in to *60 Minutes* and its Sunday night line-up. As discussed, CBS also lost some powerful affiliates in major metropolitan markets. The network dropped from first place for the 1993–94 primetime season to third in 1994–95, which included a fourth-place finish in the cherished 18–49-year-old demographic, behind even FOX.[21] When the rating for *The Late Show With David Letterman* also lagged, a CBS executive recalled that when the network wooed Letterman three years earlier, it was a pitch based on three factors: CBS was first in primetime, possessed the stronger station group, and prominent sports properties, including the NFL. In an article in *The New York Times* in September 1995, a Letterman executive offered a summation of the state of the network, stating, "All that is gone now."[22]

The struggles that CBS endured without the NFL weighed on all network executives when the next round of bidding came to a head early in 1998, none more so than CBS Sports President Sean McManus. The son of legendary ABC Sports announcer Jim McKay, McManus arrived at CBS in December 1996 amid the network's decline and set in motion a plan to reclaim a piece of the NFL. A little over a year later, in January 1998, he made the walk from CBS headquarters in Manhattan to the league's Park Avenue offices to hand deliver an offer sheet that included aggressive bids for three NFL programming packages.[23] CBS was a different conglomerate than it was four years earlier, as the merger with Westinghouse that was finalized in 1995 added owned and operated stations in four AFC markets – Baltimore, Boston, Pittsburgh, and San Francisco-Oakland – while it also acquired a station in Denver and completed an exchange for a stronger station in Miami. Those additions gave CBS-owned and operated stations in seven AFC markets, so while McManus pursued all avenues to NFL rights, it was the AFC and not the NFC that provided the best corporate fit in 1998.

A few weeks after McManus's walk, the front-page headline in *The New York Times* focused on the role that CBS assumed in the just-completed television contacts between the league and its partners: "How One Network's Urgency

Spelled Riches for the N.F.L."[24] The new contracts spanned eight seasons, from 1998 through 2005, and while that was double most of the previous deals, the focus was not on the years involved but rather on the dollars. CBS acquired the rights to the AFC for $500 million per season, more than doubling the $217 million per season NBC paid under the previous deal. FOX retained the rights to the NFC for $550 million per season, an increase over the $395 million per season it bid four years earlier. The Walt Disney Co. committed $9.2 billion to retain the rights for ABC's *Monday Night Football* and to secure the entire season of Sunday night games for ESPN, an average of $550 million per season from ABC and $600 million per season from ESPN. That meant that NBC was left on the sidelines after 33 seasons with the AFL or AFC. The increase in television rights for the NFL was staggering, with the per season total doubling from just under $1.1 billion from 1994 through 1997 to $2.2 billion from 1998 through 2005. That total did not include the rights to *NFL Sunday Ticket* on DirecTV.

Two decades later, the NFL television landscape was much as it was in 1998. The one significant change was the return of NBC in 2006 when it acquired the rights to the Sunday night package, with ESPN moving from Sunday to Monday. That meant that ABC was out of the NFL after three and a half decades. The one package that has evolved to one degree or another is *Thursday Night Football*. The NFL Network debuted an eight-game Thursday and Saturday night schedule in 2006 under the tagline "The run to the playoffs starts here," and the Thursday night package remained on the league-owned service through 2013. In 2014, the league sold the rights to eight early season games to CBS, with NFL Network simulcasting those games and holding exclusive rights to another eight Thursday games as well as two late-season Saturday night games. What was unique about the relationship was that CBS Sports produced the game with its lead announcing team of Jim Nantz and Phil Simms, even when the games were NFL Network exclusives. CBS retained the rights to that package in 2015 before splitting a ten-game package with NBC in 2016 and 2017 with a similar arrangement between the league and the networks, with the combined rights fee at $450 million per season. In 2018, 21st Century Fox reached an agreement on a five-year contract to televise 11 games between weeks 4 and 15 for an estimated $650 million per season on FOX. The NFL rights holders for 2018 and 2019 are outlined in Table 3.1.

There are two things that stood out with the television rights to the NFL at the end of the 2010s. First, the financial commitment the networks made to the league is remarkable. In 2018 and 2019, following the new Thursday deal with FOX, the combined fees for the five packages – NFC, AFC, *Sunday Night Football*, *Monday Night Football*, and *Thursday Night Football* – totaled $5.6 billion per season. That total, moreover, did not include the value of the *Thursday Night Football* games reserved for the NFL Network – no small factor behind a carriage fee that surpassed an estimated $1.50 per household per month. That total also does not include the $1.5 billion that the league received from the AT&T-owned DirecTV

TABLE 3.1 National television contracts for the NFL in the 2018 and 2019 season

	Network/Corporate Parent	Start	End	Estimated Fee (2018 and 2019)
AFC Package	CBS/CBS Corp.	2014	2022	$1.0 billion
NFC Package	FOX/Fox Corp.	2014	2022	$1.1 billion
Sunday Night	NBC/Comcast Corp.	2014	2022	$950 million
Monday Night	ESPN/Walt Disney Co.	2014	2021	$1.9 billion
Thursday Night	FOX/Fox Corp.	2018	2022	$650 million (11 weeks)
NFL Sunday Ticket	DirecTV/AT&T Inc.	2015	2022[1]	$1.5 billion

Source: League and network press releases and media reports, including John Ourand, "With major media rights deals done, how will networks grow revenue," *Sports Business Journal,* November 3, 2014.

1 The NFL had an opt-out clause in its contract with DirecTV that allowed the league to end the agreement after the 2019 season.

for *NFL Sunday Ticket*, which brought the annual total in right fees to $7.1 billion. Second, the NFL remained a fixture on broadcast television long after other sports migrated to cable. The three marquee Sunday packages, the NFC, AFC, and *Sunday Night Football*, were prized possessions of three broadcast networks: FOX, CBS, and NBC. And even when ESPN or NFL Network held exclusive rights to a regular season game, it was also broadcast on local stations in the markets of the two competing teams. ESPN televised a Wild Card playoff game for the first time in 2015, but in subsequent years, Disney simulcast playoff games on ESPN and ABC. Even the entire NFL Draft, all three days of it, was broadcast in 2019, with ABC featuring the College Game Day announcing team to complement the more hard-core coverage on ESPN. That is perhaps the clearest measure of the television power of the NFL.

From Broadcast to Cable

There was a time when the coverage of professional baseball and basketball in the United States was much like that of football. Just as NBC and CBS televised the NFL from the mid-1960s until the mid-1990s, those two networks were also the long-standing homes of Major League Baseball and the National Basketball Association, respectively. Baseball bounced from network to network as broadcast television evolved in the 1950s and early 1960s, but in 1966, the Saturday afternoon *Game of the Week* returned to NBC and it remained there through 1989, anchored by some of the greatest names in sports broadcasting, with Vin Scully and Joe Garagiola and Bob Costas and Tony Kubek forming two legendary pairings in the 1980s. ABC Sports added another parallel to football with *Monday Night Baseball* from 1976 through 1989. In the mid-1970s, CBS acquired the rights to the NBA from ABC starting with the 1973–74 season, and it remained on the network through 1989–90, with Brett Musburger and Dick Stockton two of the cornerstones of that television franchise.

There was another development in the 1970s that signaled a change that would transform television coverage of baseball and basketball. In December 1976, Ted Turner converted WTCG, an independent station in Atlanta, into the first super-station, sending its signal to local cable operators far beyond the state of Georgia. When that signal was first transmitted via satellite at 1:00 pm on a Friday afternoon, WTCG was 30 minutes into *Deep Waters*, a little-known film that was released in 1948. And while Turner would later acquire the MGM film library and old films and television shows became a staple of his superstation, two other Turner properties were indispensable in its evolution: the Atlanta Braves and Atlanta Hawks, which Turner purchased in 1976 and 1977, respectively. In 1979, Turner purchased the call letters "WTBS" from the student-run radio station at the Massachusetts Institute of Technology to better brand his station as part of the Turner Broadcasting System. Soon after, the Braves dubbed themselves America's Team as part of a promotional campaign, a label that was codified in a 1982 *Sports Illustrated* cover that carried the title "America's Team II: Eat Your Heart Out Dallas, Here Come Dale Murphy and the Atlanta Braves."[25] The debate between the Braves and Cowboys for the mantle of America's Team might be a relic of the past, but there is no disputing that the rise of WTBS signaled the start of the migration of baseball and basketball from broadcast to cable.

The state of baseball on television changed for good over a three-week period in late 1988 and early 1989. The first shockwave came in mid-December when Major League Baseball signed a four-year contract with CBS that included just 12 games during the regular season plus the All-Star Game, league playoffs, and World Series starting in 1990. The cost of those rights alone, $1.06 billion or an estimated $265 million per season, was more than the combined fees NBC and ABC paid per season under the previous agreement. There was a more significant change, however. In the final year of the previous contract, NBC alone broadcast 32 regular season games, with 30 in the traditional *Game of the Week* slot on Saturday afternoon, including four doubleheaders, with ABC adding another eight night games. Under the new contract with CBS, the number of regular season games on free-to-air networks was slated to drop from 40 to 12, although CBS increased that number to 16 in 1990. It was not long before the other shoe dropped, as three weeks after the CBS deal was signed, ESPN agreed to a four-year contract to televise 175 games per year for a rights fee estimated at $100 million per season.[26] At the time, ESPN was available in 50.1 million of the 90.4 million television households in the United States, so approximately 40 million households were limited to just 12 regular season games on national television. In the end, CBS suffered an estimated $500 million in losses from the MLB deal, and baseball has become entrenched on cable and satellite services, outside of the World Series, All-Star Game, and a handful of other games.

There have been various shifts in the television landscape since then, but the general shape of the market remained constant. After ABC and NBC teamed with MLB in an ill-fated revenue-sharing venture in 1994 and 1995, The Baseball Network (TBN), FOX, and NBC split the broadcast package from 1996 through 2000. Those deals generated $975 million in rights fees over five years, with the value for the broadcast networks being on the post-season. NBC, in fact, paid $400 million for the 1997 and 1999 World Series; 1996, 1998, and 2000 All-Star Games; and a collection of games in the league divisional and championship series. What was unique about the NBC deal was that it included no regular season games. FOX did broadcast a regionalized *Game of the Week* through the summer months, including 16 Saturdays in 1996, but it too was focused on the post-season. In September 2000, Fox Sports and Major League Baseball reached agreement on a six-year, $2.5-billion contract that gave the network the World Series and rights to the League Championship Series for both the American League and National League in each season from 2001 through 2006.

The national television contracts for Major League Baseball that cover the 2014 through 2021 seasons show the results of the migration of the sport from free-to-air to pay television platforms, a pattern that extends to regional and local telecasts. The lone connection to broadcast outlets comes through the $4.2-billion deal between MLB and FOX. That agreement gave the Fox Sports Media Group the rights to 52 national television windows on Saturdays during the regular season, with 12 of those windows exclusive to the FOX network. The other 40 were non-exclusive windows that could be televised on "another nationally distributed FOX channel."[27] Not long after that contract was signed in 2012, SPEED was converted to Fox Sports 1 and that network carried a bulk of the Fox group games when the new contract began in 2014. Fox Sports retained the rights to the World Series, All-Star Game, and one League Championship Series under the deal and added coverage of two of the four Division Series. An agreement with Turner Broadcasting followed a similar pattern. Turner received the rights to Sunday afternoon games on TBS over the last 13 weekends of the regular season, but the real value was in the post-season, where TBS retained the rights to the other League Championship Series and other two Division Series as well as one Wild Card Game. The contract with The Walt Disney Co. was the one outlier, with ESPN receiving rights to just one Wild Card Game. The value for ESPN was bulk in the regular season, with ESPN televising up to 90 regular season games per season. The details of the national MLB, NBA, and NHL television contracts are outlined in Table 3.2.

The national television revenue MLB generates pales in comparison to that of the NFL, an estimated $1.55 billion versus $5.6 billion per season in 2019 not counting various subscription services such as *MLB Extra Inning* and *NFL Sunday Ticket*, which are discussed in Chapter 6. There is another significant difference,

TABLE 3.2 National television contracts for MLB, NBA, and NHL as of 2019 or 2019–20 seasons

	Network/Corporate Parent	Start	End	Terms	Regular Season Games
Major League Baseball	FOX and FS1/Fox Corp.	2014	2021[1]	$4.2 billion/8 seasons $525 million per season	52 regular season national windows on Saturday (12 exclusive on FOX and 40 on another FOX channel)
	ESPN/Walt Disney Co.	2014	2021	$5.6 billion/8 years $700 million per season	Up to 90 regular season games
	TBS/AT&T Inc.	2014	2021	$2.6 billion/8 years $325 million per season	13 regular season games (Sunday)
National Basketball Association	ABC and ESPN/Walt Disney Co.	2016–17	2024–25	$12.6 billion/9 seasons $1.4 billion per season	Up to 100 regular season games (up to 15 on ABC and up to 85 on ESPN)
	TNT/AT&T Inc.	2016–17	2024–25	$10.8 billion/9 seasons $1.2 billion per season	64 regular season games
National Hockey League	NBC and NBCSN/ Comcast Corp.	2011–12	2020–21	$2 billion/10 years $200 million per season	100 regular season games[2]

Source: League and network press releases and media reports, including John Ourand, "With major media rights deals done, how will networks grow revenue," *Sports Business Journal*, November 3, 2014.

1 In November 2018, Fox Sports renewed its agreement with Major League Baseball through the 2028 season, with the World Series and All-Star Game remaining on the FOX network throughout that period.

2 The original deal called for 100 games per season combined between NBC and NBCSN, but in 2018–19, NBCSN televised 100 games and NBC another 12 in the regular season.

however. In the case of Major League Baseball, the revenue generated through the sale of local and regional television rights are worth far more to some teams than their respective share from national packages, major market teams in particular. The lucrative relationship between the YES Network and the Yankees in New York and the 25-year deal that pays the Dodgers more than $330 million per season in Los Angeles are perhaps the most prominent examples, but there are also teams in far smaller markets that generate significant revenue through the sale of regional television rights. Regional sports networks are discussed in more length in Chapter 5, but it is important to keep that revenue stream in mind when comparing baseball to football and even to basketball and hockey. The basic structure of the baseball deals, moreover, could remain in place for years to come. In November 2018, the Fox Sports Media Group extended its deal with MLB to keep the World Series and All-Star Game on the FOX broadcast network through 2028. At that time, 21st Century Fox was finalizing the sale of assets to The Walt Disney Co., but "New Fox" was positioning itself for a future built around live news and sports.

There was a time when the NBA was a cornerstone of broadcast network programming across the winter and spring, most notably in the 1990s, when the league became a fixture on NBC and its chairman, Dick Ebersol, worked hand-in-hand with Commissioner David Stern to move the sport forward. That relationship was fractured, at least in terms of the league and the network, in January 2002 when the NBA reached agreement on six-year contracts with The Walt Disney Co. and AOL Time Warner worth $4.6 billion starting with the 2002–03 season, a little under $800 million per season. Months earlier, Richard Sandomir of *The New York Times* had written that "NBC will very likely retain the N.B.A. as the network's defining sport," arguing,

> It would be difficult to imagine the N.B.A. being so overwhelmed by an ESPN offer that it would let the cable network team up for a broadcast deal with ABC that would yield fewer games, promotion and exposure on ABC than it gets on NBC.[28]

That prediction came less than a month after September 11, 2001, when the impact of the terrorist attacks on the economy, and the television advertising market, was not yet known. With a second revenue stream (monthly carriage fees in addition to advertising), cable programming services were better positioned to weather the economic downturn. When the league did in fact trade NBC for ESPN and ABC, the headline in the *Times* read, "The N.B.A. Takes the Money in a Fast Break to Cable."[29] Under that deal, the number of regular season games available on a broadcast network went from around 32 with NBC to around 15 on ABC, with similar ratios in the playoffs, a decline from up to 31 to 12, with *The Finals* accounting for the majority of the post-season games ABC broadcast. The NBA had indeed become a cable sport.

The contract between the NBA and Disney stipulates that ABC is home to *The Finals*, an interesting nod to the free-to-air broadcast platform, but most everything else leading up to the championship round is focused on ESPN and TNT. The success of *Inside the NBA* on TNT, with Ernie Johnson, Kenny Smith, Charles Barkley, and Shaquille O'Neal, is a testament to the symbiotic relationship between the league and its television partners, as is the fact that NBA TV now originates from Turner Broadcasting facilities in Atlanta. Those pay television relationships, moreover, are backed up with real dollars. In 2018–19, the third year of nine-year extensions signed in 2014, Disney and AT&T paid an estimated $2.6 billion for their NBA packages for ABC/ESPN and TNT, $1.4 billion and $1.2 billion respectively. That total was a 180% increase from the $930 million per season the two paid from 2008–09 through 2015–16, which was a modest 21% per season increase the two paid from 2002–03 through 2007–08. The current deal was negotiated with the existing rights holders without bids from the outside, with the NBA in an enviable position given the launch of FS1 and the fact that most other major packages were locked up for years to come. The last two contracts also included expanded digital rights for ESPN and TNT, including the Turner operation of NBA TV, NBA.com, NBA Mobile, and NBA League Pass. The most recent deal also included expanded exclusive rights for ESPN platforms in Latin America and the Pacific Rim. The rights packages are all-inclusive partnerships.

The relationship between the National Hockey League and the NBC Sports Group is like those in the NBA, although it took the league some time to develop such a bond. The NHL was a cable sport through most of the 1980s, which included coverage on USA Network and ESPN as well as an ill-fated deal with SportsChannel America, a consortium of regional sports networks. When the rights moved from ESPN to SportsChannel in 1988–89, the NHL received more coverage and more revenue, $51 million over three seasons compared to a $34 million offer from ESPN, but the households reached dropped from 48 million to just 6.5 million at the start of the initial season.[30] The NHL retained some rights in that deal, and in time, it signed an agreement with NBC to televise the All-Star Game in 1990 and 1991, which was struck shortly after NBC acquired a 50% financial interest in SportsChannel. After three seasons, SportsChannel was still in just 15 million households, but the league agreed to a fourth season at an estimated $5.5 million for 1991–92, down from $17 million per season. At the end of that contract, the league signed a five-year, $80-million deal with ESPN, and limited games were broadcast on ABC in 1992–93 and 1993–94. The NHL appeared to find a broadcast home in 1995–96, when FOX started a four-year run, although its coverage was best known for the FoxTrax, a tracking system that included a visual glow around the puck and tails to indicate the hardness and speed of shots. ESPN retained the cable rights through that period, with Disney signing a new five-year deal with the NHL for ABC and ESPN starting in 1999–2000 for $120 million per season.

The end of that contract began what proved to be a dire period for hockey in North America, but one that would forge a new partnership in the United States.

Prior to the 2004–05 season, the league signed a one-year, $60-million deal with ESPN, half of what Disney paid under the previous agreement. The new contract did not include ABC, and with no other takers, the league reached a revenue-sharing agreement with NBC for two seasons. There was little risk for NBC, since the first income generated was used to cover production costs. The return of the NHL to NBC would be delayed, however. Far more significant but related to the reduction in television revenue was the decision of the NHL owners to lock out its players in September 2004, with the owners looking to link salaries to a fixed percentage of league revenue.[31] The owners and the NHL Players Association continued to negotiate over the months that followed, but after a flurry of offers and counteroffers in mid-February, Commissioner Gary Bettman announced the cancellation of the 2004–05 season, making the NHL the first of the professional league sports leagues in North America to lose an entire season over labor strife. Before the two sides finalized a new labor agreement in July 2005, ESPN declined an option for the 2005–06 season, eventually offering less than half the $60 million per season in the previous contract to continue, which the league rejected.[32] The following month, the NHL signed a two-year agreement with Comcast to televise at least 58 regular season games on OLN, which would later be relaunched as Versus. The deal was for $65 million in the first year and $70 million in the second, but just as significant was a commitment from Comcast to support the launch of NHL Network on its cable systems that included guaranteed distribution of the service.

The marriage of the NHL and the NBC Sports Group was codified in April 2011 when the two sides inked a new ten-year, $2-billion agreement that extends through the 2020–21 season. That deal was signed three months after Comcast completed its acquisition of NBCUniversal and nine months before Versus was rebranded as NBC Sports Network. That agreement was not a change for the NHL, as NBC and Versus/OLN had held the broadcast and cable television rights, respectively, since the 2005–06 season. While the distribution platforms were indeed the same, the overall operation was quite different, as the Comcast acquisition of NBCUniversal led to the combination of the sports content operations of the two units and an integrated production plan for the league. As discussed, the leader of the combined production group was Sam Flood, a former captain of the ice hockey team at Williams College. The balance between free-to-air and pay platforms under the current deal favored the latter, with NBCSN televising 100 regular season games in 2018–19, compared to just 12 on NBC Sports. Unlike the NBA, two games in the Stanley Cup Final in 2019 were scheduled for NBCSN before finishing out on NBC. Given where the league's television package once stood, however, the fact that NBCUniversal used its collection of networks, adding CNBC and USA Network to NBC and NBCSN, to ensure that every Stanley Cup Playoff game was televised nationally, was the clearest sign of progress.

A New Day for College Sports

The power to pool television rights and enter the national marketplace as a single unitary force transformed the professional sports covered in the Sports Broadcasting Act and created incredible wealth for owners and athletes alike. Congress is often unwilling or unable to write laws that make its intent clear, but that was not true in this case, as the legislation called out the four sports immunized from antitrust scrutiny and specified that it was the professional leagues that were protected. College athletics were not covered, but that does not mean amateur sports were not a consideration. College football was a focal point in Congressional hearings before passage of the act, but the emphasis in that case was on protecting the college games from the NFL and AFL. When Commissioner Pete Rozelle testified before the House Judiciary Committee, he spoke for both leagues in assuring the members that neither the NFL nor the AFL had any interest in moving games to Saturday, insisting that the AFL was "as anxious to protect the colleges as we are." Representative William McCulloch of Ohio made clear where the colleges and universities should turn, replying, "If they did not, I would think the colleges would find some friendly and sympathetic members of this committee who would try to right any wrong that would follow." As discussed earlier, the act that was signed into law included protections for both high school and college football, and in September 1961, when ABC Sports broadcast a single national game per week, it was hard to imagine that more needed to be done. The decision to include only professional sports leagues in the act, however, contributed to dramatic changes in college athletics a quarter century later.

It would be difficult to recognize the television coverage of college football through the 1950s, 1960s, and 1970s in the present day. The technology did, indeed, advance, moving from black and white to color, from analog to digital to high definition, but the real change is in the volume of games televised and the number of networks in the mix. In 1951, the television steering committee of the National Collegiate Athletic Association issued a report that argued "television does have an adverse effect on college football attendance, and, unless brought under some control, threatens to seriously harm the nation's overall athletic and physical system."[33] The report, moreover, concluded that "the television problem is truly a national one, and requires collective action by the colleges."[34] Based on those arguments, the NCAA imposed a moratorium on telecasts in the 1951 season outside of an experimental plan that included a single game in a limited number of markets on seven Saturdays between mid-September and mid-November. There were also three Saturdays blacked out in each market across the ten-week span to measure the impact of television on gate receipts at stadiums. An individual team, moreover, could appear just twice, once at home and once on the road. The University of Pennsylvania challenged the decision, announcing that it would still televise its home games on ABC in 1951.[35] The NCAA declared Penn to be "not in good standing" with the association; some of the member institutions scheduled to be the opponents in those games said they would refuse to play, and, in time, the Quakers capitulated. The complete schedule included 19 games in the designated windows, starting with Duke at Pittsburgh on September 29, 1951.[36]

The NCAA implemented its "Television Plan" in 1952 and sold exclusive rights for that season to NBC for $1.144 million, the equivalent of just over $11 million in 2019, with General Motors signing on as the sponsor. The schedule included 11 national telecasts, with no team appearing more than once and each geographic region of the country represented. The basic structure of that contract became the blueprint for college football for the next three decades. The fact that the NCAA moved forward with a unified plan did not mean that there was unanimous agreement or that the federal government did not see antitrust issues, however. The NCAA consulted with the Department of Justice in the spring of 1951 about anti-trust statutes and the feds launched an investigation that summer. When the NCAA refused to allow the local telecast of the sold-out Tennessee-Kentucky game in Lexington the following November, the governor of the State of Kentucky, Lawrence W. Wetherby, sent a telegraph to Attorney General J. Howard McGrath, asking him to intercede. In response to that plea, the Justice Department acknowledged that it had told the NCAA that its ban on telecasts was unlawful, but the acting chief of the anti-trust division, Newell A. Clapp, referenced the ongoing litigation against the NFL and said that if the universities believed that the NCAA restrictions were illegal, then the "decision as to whether or not to permit the telecast of the game tomorrow is in their hands."[37] The two universities chose not to defy the NCAA.

That proved to be a short-lived truce, with the Big Ten Conference advocating for a regional television plan prior to the 1953 season, starting with a proposal in which each of the NCAA's regions would set their television policy, whether that was limited television, unrestricted television, or no television.[38] At the time, Big Ten Commissioner Tug Wilson described the plan as "merely our preference," but the conference became more aggressive as its proposals were rebuffed. That led to an uprising at the annual convention in 1955, with the Big Ten and Pacific Coast conferences leading the opposition. Once again, state politics were part of the discussion, with Fritz Crisler, the athletic director at the University of Michigan, telling the convention that state legislatures in the member states were exploring bills to mandate that all games be televised. Five television proposals were discussed at the convention, including one that mirrored the Big Ten regional model. When the television committee prepared to release its plan in early March, reports indicated that the plan would mirror that of the 1954 season, to which University of Illinois Athletic Director Doug Mills said that the Big Ten "may be divorced" from the NCAA.[39]

The television committee delayed the release of its plan, continued to negotiate with the Big Ten and others, and released a revised plan a few weeks later.

Rather than a slate of 13 national games, as was the case in 1954, the revised schedule included a national game-of-the-week on eight Saturdays, with regional telecasts on the other five.[40] Individual schools were limited to one national and one regional appearance or two regional dates if the national slot was relinquished. The national/regional split with strict limits on total appearances became the new template for the college football on television. A decade later, when ABC Sports reacquired the NCAA contract for the 1966 season, the start of a two-year agreement for an estimated $7.5 million per season, the network announced a schedule that included eight national telecasts and six regional windows, wherein four games were telecast in different parts of the country, with a total of 49 teams appearing at least once and 11 appearing in both a national and regional telecast.[41]

College football found a home on ABC, with the network maintaining exclusive rights to the NCAA football package for 15 years, from 1966 through 1981. In June 1977, the NCAA and ABC agreed on a new four-year, $118-million contract that covered 1978 through 1981. That contract called for an increase in the number of televised games, with each market receiving 23 games a year, including 13 national games and 10 regional windows. There were other developments in 1977 that also were significant. In June, members of the College Football Association (CFA), a group of major football conferences and independents not including the Big Ten and the Pacific-8, held their first meeting in Atlanta and began to organize and elevate their voices within the NCAA. Later that summer, Warner Cable, a unit of Warner Communications Inc., signed an agreement with Ohio State and the NCAA to televise games on QUBE, an experimental pay-per-view system in Columbus. A late-season game between Ohio State and Indiana in November 1977 that ABC did not intend to televise but fell within one of the network's afternoon broadcast windows became a sticking point in that deal.[42] ABC called upon the NCAA to disallow the cablecasts and the association acquiesced. QUBE launched that December, and the following June, Warner Communications filed an antitrust suit against ABC and the NCAA, arguing that the two had "monopolized the telecasting of all popular regular-season college football game" in violation of the Sherman Act.[43] In time, the parties settled, which included an agreement not to file suit for two years, and Warner was allowed to cablecast five games in 1978 and another five in 1979. The two parties returned to court once again in 1980, but in that case, the NCAA television plan emerged unscathed.[44]

That period, however, was the beginning of the end for the relationship between the NCAA and college football. In July 1981, the NCAA reached agreement with ABC and CBS on a new four-year contract that was to cover the 1982 through 1985 seasons. For $263 million combined over a four-year term, the two networks received a total of 28 broadcast windows, 14 each for national or regional games. That represented a significant increase over the rights fee that ABC paid under the previous agreement. The contract also allowed for more appearances for the marquee teams, three per season, with up to two of those on national television. There were hopes that the increased payouts and appearances in the new contract would stem the rise of the CFA, but those prospects were soon squashed. A week after the NCAA announced its agreement with ABC and CBS, the CFA signed a four-year agreement of its own with NBC for $180 million. In response, the NCAA announced that it would take disciplinary action against member institutions that participated in the CFA television contract and that the sanctions would not be limited to football programs. In the face of those threats, most CFA members were not willing to support the contract with NBC, and the deal was never finalized, but those warnings proved to be significant.

In September 1981, the University of Oklahoma and University of Georgia filed suit in the U.S. District Court for the Western District of Oklahoma and were granted a preliminary injunction blocking the NCAA from initiating disciplinary action or otherwise interfering with CFA negotiations with NBC Sports. When the case was heard in Oklahoma City, U.S. District Court Judge Luther Eubanks said, "I want to create an atmosphere so you can settle this family dispute yourselves. I would like the court to fade into the shadows."[45] That hope was not realized; far from it. In September 1982, almost a year to the day later, Judge Juan Burciaga ruled that the NCAA was in violation of the Sherman Act and that the "veiled threats which came from NCAA officials and NCAA's entire course of conduct constituted classic cartel behavior."[46] Judge Burciaga's conclusion was most chilling, as he stated that the NCAA had suffered from a "self-inflicted wound" and that the court did not need to determine whether the NCAA was "motivated by genuine concern for NCAA members, by lust for power, or by rank greed. What is clear is that NCAA has violated the antitrust laws, and that the Court's duty is to restore competition to this monopolized market."[47]

The NCAA appealed the decision to the U.S. Court of Appeals for the Tenth Circuit, and while that court argued that the lower court might have gone too far and its ruling might be "construed to prevent the NCAA from imposing television sanctions on schools that violate regulations unrelated to the television plan," it did affirm in a 2–1 decision that the television plan was illegal.[48] The NCAA appealed that decision to the Supreme Court, and Associate Justice Byron White, a star running back at Colorado and the Heisman Trophy runner-up in 1937, granted a stay in the summer of 1983, which, in effect, granted the NCAA one more year of control. That ended in June 1984 when the Supreme Court affirmed the ruling from the Court of Appeals, arguing that the NCAA had "restricted, rather than enhanced, the place of intercollegiate athletics in the Nation's life."[49]

The impact of that decision was immediate and profound. The NCAA made a last-ditch attempt to broker a deal with the major football conferences, but that failed. The College Football Association then signed with ABC Sports for 20 national games, while the Big Ten and Pacific-10 conferences reached an agreement with CBS Sports for 14 national games. Both of those deals focused on the marquee time slots, with colleges empowered to sell the rights to games outside those telecast windows. What was significant about those contracts is that the major football powers did not find the rich payouts they envisioned, with the per-game, per-team average for national telecasts dropping from $700,000 under the NCAA deal to $300,000 under the CFA deal. And, in time, the deals created issues for ABC and CBS as well, with the ratings dropping from an average of 9.8 in 1983 to 7.2 in 1984 for the two networks, with each ratings point representing 10% of the television households nationwide, which Nielsen pegged at 84.5 million in January 1984.[50] There was a direct correlation between those declines and advertising revenue, with ABC reducing the price of a 30-second commercial from $57,300 in 1983 to $30,000 in 1984 and CBS dropping its prices from $59,000 to $38,000.[51] While the value of each broadcast decreased, the number of games available increased. The CFA signed another agreement with ESPN for 15 games, most of which were on Saturday night, while the Southeastern Conference created a 12-game slate for WTBS, which had aired a supplemental schedule through the NCAA in 1982 and 1983. That volume was a precursor of what was to come.

The television marketplace for sports television continued to evolve over the years, and decades, that followed. In late 1989 and early 1990, Capital Cities/ABC Inc. reached agreement with the CFA on two new contracts to commence with the 1991 season, the first a four-year contract with ESPN and the second a five-year contract with ABC. The terms of those deals were renegotiated just weeks after the ABC deal was inked in January 1990 when Notre Dame broke from the CFA and signed its own five-year contract with NBC that gave that network exclusive rights to all its home game from 1991 through 1995. The ABC deal with the CFA was reduced from $210 million to $175 million over five years, moving from an average of $42 million per season to $35 million, while a fifth year was added to the ESPN contract, but the per year average was reduced from $27.5 million to $25 million.[52]

At the time, ABC Sports was in the midst of an agreement with the Big Ten-Pacific-10 television alliance that ran through 1996, so the two deals gave Capital Cities/ABC first choice over what games would receive exposure – on both broadcast and cable – for most of college football's premier teams. That combination led the Federal Trade Commission to file a complaint against both the College Football Association and Capital Cities/ABC Inc. in September 1990, arguing that the two parties had "unreasonably restrained competition in the marketing of college football telecasts and among telecasters of college football games."[53] The complaint mirrored the issues raised in the case against the NCAA, but the Commission never ruled on the antitrust questions involved, dismissing the case in 1994 on the argument that it did not have purview over a non-profit.

There were other developments in this period that had a long-term impact on college football. In 1990, the Southeastern Conference announced that Arkansas and South Carolina would join the SEC, first with basketball in 1991–92 and then with football in 1992. That brought the conference to 12 teams and resulted in the creation of two six-team divisions, the East and the West. In 1987, the NCAA passed a bylaw that allowed conferences with 12 or more teams to split into two divisions and hold a one-game playoff without the championship game counting against limits on regular season games. The bylaw was designed to accommodate two Division II conferences – the Pennsylvania State Athletic Conference and the Central Intercollegiate Athletic Association – but there were no limits placed on the rule. The SEC used that loophole to become the first Division I conference to hold a championship game in 1992 and generate millions more in television revenue. In 1994, the conference announced that it would step away from the College Football Association that it had helped create and sign its own television contract with CBS. The five-year agreement was valued at $85 million and covered the 1996 through 2000 football seasons but it also included men's and women's basketball. The CFA announced in June 1996 that it would disband the following summer.

The model that the SEC established in the 1990s, including a championship game in football and comprehensive media rights that covered both football and basketball, became the model other conferences followed. And while the addition of Arkansas and South Carolina was predicated on the bid to reach 12 members, the addition of Texas A&M and Missouri in 2012 had more to do with conference footprint and television households reached. That was also evident when the Pac-10 transformed into the Pac-12 as the conference moved east away from the Pacific Ocean with the addition of Colorado and Utah in 2011, which brought the Denver and Salt Lake City markets within the conference. The Big Ten reached 12 teams and created a championship game with the addition of Nebraska in 2011, which was 21 years after Penn State gave the Big Ten a total of 11 teams in 1990, but the conference still moved east and expanded along the Atlantic seaboard with the addition of Rutgers and Maryland in 2014, moving it even closer to New York City and Washington, DC. The Atlantic Coast Conference was the most transformed of the super conferences, as it moved from an eight-team group concentrated in the Carolinas and Virginia in 1990 to a 16-team conference that extends from Miami to Boston and as far west as Louisville in football and Notre Dame in basketball. The media rights deals for the major football conferences are detailed in Table 3.3.

The transformation of television coverage of college football was most evident on the first weekend of the 2018 season, which extended from Thursday to Monday. In 1983, the final season in which the college football television schedule was under the purview of the NCAA, there were a total of 28 national and regional windows for ABC and CBS across the entire season, not counting bowl games. On the opening weekend in 2018, Disney alone televised a total of 20 games on its linear national networks – ABC, ESPN, ESPN2, ESPNEWS, and ESPNU. There were another six on the ESPN-owned SEC Network, which was regional in terms of the conference footprint but was built to be a national network, with around 60 million households in 2018. That collection of Disney networks alone offered almost as many telecasts over five days (26) as ABC and

TABLE 3.3 National media rights contracts for Power Five conferences as of June 30, 2019

Conference	Network/Corporate Parent	Start	End	Terms
Atlantic Coast	ABC and ESPN/ Walt Disney Co.	2012–13	2026–27	$4.2 billion/15 years ($280 million per year)
Big Ten	ABC and ESPN/ Walt Disney Co.	2017–18	2022–23	$1.14 billion/6 years ($190 million per year)
	CBS/CBS Corp. (basketball only)	2017–18	2022–23	$60 million/6 years ($10 million per year)
	FOX/FS1/Fox Corp.	2017–18	2022–23	$1.440 billion/6 years ($240 million per year)
	BTN/Fox Corp. (51%)	2007–08	2031–32	$2.8 billion/25 years ($112 million per year)
Big 12	ABC and ESPN/ Walt Disney Co.	2012–13	2024–25	$1.3 billion/13 years ($100 million per year)
	FOX and FS1Fox Corp.	2012–13	2024–25	$1.2 billion/13 years ($92.3 million per year)
Pac-12	ABC and ESPN/ Walt Disney Co.	2012–13	2023–24	$3 billion/12 years ($250 million per year)
	FOX and FS1/Fox Corp.	2012–13	2023–24	
Southeastern	ABC and ESPN/ Walt Disney Co.	2014–15	2033–34	$6 billion/20 years ($300 million per year)
	CBS/CBS Corp.	2009–10	2023–24	$825 million/15 years ($55 million per year)

Source: League and network press releases and media reports, including John Ourand, "With major media rights deals done, how will networks grow revenue," *Sports Business Journal,* November 3, 2014.

CBS broadcast together in 1983 (28). There were another 34 games streamed on one of the ESPN services – ESPN+, ESPN3, or ACC Network Extra – bringing the Disney total to 60. And that does not include the games carried on CBS and CBS Sports Network, FOX and FS1, or the conference networks ESPN did not own, including the Big Ten Network (BTN) and Pac-12 Networks. What is perhaps more remarkable is the financial commitment ESPN has made to college sports, over $20 billion counting the contracts for the Power Five conferences as well as the college football playoffs, more than $1.5 billion in 2019 alone. Those deals, moreover, do not include ESPN agreements with other conferences or the 14-year, $500-million deal ESPN and the NCAA signed for 24 collegiate championships outside of football and men's basketball that extends through 2023–24, including the Women's Final Four.

Most of the deals in question are rather complex, covering a range of media rights in most cases, and rather long, oftentimes covering 15 to 20 years. Both of those trends were evident with the extension of the deal between Southeastern

Conference and ESPN that was announced in 2013. That agreement, which extends through 2033–34, covers football and basketball and provided the foundation for the launch of the SEC Network in 2014. That network is owned and operated by ESPN as part of its agreement with the conference. The one outlier was one of the most recent deals signed, the six-year agreement the Big Ten Conference signed with ABC, CBS, and FOX. That media rights deal, which totals $2.64 billion, averages $440 million a year, nearly three times as much as the previous contracts, which is remarkable given the fact that it was finalized in 2016 when ESPN and other media were struggling with cord cutting and other economic challenges. What is also significant is that the Big Ten will be back on the marketplace prior to the 2022–23 season, before the Pac-12 (2023–24), Big 12 (2024–25), and ACC (2026–27), so it could be positioned to reap the benefits of a revitalized market.

Money Matters

There are various anomalies that arise in the analysis of national multi-sport television networks. Perhaps the most glaring relates to the National Football League. In 2018, *Sunday Night Football* finished the season averaging 19.3 million viewers, live plus same day data, making it the top-rated primetime show for a record eighth consecutive season. In terms of viewership, from September through December, it beat the second ranked show, *Thursday Night Football* on FOX, by 35% (14.3 million) and the third ranked show, *The Big Bang Theory*, by 52% (12.7 million).[54] That translated into the highest average price for a commercial for any show during the 2018–19 television season, an estimated average of $665,000 for a 30-second spot.[55] The story of *Monday Night Football* on ESPN was similar but at the same time different. In 2018, the average audience for *MNF* was 11.6 million, making it the most-watched series on cable and enabling ESPN to rank first among all networks – broadcast or cable – on Monday nights through the fall. The average viewers marked an 8% increase over 2017, but that number was still almost eight million per game, fewer than NBC on Sunday night, and contributed to far lower ad rates. And therein lies the oddity, for while NBC pays $950 million for a season of *Sunday Night Football*, ESPN shells out twice as much: $1.9 billion per season. The math, at least on the surface, does not add up.

The size of that contract was at least a factor in a series of layoffs at ESPN that culminated in 2017 with cuts that hit close to NFL programming, including analysts Jerome Bettis and Trent Dilfer, and reporters and writers John Clayton and Ed Werder. The analysis of the revenue generated from carriage fees from multichannel video programming distributors sheds some light on the topic. The average subscribers and average revenue per month for six multi-sport cable and satellite networks are detailed in Table 3.4. The ESPN business model was long predicated on inclusion in the most widely distributed bundles or tiers and negotiated annual increases in carriage fees, an approach that generated billions of

TABLE 3.4 Average subscribers and affiliate revenue per month for six multi-sport services: ESPN, ESPN2, Fox Sports 1, Fox Sports 2, NBC Sports Network, and CBS Sports Network, 2012 through 2018. Subscriber totals in millions

	2012	2013	2014	2015	2016	2017	2018
ESPN	98.8	97.8	95.8	93.0	89.9	87.7	86.4
	$5.00	$5.40	$5.94	$6.42	$6.61	$6.91	$7.12
ESPN2	98.7	97.7	95.8	92.9	89.8	87.5	86.3
	$0.67	$0.70	$0.77	$0.83	$0.85	$0.88	$0.91
FS1	79.9	84.5	86.6	84.9	84.9	84.9	83.9
	$0.22	$0.24	$0.35	$0.48	$0.60	$0.64	$0.67
FS2	36.4	36.2	40.3	47.8	50.7	51.3	54.7
	$0.15	$0.16	$0.16	$0.17	$0.19	$0.21	$0.22
NBCSN	77.0	77.7	79.5	82.4	83.3	83.8	83.7
	$0.25	$0.26	$0.29	$0.30	$0.33	$0.34	$0.40
CBSSN	45.2	48.6	53.0	55.0	55.0	53.5	51.5
	$0.11	$0.11	$0.12	$0.12	$0.12	$0.13	$0.14

Source: Kagan, a media research group within S&P Global Market Intelligence, accessed November 22, 2019.

dollars for the acquisition of packages such as *Monday Night Football*. In 2018, ESPN surpassed an average of $7 per household per month, which generated over $7 billion in affiliate revenue. That was in addition to over $2.5 billion in gross advertising revenue. Those figures also point to the impact of cord cutting, as the average number of subscribers in 2018 were almost 15 million fewer than when ESPN signed its deal with the NFL in 2011. At $7 per household, that amounted to over $100 million less in potential affiliate revenue per month in 2018.

Those carriage fees also point to significant differences between ESPN and the other multi-sports services on the cable and satellite platforms, with the perceived battle between ESPN and Fox Sports 1 the prime example. That becomes clear when one examines the data behind the two networks. The number of subscribers for four of the networks – ESPN, ESPN2, FS1, and NBCSN – were more or less equal in 2018, between an average of 86.4 million and an average of 83.7 million, which was the result of modest increases since 2012 for FS1 and NBCSN and significant declines for ESPN and ESPN2 over that same period. What is not equal is the average revenue per average subscriber the networks received from carriers. Fox Sports was able to double the average carriage fee around the launch of FS1, from an average of 24 cents in 2013 to an average of 48 cents in 2015, with more modest increases since then. Even with the increases, the FS1 fees are miniscule compared to those of ESPN, which received an estimated average of $7.12 per subscriber per month in 2018. FS1 was also well behind ESPN2, 67 cents a month compared to 91 cents a month in 2018, a 24-cent difference that amounts to over $240 million a year in affiliate revenue when applied to 85 million subscribers over a 12-month period. And that is where the notion of a head-to-head competition falters. ESPN generated an estimated $7.4 billion in affiliate revenue in 2018 compared to just $678.9 million for FS1. That was more than three times as much as SPEED generated in its final full year, but it did not give FS1 the resources to truly compete with ESPN for expensive sports properties.

There is another change in the television marketplace that impacts the competition between national networks. As discussed earlier, when the Cable Act of 192 first required cable operators to receive "retransmission consent" from broadcast stations, most media conglomerates used that to leverage increased carriage and/or fees for programming services, including ABC and ESPN2. Since the mid-2000s, however, station groups have increasingly focused on direct fees in exchange for carriage. In 2006, Kagan estimated total broadcast retransmission fees at $214.6 million, a dollar value that had increased to more than $10 billion in 2018.[56] For a conglomerate such as Fox Corp., those numbers are now quite significant and assume a prominent role in the acquisition of sports rights. In media and communication summit in May 2019, Lachlan Murdoch said that Fox no longer needed to "spread out the leverage we get from retransmission" to support "many of our emerging cable channels."[57] That would enable Fox to "focus it on revenue back to us" and Murdoch estimated that it could increase retransmission revenue by a billion dollars by 2022, stating that "critical sports right, the best sports rights" was the "best content on television."[58]

Summary

The analysis of national multi-sport networks over the last three-plus decades reveals the importance of content in the sports television marketplace, albeit with important caveats. First, there is a clear pattern in which the fortunes of national networks rise or fall with the addition or subtraction of major contracts. That was clear with the ascent of FOX and decline of CBS when the NFC package switched networks in 1994. Second, the fees required to secure those rights rose to a dramatic degree over time, most evident with the increase from the $900 million the NFL collected from four packages in 1993 – AFC, NFC, *Sunday Night Football*, and *Monday Night Football* – to the $4.95 billion those same rights earned per season starting in 2014. Third, those fees point to a delicate balancing act for the conglomerates that own these networks and services: being aggressive in the pursuit of such rights without extending past the point that hurts the bottom line. As discussed in Chapter 2, CBS wrote off $600 million in pre-tax losses from the sports contracts it signed in the late 1980s and early 1990s. Disney committed billions for marquee rights for professional football, baseball, and basketball and college football, only to see cord cutting reduce projected increases in affiliate revenue for ESPN, which contributed to significant staff cuts between 2015 and 2017. And, fourth, there are limits to the costs that conglomerates such as Disney and programming services such as ESPN can pass along to operators and subscribers without inducing even more cord cutting and making the situation even worse.

Notes

1. Leonard Shapiro, "And the Forth Shall Be First: How Fox Stalked the NFL and Bagged TV Deal," *The Washington Post,* December 26, 1993, D1.
2. "And the Forth Shall Be First."
3. Diane Pucin, "ESPN and BCS Confirm Agreement on Four-Year Deal," *Los Angeles Times,* November 19, 2008, D6.
4. Cynthia Littleton, "ESPN Bowls Over Fox," *Daily Variety,* November 18, 2008, 4.
5. "ESPN Bowls Over Fox."
6. Nielsen Co., "Number of US TV Households Climbs by One Million for 2010–11 Season." Press release, August 27, 2010.
7. Quoted in Cecilia Kang, "ESPN, BCS Deal Raises Questions," *The Washington Post,* November 26, 2008, E5.
8. Atif Zubair, "Economics of Broadcast TV Retransmission Revenue 2019," S&P Market Intelligence, September 10, 2019.
9. "Economics of Broadcast TV Retransmission Revenue 2019."
10. Fox Corp., Annual Report, Form 10-K, Filed August 9, 2019.
11. United States v. National Football League, 116 F. Supp. 319 (E.D. Pa. 1953) at 322–323.
12. *US v. NFL,* 116 F. Supp. 319 at 323.
13. United States v. National Football League, 196 F. Supp. 445 (E.D. Pa. 1961) at 447.
14. Telecasting of Professional Sports Contests, Public Law 87–331, 15 USC. 32 (1961).
15. *Professional Football League Merger: Hearings Before Antitrust Subcommittee of the Committee on the Judiciary,* 89th Cong., 2nd Sess. (1966), 33.
16. Suspension of Credit Act, Public Law 89–800, 68A Stat. 163 (1966).
17. *Professional Football League Merger,* 102.
18. *Professional Football League Merger,* 209 and 246.
19. United States Football League v. National Football League, 842 F.2d 1335 (2nd Cir. 1988) at 43.
20. *USFL v. NFL,* 842 F.2d 1335 at 43.
21. Richard Brunelli, "CBS: A Season to Forget," *Mediaweek,* April 17, 1995, 6.
22. Bill Carter, "'Letterman' Not Amused as CBS Ratings Fizzle," *The New York Times,* September 25, 1995, D1.
23. Richard Sandomir, "How One Network's Urgency Spelled Riches for the N.F.L.," *The New York Times,* January 17, 1998, A1.
24. "How One Network's Urgency Spelled Riches for the N.F.L."
25. "America's Team II: Eat Your Heart Out, Dallas, Here Come Dale Murphy and the Atlanta Braves," *Sports Illustrated,* August 9, 1982.
26. Jeremy Gerard, "ESPN Will Pay $400 Million for Baseball-Game Rights," *The New York Times,* January 6, 1989, D1.
27. Major League Baseball, "MLB, Fox and Turner Reach New Eight-Year Television Agreements." Press release, October 2, 2012.
28. Richard Sandomir, "The N.B.A. Negotiates in a Changed World," *The New York Times,* October 5, 2001, D14.
29. Richard Sandomir, "The N.B.A. Takes the Money in a Fast Break to Cable," January 23, 2002, D3.
30. Norman Chad, "NHL and SportsChannel: More Is Less," *The Washington Post,* November 26, 1988, D6.

31. Joe Lapointe, "Expected N.H.L. Lockout Curbs the Enthusiasm," *The New York Times,* September 14, 2004, D4.
32. Duncan Currie, "The NHL on Ice; ESPN Bids the NHL Adieu. Could Things Get Any Worse for Pro Hockey?" *The Daily Standard,* June 10, 2005.
33. National Collegiate Athletic Association v. Board of Regents of the University of Oklahoma, 468 US 85 (1984), at 89–90.
34. *NCAA v. Board of Regents,* 468 U.S at 90.
35. *NCAA v. Board of Regents,* 468 U.S at 90.
36. Paul Zimmerman, "Four Major Grid Tilts to Be Television Here," *Los Angeles Times,* September 6, 1951.
37. Associated Press, "Government Says TV Restrictions Are Illegal," *The Washington Post,* November 24, 1951, 10.
38. Associated Press, "Big Ten Proposed Control of Football TV Regionally," *The New York Times,* December 7, 1952, S1.
39. Associated Press, "NCAA Delays TV Plan," *The New York Times,* March 3, 1955, 33.
40. United Press International, "NCAA Members Adopt Plan for Football TV 'Compromise'," *The New York Times,* March 25, 1955, 29.
41. Gordon S. White Jr., "NCAA TV Games to Start Sept. 10," *The New York Times,* June 7, 1960, 50.
42. Ellen Graham, "Proposed Cablecast of Football Contest Brings ABC Protest," *The Wall Street Journal,* September 26, 1977, 24.
43. Warner Amex Cable v. American Broadcasting, 499 F. Supp. 537 (S.D. Ohio 1980).
44. Brian L. Porto, *The Supreme Court and the NCAA* (Ann Arbor, MI: The University of Michigan Press, 2012), 37–39.
45. United Press International, "Judge Bars NCAA Action," *The Washington Post,* September 19, 1981, D5.
46. Board of Regents of the University of Oklahoma and the University of Georgia Athletic Association v. National Collegiate Athletic Association, 546 F. Supp. 1276 (W.D. Okla. 1982), 1295.
47. *Board of Regents v. NCAA,* 546 F. Supp. at 1328.
48. Board of Regents v. National Collegiate Athletic Association, 707 F. 2d 1147 (10th Cir. 1983).
49. *NCAA v. Board of Regents,* 468 US 85.
50. Steve Wieberg, "Flop Go the Ratings," *USA Today,* August 23, 1994, 8C.
51. Peter Kerr, "Madison Ave.'s Football Woes," *The New York Times,* September 22, 1984, 39.
52. Robert McG. Thomas, "College Football Contracts for Television Are Reduced," *The New York Times,* February 1, 1990, 26.
53. Federal Trade Commission, College Football Association, et al, Final order, opinion, etc., in regard to alleged violation of Sec. 5 of the Federal Trade Commission Act, 117 F.T.C. 971 (1994).
54. NBC Sports Group, "NBC 'Sunday Night Football' on Pace to Be TV's #1 Primetime Show for Unprecedented 8th Consecutive Year; Viewership up 7% From '17." Press release, January 2, 2019.
55. Jeanine Poggi, "Here's How Much It Costs to Advertise in TV's Biggest Shows," *AdAge.com,* October 2, 2018. https://adage.comarticle/media/tv-pricing-chart /315120
56. Justin Nielsen, "Retrans Projections Update: Sub Rates Continue to Rise," S&P Global Market Intelligence, June 13, 2019. Accessed June 18, 2019.
57. Lachlan Murdoch, "Fox Corporation at the MoffettNathanson 6th Annual Media & Communication Summit," May 14, 2019. https://investor.foxcorporation.com/ events/event-details/moffettnathanson-conference
58. "Fox Corporation at the MoffettNathanson."

Further Reading

Cressman, Dale L., and Lisa Swenson. "The Pigskin and the Picture Tube: The National Football League's First Full Season on the CBS Television Network." *Journal of Broadcasting & Electronic Media* (September 2007): 479–497.

Fortunato, John A. "Agenda-Setting Through the Television Programming Schedule: An Examination of Major League Baseball on Fox." *International Journal of Media Management* 18, nos. 3–4 (2016): 163–180.

Grow, Nathanial. "The Enduring Power of the Sports Broadcasting Act." In *The Oxford Handbook of American Sports Law*, edited by Michael A. McCann. New York: Oxford University Press, 2018.

Leibovich, Mark. "Undefeated." *The New York Times Magazine*, February 7, 2016, 38–45.

Mitten, Matthew J., and Aaron Hernandez. "The Sports Broadcasting Act of 1961: A Comparative Analysis of Its Effects on Competitive Balance in the NFL and NCAA Division I FBS Football." *Ohio Northern University Law Review* 39 (2013): 745–772.

Tolbert, Mary H., and D. Kent Meyers. "The Lasting Impact of *NCAA v Bd. Of Regents of the University of Oklahoma:* The Football Fan Wins." *The Oklahoma Bar Journal* 89, no. 26 (October 2018): 22–25.

Chapter Bibliography

Associated Press. "Government Says TV Restrictions Are Illegal." *The Washington Post*, November 24, 1951, 10.

————. "Big Ten Proposed Control of Football TV Regionally." *The New York Times*, December 7, 1952, S1.

————. "NCAA Delays TV Plan." *The New York Times*, March 3, 1955, 33.

Board of Regents of the University of Oklahoma and the University of Georgia Athletic Association v. National Collegiate Athletic Association. 546 F. Supp. 1276 (W.D. Okla. 1982).

Board of Regents v. National Collegiate Athletic Association, 707 F.2d 1147 (10th Cir. 1983).

Brunelli, Richard. "CBS: A Season to Forget." *Mediaweek*, April 17, 1995, 6.

Carter, Bill. "'Letterman' Not Amused as CBS Ratings Fizzle." *The New York Times*, September 25, 1995, D1.

Chad, Norman. "NHL and SportsChannel: More Is Less." *The Washington Post*, November 26, 1988, D6.

Cressman, Dale L., and Lisa Swenson. "The Pigskin and the Picture Tube: The National Football League's First Full Season on the CBS Television Network." *Journal of Broadcasting & Electronic Media* (September 2007): 479–497.

Currie, Duncan. "The NHL on Ice; ESPN Bids the NHL adieu. Could Things Get Any Worse for pro Hockey?" *The Daily Standard*, June 10, 2005.

Federal Trade Commission. College Football Association, et al, Final order, opinion, etc., in regard to alleged violation of Sec. 5 of the Federal Trade Commission Act. 117 F.T.C. 971 (1994).

Fortunato, John A. "Agenda-Setting Through the Television Programming Schedule: An Examination of Major League Baseball on Fox." *International Journal of Media Management* 18, nos. 3–4 (2016): 163–180.

Fox Corp. Annual Report, Form 10-K. August 9, 2019.

Gerard, Jeremy. "ESPN Will Pay $400 Million for Baseball-Game Rights." *The New York Times*, January 6, 1989, D1.

Graham, Ellen. "Proposed Cablecast of Football Contest Brings ABC Protest." *The Wall Street Journal*, September 26, 1977, 24.

Grow, Nathanial. "The Enduring Power of the Sports Broadcasting Act." In *The Oxford Handbook of American Sports Law*, edited by Michael A. McCann. New York: Oxford University Press, 2018.

Kang, Cecilia. "ESPN, BCS Deal Raises Questions." *The Washington Post*, November 26, 2008, E5.

Kerr, Peter. "Madison Ave.'s Football Woes." *The New York Times*, September 22, 1984, 39.

Lapointe, Joe. "Expected N.H.L. Lockout Curbs the Enthusiasm." *The New York Times*, September 14, 2004, D4.

Leibovich, Mark. "Undefeated." *The New York Times Magazine*, February 7, 2016, 38–45.

Littleton, Cynthia. "ESPN Bowls Over Fox." *Daily Variety*, November 18, 2008.

Major League Baseball. "MLB, Fox and Turner Reach New Eight-Year Television Agreements." Press release, October 2, 2012.

Mitten, Matthew J., and Aaron Hernandez. "The Sports Broadcasting Act of 1961: A Comparative Analysis of Its Effects on Competitive Balance in the NFL and NCAA Division I FBS Football." *Ohio Northern University Law Review* 39 (2013): 745–772.

Murdoch, Lachlan. "Fox Corporation at the MoffettNathanson 6th Annual Media & Communication Summit." May 14, 2019. https://investor.foxcorporation.com

National Collegiate Athletic Association v. Board of Regents of the University of Oklahoma. 468 US 85 (1984).

NBC Sports Group. "NBC 'Sunday Night Football' on Pace to Be TV's #1 Primetime Show for Unprecedented 8th Consecutive Year; Viewership up 7% From '17." Press release, January 2, 2019. https://nbcsportsgrouppressbox.com

Nielsen Co. "Number of US TV Households Climbs by One Million for 2010–11 Season." Press release, August 27, 2010.

Nielsen, Justin. "Retrans Projections Update: Sub Rates Continue to Rise." S&P Global Market Intelligence, June 13, 2019. Accessed June 18, 2019.

Ourand, John. "With Major Media Rights Deals Done, How Will Networks Grow Revenue." *Sports Business Journal*, November 3, 2014.

———. "ESPN Stays in the Game." *Sports Business Journal*, June 20, 2016.

Poggi, Jeanine. "Here's How Much It Costs to Advertise in TV's Biggest Shows." *AdAge. com*, October 2, 2018. https://adage.comarticle/media/tv-pricing-chart/315120.

Porto, Brian L. *The Supreme Court and the NCAA*. Ann Arbor, MI: The University of Michigan Press, 2012.

Professional Football League Merger: Hearings Before Antitrust Subcommittee of the Committee on the Judiciary, 89th Cong., 2nd Sess. (1966).

Pucin, Diane. "ESPN and BCS Confirm Agreement on Four-Year Deal." *Los Angeles Times*, November 19, 2008, D6.

Sandomir, Richard. "How One Network's Urgency Spelled Riches for the N.F.L." *The New York Times*, January 17, 1998, A1.

———. "The N.B.A. Negotiates in a Changed World." *The New York Times*, October 5, 2001, D14.

———. "The N.B.A. Takes the Money in a Fast Break to Cable." *The New York Times*, January 23, 2002, D3.

Shapiro, Leonard. "And the Forth Shall Be First: How Fox Stalked the NFL and Bagged TV Deal." *The Washington Post*, December 26, 1993, D1.

Sports Illustrated. "America's Team II: Eat Your Heart Out, Dallas, Here Come Dale Murphy and the Atlanta Braves." Cover, August 9, 1982.

Suspension of Credit Act. Public Law 89–800, 68A Stat. 163 (1966).

Telecasting of Professional Sports Contests. Public Law 87–331, 15 USC. 32 (1961).

Thomas, Robert McG. "College Football Contracts for Television Are Reduced." *The New York Times*, February 1, 1990, 26.

Tolbert, Mary H., and D. Kent Meyers. "The Lasting Impact of *NCAA v Bd. Of Regents of the University of Oklahoma:* The Football Fan Wins." *The Oklahoma Bar Journal* 89, no. 26 (October 2018): 22–25.

United Press International. "NCAA Members Adopt Plan for Football TV 'Compromise'." *The New York Times*, March 25, 1955, 29.

———. "Judge Bars NCAA Action." *The Washington Post*, September 19, 1981, D5.

United States Football League v. National Football League. 842 F.2d 1335 (2nd Cir. 1988).

United States v. National Football League. 116 F. Supp. 319 (E.D. Pa. 1953).

———. 196 F. Supp. 445 (E.D. Pa. 1961).

Warner Amex Cable v. American Broadcasting. 499 F. Supp. 537 (S.D. Ohio 1980).

White Jr., Gordon S. "NCAA TV Games to Start Sept. 10." *The New York Times*, June 7, 1960, 50.

Wieberg, Steve. "Flop Go the Ratings." *USA Today*, August 23, 1994, 8C.

Zimmerman, Paul. "Four Major Grid Tilts to Be Television Here." *Los Angeles Times*, September 6, 1951, C1.

Zubair, Atif. "Economics of Broadcast TV Retransmission Revenue 2019." S&P Market Intelligence, September 10, 2019.

4

NATIONAL SINGLE SPORT, LEAGUE, AND CONFERENCE NETWORKS

The stated purpose of the Cable Television Consumer Protection and Competition Act of 1992 was to "promote the availability to the public of a diversity of views and information through cable television and other video distribution media" and "ensure" the expansion of "capacity and programs offered" over cable systems.[1] Toward that end, Congress "imposed" on the Federal Communications Commission annual reporting requirements, mandating that the Commission study the state of competition in the video marketplace. There are numerous flaws with the FCC reports, including an over-reliance on trade associations for data, but these studies also provide documentation of the ideas that circulated as cable and satellite technologies evolved.[2] The list of "Planned National Programming Services" in the Fourth Annual Report, released in January 1998, included networks targeted at corporate executives (CEO Channel), hobbyists (Sewing and Needle Arts Network), moviegoers (The B-Movie Network), museumgoers (M1-The Museum Channel), and shoppers (The Outlet Mall Network).[3] The lists were an annual tribute to perceived niches in the marketplace and the entrepreneurs hoping to reach them. Not surprisingly, services focused on sports were prominent on those lists. The Tenth Annual Report, released in 2004, included the Boxing Channel, Ice Channel, and Martial Arts Action Network on the list of planned channels, while TFN: The Football Network was on the list of operating unaffiliated national services (those without a connection to multichannel video programming distributors).[4]

TFN: The Football Network did appear in a few hundred thousand homes for a matter of months in 2003. In the end, however, it became little more than a footnote to an onslaught of niche networks that were aligned with distributors, such as the Golf Channel; were connected with integrated media conglomerates through ownership, such as the SEC Network; or were connected to high value content, such as the NFL Network. The evolution of such services and the conditions that appear to promote success are worth considering. The Outdoor Channel launched in 1993 with a mix of hunting, fishing, and shooting sports and related lifestyle programming. That was two years before the Outdoor Life Network (OLN) debuted with similar programming. The Outdoor Channel remained true to its programming roots but struggled to gain subscribers, reaching only 24.4 million households more than a decade later in March 2005.[5] OLN followed a far different pattern, surpassing 25 million subscribers within five years and 50 million within ten years.[6] The biggest difference was that three prominent cable operators, Comcast, Continental, and Cox, launched OLN, while the Outdoor Channel went out on its own. The name and genre of the network would change, from OLN to Versus to NBC Sports Network, and from hunting, fishing, and shooting to more mainstream sports. The one constant, however, was more significant, as over time it became an important part of the Comcast collection of services, with that corporation acquiring the 82.3% of OLN that it did not own in October 2001 in a deal with the News Corp.-owned Fox Entertainment Group.[7] In a separate but related transaction, News Corp. acquired the Comcast interest in Speedvision and rebranded the service as SPEED, which it converted to Fox Sports 1 in 2013. The question that remained unanswered was whether single sport, league, and/or conference networks could succeed without such links.

Single Sport Networks

The Golf Channel and Tennis Channel were two of the services included in the lists of national video programming services in the Tenth Annual Report on the video marketplace when it was released in 2004.[8] The two services, however, were on different lists. The Golf Channel was on the list of programming services in which multiple system operators held a financial interest. The Comcast stake reached 99.9% in December 2003 when it acquired 8.6% of the Golf Channel from the Tribune Co., which coincided with a deal to create Comcast SportsNet Chicago with a group of Chicago team owners that included the *Tribune*, the parent corporation of the Cubs at that time. The Tennis Channel, on the other hand, was on the list of video programming services "not affiliated with a cable operator." The evolution of the Golf Channel and Tennis Channel provides some insight into the value of conglomeration in the television marketplace, although pure luck could assume an important role as well.

The Golf Channel debuted in 1995, one year before Tiger Woods turned pro and became the dominant figure in his sport for more than a decade, winning 14 major titles from 1997 through 2008 before adding number 15 in 2019. The official launch of the Tennis Channel in May 2003, on the other hand, came eight months after Pete Sampras won the last of his 14 Grand Slam titles at the U.S. Open and four months after Andre Agassi collected his eighth at the Australian Open. Andy

Roddick won the U.S. Open in September 2003, four months after the Tennis Channel launched, but the American men did not win another singles title in the 16 years that followed, a period that was dominated by three of the all-time greats, Switzerland's Roger Federer, Spain's Rafael Nadal, and Serbia's Novak Djokovic. During that same period, Woods collected seven majors, and he was one of 17 different Americans to win a total of 34 major golf titles. The United States, of course, fared far better on the women's side of the tennis draw, as Serena and Venus Williams combined for 20 titles from 2004 through 2019, while Sloane Stephens claimed her lone Slam title at the U.S. Open in 2017, and Sofia Kenin captured the first Slam title of the 2020s at the Australian Open. The decline of the American men no doubt contributed to the struggles of the Tennis Channel to gain a foothold on cable and satellite systems, but there were other significant challenges.

When media entrepreneur Joseph Gibbs and golf legend Arnold Palmer launched the Golf Channel on January 17, 1995, they did so with the financial backing of prominent cable multiple system operators. Comcast Corp., Continental Cablevision, Newhouse Broadcasting, and Times Mirror Co. were among the initial investors in the channel. Comcast and Continental entered 1995 as the third- and fourth-ranked cable operators in the United States, with over 3 million subscribers each, including pending sales and acquisitions.[9] For Newhouse, the investment came as it entered into a management deal with Time Warner Cable, the second largest operator at the time, while for Times Mirror, it came as it merged with Cox Communications to create a top five MSO. Those investments and vertical connections fueled the Golf Channel launch in the United States in 1995, while a $50-million investment from News Corp. for a one-third stake in 1996 allowed it to expand overseas, starting in Japan.

The ownership link between the Golf Channel and prominent cable operators proved to be the most valuable connection, since it came at a transformative moment for the industry. Passage of the Telecommunications Act of 1996 ushered in an era of unmatched investment in telecom infrastructure, with the cable industry spending an estimated $43.4 billion on capital expenditures from 1996 through 2001.[10] Most of that was dedicated to digital upgrades to cable systems, which created bandwidth for new content. The Golf Channel originated as a premium service, but it converted to a basic service soon after and Comcast Corp. became its strongest advocate. In the first quarter of 1998, Comcast invested $76 million in the Golf Channel to increase its share from under 15% to more than 40%.[11] It invested $99.0 million more in February 2000 to increase its stake to more than 54% and another $137.8 million later that year to bring its ownership interest to more than 60%.[12] Comcast then acquired the 30.8% of the Golf Channel that News Corp.'s Fox Entertainment Group controlled for $364.9 million to bring its ownership interest to 91.0%.[13] Just as significant as the investment was the reach of the Golf Channel, growing from an estimated 1.5 million households in 1995 to more than 30 million in 2000 to 60 million in 2004, less than a decade after its launch.[14]

The story of the Tennis Channel is similar but at the also different. As was the case with the Golf Channel, the vision came from a media entrepreneur, Steve Bellamy, with investments from not one but two legends of the sport, Sampras and Agassi. The critical difference was in the other investors. While it launched with carriage agreements with two prominent MSOs, Time Warner Cable and Cox Communications, neither held a financial interest in the service. The main backing for the Tennis Channel came from a collection of eight private equity groups. One of those, DND Capital Partners, was co-chaired by two long-time senior Viacom executives, Philippe Dauman and Thomas Dooley, while a third, Kenneth Gorman, led another investor, Apollo Partners. While those equity groups could provide capital and media management expertise, they could not expedite the carriage of the Tennis Channel on cable and satellite systems, and that became a major obstacle. The service launched in 2003 and reached 3.2 million households in a single month in that year but was still under 10 million in 2006 and just over 25 million in 2010.[15] In 2013, when it marked its tenth anniversary, a point at which the Golf Channel surpassed 67 million households, the Tennis Channel was still in fewer than 30 million households.[16]

There is another important link between the two services. In 2010, Tennis Channel Inc. filed a complaint with the FCC against Comcast Cable Communications.[17] In that action, the Tennis Channel alleged that Comcast discriminated against its service in violation of FCC rules implemented in response to the 1992 Cable Act. Section 16 of the act called for regulations that would prevent an MSO from conduct that would "unreasonably restrain the ability of an unaffiliated video programming vendor to compete fairly by discriminating . . . on the basis of affiliation or non-affiliation of vendors."[18] In short, the Tennis Channel claimed that the cable MSO was in violation for carrying the tennis-focused service on a sports tier that required an additional fee while placing two Comcast services, Golf Channel and Versus, on an expanded basic tier. The difference was significant, since Comcast had 22.8 million video customers at the end of 2010, with 19.7 million of those households receiving the digital starter service that included the Golf Channel and Versus.[19] On the other hand, subscriptions to Comcast's sports package, which included the Tennis Channel, were estimated to be around 3 million households in 2010.

The path of *Tennis Channel Inc. v. Comcast Cable Communications* through the Commission and the courts follows an interesting trail. An administrative law judge ruled in favor of the Tennis Channel on the complaint to the FCC, arguing that "the weight of reliable record evidence demonstrates that the differences in channel placement and penetration level are based on affiliation."[20] That argument included a quote from Comcast President Steven Burke that affiliated networks "get treated like siblings as opposed to like strangers."[21] The presiding judge ordered Comcast to pay the government $375,000 and to carry the Tennis Channel on the same level of distribution as the Golf Channel and Versus.[22] In time, the Commission upheld that decision, although it rejected the channel placement remedy and issued a limited stay in regard to Comcast systems with limited bandwidth.[23] Comcast appealed that decision to the U.S. Court of Appeals for the DC Circuit, questioning the ascribed meaning of Section 16 of the act as well as claiming that the evidence did not support the conclusion that Comcast discriminated against the Tennis Channel.[24] The Court of Appeals did not rule on the questions related to the meaning of Section 16, but it ruled in favor of Comcast on the claim of discrimination, concluding that there was no evidence that the distribution of the Tennis Channel more broadly offered commercial benefit to Comcast and, in turn, there was no evidence of discrimination based on affiliation.[25] The Supreme Court refused to review the lower court decision, and the Commission later rejected a Tennis Channel request for reaffirmation of the original decision.[26]

The financial impact of distribution agreements, both in terms of the number of households reached and the carriage fees collected, becomes clear in the comparison of the Golf Channel and Tennis Channel. The Golf Channel averaged 58.4 million subscribers in 2003, the year the Tennis Channel launched, so it started with a significant advantage, but the comparison is still illuminating. The average subscribers, average fee per month, and annual affiliate fees for the two services are documented in Table 4.1. The Tennis Channel surpassed an average of 10 million subscribers in 2007 after reaching an agreement with Dish Network and 20 million subscribers in 2008 after a similar agreement with DirecTV, with subscribers on the Sports Tier of Comcast systems contributing to those numbers. The Tennis Channel, however, could not even approach the penetration of the Golf Channel in the years that followed. In 2010, when it filed its carriage

TABLE 4.1 Average subscribers and affiliates revenue per month for the Golf Channel and Tennis Channel, selected years, 2000–2018

Year	Golf Channel			Tennis Channel		
	Average Subscribers (in millions)	Affiliate Revenue per Average Subscribers/ Month	Total Affiliate Revenue (in millions)	Average Subscribers (in millions)	Affiliate Revenue per Average Subscribers/ Month	Total Affiliate Revenue (in millions)
2000	29.0	$0.15	$53.4	–	–	–
2005	67.4	$0.21	$165.7	5.6	$0.13	$8.9
2010	82.5	$0.27	$264.6	24.7	$0.16	$46.1
2015	78.3	$0.35	$333.0	29.6	$0.20	$69.4
2016	77.3	$0.40	$368.5	36.6	$0.12	$50.8
2017	75.3	$0.41	$373.4	49.5	$0.16	$92.2
2018	71.6	$0.48	$408.4	56.0	$0.15	$97.8

Source: Kagan, a media research group within S&P Global Market Intelligence, accessed September 3, 2019.

complaint with the FCC, the Tennis Channel had an average of 24.7 million subscribers, compared to 82.5 million for the Golf Channel, a variance that contributed to a difference in affiliate revenue in excess of $200 million. In 2015, the Tennis Channel averaged 29.6 million subscribers with an average monthly fee of 20 cents per household. That generated affiliate revenue of $69.4 million. The Golf Channel received an average monthly subscriber fee of 35 cents that same year. Far more significant, however, was the fact that it had an average of 78.3 million subscribers in 2015, which generated total affiliate revenue of $333.0 million, more than four times as much as the Tennis Channel. Those differences also contributed to the net advertising revenue the networks were able to generate in 2015: $155.3 million for the Golf Channel compared to $52.9 million for the Tennis Channel.[27]

The fortunes of the Tennis Channel would soon change. In January 2016, Sinclair Broadcast Group, one of the largest owner of local broadcast stations in the United States, announced the acquisition of the service for $350 million.[28] Even before the deal was finalized, Sinclair stated in corporate documents that it had negotiated agreements to increase carriage for Tennis Channel from approximately 30 million to approximately 50 million homes.[29] Therein lies the power of conglomeration, since Sinclair included the Tennis Channel in its retransmission negotiations with cable, satellite, and telco distributors. At the end of 2018, Sinclair owned or operated over 191 local affiliates in 89 different markets, including 59 with FOX, 41 with ABC, 30 with CBS, and 24 with NBC, creating tremendous leverage in negotiations.[30] In 2018, Sinclair announced retransmission renewals for various local stations with Cox Communications, Dish Network and Sling TV, and Verizon Vios, all of which included carriage of the Tennis Channel, as well as an agreement with PlayStation Vue that included the launch of the Tennis Channel on that system.[31] In 2018, the Tennis Channel had an average of 56.0 million subscribers, compared to 71.6 million for the Golf Channel, although Golf generated over $300 million more in affiliate revenue in 2018 thanks to average affiliate fees that were three times as much, $0.48 compared to $0.15.

The ownership and conglomeration of the Golf Channel and Tennis Channel has impacted the two services in other ways. In 2006, the Golf Channel signed a 15-year rights deal with the PGA Tour that covered the early rounds for events on CBS and NBC, as well as 72-hole coverage of tournaments in the late fall and early winter, so it had established a foothold before its marriage with NBC Sports. The combination of the broadcast network and cable service within the NBC Sports Group, however, elevated the Golf Channel even further, both in terms of prominence and properties. Comcast received final approval for the acquisition of NBCUniversal in January 2011, and the integration of the Golf Channel into the NBC Sports Group began that February with the appointment of a new president, Mike McCarley, formerly the senior vice president for communication, marketing, and promotion at NBC Sports and the Olympics. The connection became most evident that same month when NBC's on-air coverage of the WGC-Accenture Match-Play Championship was branded as *Golf Channel on NBC*. The benefits came through various channels. In 2014, the Golf Channel debuted as the first-day home for the Ryder Cup competition between the United States and Europe, rights NBC reclaimed from ESPN in a deal that included increased access to highlights from the Olympic Games and English Premier League and the release of Michelle Beadle from her contract with NBC Sports Group. ESPN had gained the rights to the first day of the biennial competition from 2006 through 2014 in a deal that allowed Al Michaels to join NBC for *Sunday Night Football* and facilitated the return of the animated cartoon *Oswald the Lucky Rabbit* to Disney, which Walt Disney and Ub Iwerks created for Universal Pictures in 1927.

The impact of ownership was most evident in the summer and fall of 2016. The Tennis Channel had a presence at that sport's last two majors of the year, Wimbledon and the U.S. Open, with shoulder programming that featured analysis and highlights. ESPN, however, held the exclusive rights to televise all matches at the two events. The Golf Channel was limited to the studio shows at the U.S. Open and PGA Championship, but that was not the case at the other marquee events. In July, at Royal Troon Golf Club in Scotland, NBC Sports Group debuted as the U.S. rights holder to the British Open, with the Golf Channel assuming a prominent role in the plans, including live coverage the first two days of the tournament. In September, the Golf Channel was once again home to the first day of matches at the Ryder Cup. The true jewel, and the one most tied to ownership, came in August when golf returned to the Olympic Games after 112 years and the Golf Channel carried all four days of both the men's and women's tournaments from Rio de Janeiro.

Professional League Networks

The evolution of sport-specific cable and satellite networks assumed a new form at the start of the new millennium, with the advent of networks devoted to the major professional team sports. There were efforts to launch outlets devoted to team sports prior to 2000, with the aforementioned TFN: The Football Network being a prominent example. Entrepreneur Jantonio Turner founded TFN in 1996 and worked to raise the capital needed to launch an around-the-clock service focused on football. TFN started slow, packaging football-related programming for basic cable outlets, including two series on Spike and specials on USA Network, and syndicating college football games, including the Atlantic 10. In time, Turner hired the same media consultants that developed the business plan for the Golf Channel and retained an investment banker with an eye toward the sale of stock and a launch in 2003.[32] The Football Network did launch in fewer than 300,000 households in September of that year, funded in part through incentives from the state of Louisiana, including cash, tax credits, and access to state-of-the-art facilities in Baton Rouge.[33] TFN obtained the rights to lower-level football, such as the Canadian Football League, NCAA Division I-AA, high school, and even flag football leagues, but it did not have access to even the highlights of the National Football League. It went dark in mid-December, having burned through $10 million.

The ownership of content was one of the common threads for the networks launched in this period, as was cross-promotion. In 1999, the National Basketball Association created NBC.com TV as a platform for news and highlights to promote NBA League Pass, a subscription-based service for out-of-market games. In 2003, the National Football League followed suit, launching the NFL Network primarily on DirecTV. The satellite carrier was home to the NFL out-of-market package *NFL Sunday Ticket*, so there was a lucrative partnership between the two parties. The same was true with the launch of the NHL Network in 2007 and MLB Network in 2009. In the case of the NHL Network, the development began as an offshoot of the Canadian version of the channel. The creation of the U.S.-based network was part of a national rights deal signed with Comcast-owned cable programmer OLN, now NBC Sports Network, with the cable giant receiving a minority ownership interest in the network. MLB Network followed a similar pattern, with distributors DirecTV, Comcast, Cox Communications, and Time Warner Cable being partners in the *Extra Innings* out-of-market service, all holding minority interests in the channel.

There were similarities with the four league-owned networks, but there were also differences, at least in the beginning. When NBA TV launched in November 1999, it was built around studio shows featuring news, interviews, and highlights, supplemented with vintage games and NBA Entertainment-produced programming, including *NBA Inside Stuff*, which debuted on NBC in 1990. What NBA TV did not offer, at least in its first three seasons, were telecasts of live games. The same was true with NFL Network when it debuted four years later in November 2003. When it launched, the service was also built around a signature studio show, *NFL Total Access*, but 101 of its 168 hours per week came from the vaults of NFL Films.[34] NBA TV added live game coverage in the middle of the 2002–03 season, while NFL Network introduced *Thursday Night Football* in 2006. MLB Network followed a different path. It too built its schedule around a studio show, *MLB Tonight*, which in its inaugural season started at 5:00 pm Eastern time on most nights and stayed on until the end of West Coast night games some eight hours later. The difference was that MLB Network started with a signature game telecast, *Thursday Night Baseball*, starting in its first season.

There was another important difference. MLB Network launched in an estimated 50 million households. It accessed most of those households through a digital or expanded basic tier rather than a more limited sports tier. That was a radical departure from NBA TV, which reached an estimated 1.5 million households through DirecTV's Total Choice Gold package when it debuted in 1999. Many cable operators, including Comcast and Time Warner Cable, developed sports tiers in the mid-2000s to limit the impact of sports programming on subscription rates, and NBA TV and NHL Network became anchors of such tiers, limiting distribution and revenue for those services. In mid-2007, NBA TV and NHL Network had 10 to 15 million subscribers in the United States.[35] The NFL took a different path. From the outset, NFL Network demanded carriage on digital or expanded basic tiers and was limited to an estimated 10 million households through DirecTV when it debuted in 2003. The network began to gain access to cable networks in 2004, signing first with Charter Communications for carriage at $0.20 per month per household.[36] NFL Network was launched on a digital sports tier on Charter systems, but there was an obligation for the MSO to reach a minimum number of households over a five-year period.

In addition to its tier demands, the NFL also was not willing to offer ownership in the network in exchange for carriage, and it struggled to gain household penetration. The NFL reached a compromise with Comcast later in 2004, with the NFL Network placed on the Digital Plus platform as opposed to the sports tier. The Digital Plus tier did not have the same reach as Digital Classic, but it still gave the NFL access to a majority of the 8.7 million digital customers on Comcast systems at the end of 2004, although still well short of the total 21.5 million Comcast subscribers.[37] That was one piece of complicated negotiations between the league and the largest cable operator, which included possible access to *NFL Sunday Ticket* as well as a package of Thursday night games for Comcast-owned OLN, with an offer of $450 million a year. When exclusive rights to *NFL Sunday Ticket* remained with DirecTV and the league opted to keep the Thursday night games in house and place them on NFL Network, Comcast felt betrayed, invoked a clause in its contract, and moved the network to a sports tier and the NFL went to court.[38] The NFL filed suit in New York Supreme Court to block Comcast from moving the network to a sports tier, later appealing when a summary judgment went against the network. The NFL also launched a public "Make the Switch" campaign against Comcast, encouraging costumers to switch to satellite providers, which led the cable operator to file a breach of contract suit against the league.

The placement of the Thursday night package on NFL Network had widespread implications and not just for Comcast. The move triggered a clause in contracts with distributors that resulted in steep carriage fee increases for the network, from an estimated 12 cents per household per month in 2005 to 60 cents in 2007.[39] The failure of the NFL Network to gain widespread distribution also impacted fans, although it was not a major issue until the 2007 season. That November, the Green Bay Packers and Dallas Cowboys met for a Thursday night game at Lambeau Field, the first meeting of 10–1 teams since the 1990 season. The game was available on broadcast stations in the local markets of the two teams, but it was not available in much of the country, with the NFL Network only carried in just over 40 million homes at that point in the season. In December, the NFL Network featured the New England Patriots in their pursuit of a perfect regular season record against the New York Giants. As the games approached, the NFL tried various tactics to increase carriage, including an invitation from Commissioner Roger Goodell to Time Warner Cable to enter binding arbitration to determine the tier and carriage price for the service. Time Warner Cable declined that offer. Politicians also entered the fight, with Massachusetts Senator John Kerry and Representative Ed Markey calling on the league and cable operators, Time Warner Cable and Cablevision in particular, to end their impasse. The NFL failed to resolve those issues and resorted to a three-network simulcast on CBS, NBC, and NFL Network.

That was not the end of the story or the litigation. Not finding success in the New York court system against Comcast, the NFL filed a complaint with the Federal Communications Commission in 2008, accusing the cable giant of discrimination.[40] NFL Network President Steve Bornstein accused Comcast of placing the network "on a costly sports tier" while "making sports channels it owns available to all viewers on a less costly basis."[41] Bornstein was focused on the two Comcast-owned and operated services, Golf Channel and Versus, both of which were carried on the expanded basic tier. As discussed earlier, the 1992 Cable Act mandated that operators could not discriminate "on the basis of affiliation and non-affiliation of vendors in the selection, terms or conditions of carriage of video programming."[42] Comcast, in turn, argued that the Golf Channel and Versus had year-round programming with live events far in excess to the eight games on NFL Network per year. The Cable Act also included provisions that prohibit a distributor from requiring a financial interest as a "condition for carriage." In this case, the NFL claimed that Comcast dropped the NFL Network in retaliation to the decision "not to grant Comcast telecast rights – a financial interest – in a valuable program package of eight, live NFL football games."[43] In the debate over carriage on Comcast, Dallas Cowboys owner and NFL Network Committee Chairman Jerry Jones argued, "The company we are talking about here [Comcast], I guess I should go ahead and say it, is a company that depends upon privileges at the government level. And they shouldn't use those privileges to keep fans here from seeing the NFL."[44] The NFL, clearly, was also active in soliciting support inside the Washington beltway. The NFL and Comcast reached an agreement on a new, long-term carriage agreement for NFL Network and added *NFL RedZone* before the start of the 2009 season.

The changing dynamics in the relationship between the NFL and Comcast provides another tale in the annals of media conglomeration. Less than nine months after signing the agreement to carry the NFL Network, Comcast announced in December 2009 its intent to acquire a majority interest in NBCUniversal, the parent corporation of NBC, which was in the midst of a six-year contract with the NFL for *Sunday Night Football*. That was one of the most valuable properties in the NBC arsenal and transformed the NFL and Comcast from rival litigants to important business partners. The federal government approved the Comcast-NBCUniversal deal in January 2011, and that December the two parties announced a new nine-year deal for *Sunday Night Football* that was worth billions. The connection between NFL Network and NBC became even more intertwined in 2016 when the NFL signed a two-year agreement to share *Thursday Night Football* with NBC and CBS.[45] The two broadcast networks split ten games, all of which were simulcast on NFL Network, with another eight games televised exclusively on the pay service.

There was another dimension of the deal between the NFL and the broadcast networks that was a clear sign of the times. Prominent announcers were once aligned with a specific network, and the sharing of well-known talent was rare, but that changed with the decline of the broadcast networks. The NFL first shared the package with a broadcast partner in 2014, with eight games simulcast on CBS and NFL Network and another eight exclusively on NFL Network. What was most interesting about the deal was that the marquee CBS announcing team of Jim Nantz and Phil Simms and sideline reporter Tracy Wolfson handled the commentary for all 16 games, with a CBS production crew behind the cameras. Perhaps most striking was that James Brown and analysts from the long-running CBS pre-game show *The NFL Today* also handled the pre-game show on CBS and NFL Network, *NFL Thursday Night Kickoff*. Rich Eisen and his colleagues from the NFL Network had their own shows from the stadium, but the immediate pre-game, halftime, and post-game shows were handled by CBS. The supposed separation between the NFL and CBS became important on the first telecast in 2014 when Brown and Scott Pelley, the anchor of the *CBS Evening News*, led the coverage of the Ray Rice scandal, days after the TMZ website released footage of the Baltimore Ravens running back hitting his then-fiancée inside an elevator at an Atlantic City casino.

The marriage of NBA TV and Turner Broadcasting provides another example of the tangled relationships between media conglomerates and the professional leagues they cover. In the early 2000s, Turner explored the creation of a new sports network with the NBA as part of its contract with the league, but when that endeavor did not come to fruition, Time Warner made a multi-million-dollar investment in NBA TV in exchange for a 10% equity interest in the service. In 2007, Time Warner returned that ownership stake to the league as part of a deal that moved NBA TV from a sports tier to a digital basic tier on Time Warner-owned systems.[46] That deal might have changed the ownership of the service, but an agreement two months later created a much tighter connection, as the NBA announced that NBA TV, NBA.com, and other digital services would move to Atlanta, with Turner Sports operating the services, responsible for content and sales. That move gave NBA TV easy access to the cast of *Inside the NBA* (Ernie Johnson, Kenny Smith, Charles Barkley, and Shaquille O'Neal), but it also made its studio operations eligible for tax credits through the state of Georgia.

The four networks aligned with the U.S. professional sports leagues can be broken into two clusters, with NFL Network alone in one group, and the other three together in the other. In 2018, the average carriage fees for MLB Network, NBA TV, and NHL Network were comparable: 30 cents, 32 cents, and 36 cents, respectively, with some variance in the number of subscribers: 59.5 million, 46.7 million, and 32.7 million, respectively.[47] There were also some common elements in the ownership of the networks, as operators AT&T Inc., Comcast, Charter Communications, and Cox Communications all owned a share of MLB Network, while Comcast owned 15.6% of NHL Network. As noted earlier, while the NBA owned 100% of NBA TV, the links to Turner were undeniable. In one way, NFL Network was similar to NBA TV since the National Football League held 100% ownership, but in others, it was quite different. In 2018, NFL Network had an average of 68.0 million subscribers, but the most significant difference was the estimated $1.58 average affiliate it received each month per household.[48] That fee resulted in $1.289 billion in affiliate revenue in 2018, over $1 billion more than MLB Network. What made that fee more remarkable is that NFL Network had very little exclusive live game coverage. In 2018, it televised 13 games for *Thursday Night Football*, 11 of which were simulcast on FOX as part of a new $550-million per-year deal, an early morning game from London in late October, and Saturday doubleheaders on the last two weekends of the season in December. MLB Network, in contrast, had over 40 live game windows during the pennant race in September 2018 alone.

Collegiate Athletic Conference and University Networks

The emergence of networks devoted to a specific collegiate conference or even a single university is one of the newer additions to the sports programming landscape, but the basic idea has been there since the beginning. When Bill Rasmussen started to build the foundation for ESPN in the late 1970s, he first envisioned it as a regional network carried on cable systems in the state of Connecticut with content from the University of Connecticut (UConn) figuring prominently in that plan. John Toner, the athletic director at UConn at that time and later the president of the NCAA, became an important intermediary as Rasmussen tried to secure rights for his proposed network. In November 1978, close to a year before the launch of ESPN, two events on the UConn campus were used to demonstrate the "E.S.P. Network" for cable operators, a men's basketball exhibition game against Athletes in Action and an Eastern College Athletic Conference soccer playoff game. The vision of intercollegiate athletics on ESPN was evident in an October 1978 proposal to the NCAA that proclaimed, "All of the elements are now in place to originate an NCAA National Network" and proposed to televise "several hundred NCAA Division I, II and III men's and women's athletic events."[49] Five months later, in March 1979, NCAA Executive Director Walter Byers signed a two-year contract with the "E.S.P. Network" for all NCAA Championship events not committed to other networks.

The factors that made natural a marriage between the NCAA and ESPN are still evident in the programming networks focused on a single conference or a single university. The rights to championships not committed to other networks in the original ESPN deal spoke to the untapped inventory that the NCAA, conferences, and teams controlled. The Supreme Court decision in *NCAA v. Board of Regents* in 1984 discussed in Chapter 3 set the stage for the explosion of college football games across broadcast networks and cable platforms, but it did little to dilute available volume in other sports. That catalog increased to a dramatic degree with the growth in women's athletics that evolved after the passage of Title IX in 1972. The increase in participation is staggering, from 16,000 women in 1972 to 200,000 in 2014.[50] The average number of women's teams at NCAA member schools increased from 2.5 in 1970 to 8.83 in 2014.[51] The number is even higher, an average of 10.16, in the Football Bowl Subdivision schools, which includes the ten most prominent conferences and major independents. Those increases are most evident in team sports, such as basketball, soccer, softball, and volleyball. While basketball and volleyball participation were common a year prior to mandatory Title IX compliance in 1977, with participation of NCAA member schools at 90.4% and 80.1%, respectively, the growth of soccer and softball is dramatic: an increase from 2.8% in 1977 to 93.3% in 2014 in the case of women's soccer and 48.4% to 89.2% in the case of softball. While the NCAA tournaments for those four sports are now featured on ESPN, regular season games have become the foundation of conference networks.

The development of programming services dedicated to a single conference was a logical next step after the introduction of NBA TV and NFL Network, although the first forays into services dedicated to intercollegiate athletics focused on national and/or regional networks. In April 2003, CSTV (College Sports Television) debuted as an independent network in about 11 million households through DirecTV with programming and marketing agreements with more than two dozen athletic programs. In September 2004, Fox Sports Networks converted three digital services that carried programming from its regional sports networks and reached about three million households into three services under the Fox College Sports (FCS) name: FCS Atlantic, FCS Central, and FCS Pacific. In March 2005, ESPN launched its own college sports network, ESPNU, and later that year, in November 2005, CBS acquired CSTV and rebranded the service as CBS College Sports Network. With that sale, the new college sports services all became part of major media conglomerates: CBS Corp., Disney, and News Corp.

Conglomerates assumed a prominent role in the emergence of conference-specific networks that followed. From 2006 through 2014, four conferences launched stand-alone networks: Mountain West Conference in September 2006, Big Ten Conference in August 2007, Pac-12 Conference in August 2012, and Southeast Conference (SEC) in August 2014. Three of the four were tied to conglomerates from the outset, with Pac-12 Networks the lone independent within that group. CBS Corp. and Comcast held interests in the Mountain West Sports Network (The mtn.), and News Corp. controlled 51% of the Big Ten Network (BTN), while the ESPN unit of Disney owned the SEC Network. The corporate connections did not guarantee success, however, as the Mountain West shuttered its network in 2012 after two of its charter members, Brigham Young University and the University of Utah, left the conference, with BYU becoming an independent school in football and Utah joining the Pac-12. The partnership between the conference and the two conglomerates included an out clause that allowed either party to exit after the two schools departed.[52] The Mountain West added Boise State, Fresno State, and Nevada, but the loss of Salt Lake City and Provo, Utah, where Comcast is dominant, was too much to overcome.

The collection of in-conference markets became critical to the financial success of such networks and a driving force in expansion. When the Southeast Conference expanded from 12 to 14 schools in 2012, it added Texas A&M University and the University of Missouri, which allowed the conference to expand into two additional states. The same was true with the Big Ten expansion from 12 to 14 in 2014 when the conference added the University of Maryland and Rutgers University. What was critical about that move was that the Big Ten added schools in the states of Maryland and New Jersey but also connected with two major markets, Washington, DC, and New York City, respectively. Unlike the Big Ten, which retains its long-standing name with 14 members, the Pacific-10 Conference changed its name to the Pac-12 in 2012 when it added the University of Colorado and the University of Utah. What was most critical about these additions is that it gave the conference access to one more market among the 20 largest in the country, Denver, and another in the top 35, Salt Lake City. Comcast was the dominant cable operator in both markets, as it was in the San Francisco Bay Area, Portland, and Seattle. That allowed the conference to negotiate a carriage agreement with one MSO that covered a significant percentage of its footprint, and the original deal covered parts of six states. The list of in-market states and estimated carriage fees are listed in Table 4.2.

The importance of such expansion is found in the fee structure for these networks. When ESPN launched the SEC Network in 2014, its fee card for the service was $1.30 per household per month in-market, and $0.25 out-of-market, and reports at the time indicated that it was successful in locking in those rates. Making Texas and Missouri in-market states for the network through the addition of A&M and Mizzou added more than 11.5 million potential subscribers at the higher rate, 9.2 million and 2.3 million, respectively.[53] With carriage on the expanded digital tiers and average national penetration rates for cable and alternative delivery systems around 90% at the time, that could mean an additional $1 per month in over 10 million households. And unlike the other conference networks, the SEC Network was on DirecTV and Dish Network from the date of its launch. The financial rewards from expansions were similar with the Big Ten. In 2014, the Big Ten Network received an estimated $1 per household per month within the conference footprint, compared to less than 20 cents outside of those states. The addition of Rutgers alone brought the New York-designated market area and its 7.4 million television households inside the Big Ten region, and the network signed carriage agreements with Cablevision, Comcast, and Time

TABLE 4.2 Average subscribers and affiliate revenue per month for major collegiate conferences television services and comparative data, 2018

	Launch Date	Total Schools (2018)	Average Subscribers per Month (in millions) (2018)	Average Affiliate Revenue per Average Subscriber per Month (2018)	Affiliate Revenue (in millions) (2018)	In Market States
Big Ten Network	August 2007	14	57.6	$0.50	$347.8	11: Illinois, Indiana, Iowa, Maryland, Michigan, Minnesota, Nebraska, New Jersey, Ohio, Pennsylvania, Wisconsin
Pac-12 Networks	August 2012	12	18.6	$0.11	$25.3	6: Arizona, California, Colorado, Oregon, Washington, Utah
Southeast Conference Network	August 2014	14	59.9	$0.78	$563.2	11: Alabama, Arkansas, Florida, Georgia, Kentucky, Louisiana, Mississippi, Missouri, South Carolina, Tennessee, Texas

Source: Subscriber and affiliate revenue data derived from Kagan, a media research group within S&P Global Market Intelligence, accessed September 3, 2019.

Warner Cable in the spring of 2014 for systems in the New York/New Jersey television market. That was significant, since the conference struggled to gain carriage with Comcast and Time Warner Cable when it debuted in 2007 and did not sign agreements with those MSOs until 2008.

The addition of the Denver and Salt Lake City markets expanded the footprint of the Pac-12 Conference, but its network struggled through the 2010s. As noted previously, it was the one network among the big three that went out on its own, not adding a media conglomerate as an equity owner. It also created a collection of six regional networks – Pac-12 Arizona, Pac-12 Bay Area, Pac-12 Los Angeles, Pac-12 Mountain, Pac-12 Oregon, and Pac-12 Washington – in addition to its national network. That allowed the network to cover far more events on a regional basis, an important consideration for the conference that captured 330 NCAA titles between 1981–82 (when it started sponsoring women's sports) and 2018–19, but it also increased production costs. Far more significant was the inability of the Pac-12 to reach a carriage agreement with DirecTV, an impasse that saw no signs of resolution at the end of the 2019 football season. The Pac-12 Networks had under 20 million average subscribers in 2018, about one-third of the BTN and SEC Network. The Pac-12 Networks increased from 14.6 million subscribers at the end of 2015 to 18.6 million at the end of 2018, but the estimated average price, a mix of in-market and out-of-market rates, over that same period dropped from 35 cents to 11 cents. And that put the conference at a disadvantage against the Big Ten and SEC.

The allocation of rights through multiple agreements becomes an important part of the conference financial equation, with the Big Ten providing a clear example. In 2006, the Big Ten signed a ten-year, $1-billion media agreement with The Walt Disney Co. that included first- and second-tier football rights for ABC and ESPN as well as rights for men's and women's basketball and women's volleyball. The conference later signed another basketball-only agreement with CBS for $72 million over six years. All those agreements ran through the 2016–17 season. The total haul for the conference starting in 2017–18 increased to an average of $440 million a year as part of six-year, $2.64-billion deals with Fox and Disney for football and basketball, as well as a basketball-only deal with CBS. Fox and Disney shared the top-tier rights, with each party showing 27 games on their collection of networks in the 2017 football season, with FOX also airing the conference championship game. That still left 40 regular reason football games for BTN as part of the third-tier rights the conference did not sell. News Corp. signed a 20-year contract with the Big Ten when the network launched in 2007, with an option for five more years, which included escalating rights fees as well as profit participation. In 2007–08, the network paid the conference $66 million as a rights fee, but at that time, the News Corp. financial projections estimated a total pay-out of $2.8 billion over 25 years, an average of $112 million per year.[54] BTN was one of the sports-related services that Fox Corp. retained after entertainment assets were sold to Disney in 2019.

The story was less uniformed in the Big 12. The conference signed a new 13-year deal with Disney in 2012, in which ABC and ESPN share first- and second-year rights with Fox through a deal it signed in 2011. The sharing of rights between Disney and Fox was consistent with the approach the two conglomerates took with the Pac-12 Conference, and the combined rights fee of $2.6 billion over 13 years was consistent with that deal as well. Where the Big 12 differed was in the allocation of third-tier rights. While the Pac-12 pooled those rights and used them to create the Pac-12 Networks, member schools in the Big 12 retained their rights. The University of Texas transferred them to ESPN to create a dedicated, stand-alone network featuring that one sports program 24 hours a day, signing a 20-year, $300-million deal for the Longhorn Network in 2010. The network is a financial boon for Texas, generating a guaranteed annual minimum royalty of $10.9 million in the first year with 3% annual increases, with profit sharing once ESPN generates $295 million in gross revenue.[55] The network struggled to gain carriage in the state and nationwide, however, with DirecTV among the distributors remaining on the sidelines in the early years, but the network was part of a massive agreement DirecTV reached with Disney for carriage of its broadcast stations and cable networks in late 2014. The network also created tensions within the conference. The contract with ESPN prohibits Texas from contributing to a Big 12 network, which limits the third-tier revenue of the other schools and establishes an exclusive negotiating period in the event the school decides to become an independent, which raised doubts about its commitment to the conference.

The Atlantic Coast Conference was the last of the Power 5 conferences to develop a plan for television. In 2010, the conference announced a 12-year deal with ESPN that gave it exclusive rights starting with the 2011–12 season, although long-time ACC outlet Raycom Media sublicensed the rights to some games as part of that deal. In 2013, the ACC completed a grant of media rights agreement, which gave the conference control of its member's television rights. Then, in 2016, ESPN and the ACC announced the creation of the ACC Network, with a streaming service, ACC Network Extra, debuting in 2016 and a linear service, ACC Network, launching in August of 2019. The importance of being backed by Disney was evident in the months leading up to the launch of the ESPN-owned network. That summer, Disney made carriage of the ACC Network a centerpiece of its negotiations with Charter Communications, the second-largest cable MSO at the time. That meant the ACC Network was bundled not only with the ESPN linear networks but also with other Disney services and others it acquired from Fox.

Summary

The analysis of single sport, league, and conference networks makes a number of trends quite clear. First, horizontal or vertical integration are vital to success in the marketplace, whether that is the connections to cable operators that fueled the growth of the Golf Channel or the relationship to ESPN that supported the SEC Network. To be clear, NFL Network has succeeded without such connections, but it is a rare case. Far more illustrative are the struggles of the Pac-12 Networks and the successes of the ACC Network, which had a deal in place with DirecTV four months before launch, something the Pac-12 was still looking for as it completed its eighth football season, with no resolution in sight. Second, league and corporate executives that oftentimes advocate for free market solutions are not reticent to turn to the Federal Communications Commission or the federal courts when the marketplace does not yield the desired outcome. That was most evident in the lawsuits of the National Football League and Tennis Channel against Comcast. What made those cases even more interesting is how the situation changes once ownership does, how the NFL and Comcast became business partners rather than rival litigates after the latter acquired NBCUniversal, and how the Tennis Channel gained needed leverage when it paired with Sinclair Broadcast Group in negotiations with MSOs, including Comcast.

Notes

1. Cable Television Consumer Protection Act of 1992, 102d Congress, Public Law 102–385 (1992).
2. William M. Kunz, "FCC Studies of the Television Marketplace Under George W. Bush: Flawed Measurements and Invalid Conclusions," *Democratic Communiqué* 25, no. 2 (2012): 1–21.
3. Federal Communications Commission, Annual Assessment of the Status of Competition in Markets for the Delivery of Video Programming, Fourth Annual Report, FCC 97–423, CS Docket No. 97–141 (1997), F11–F13.
4. Federal Communications Commission, "Annual Assessment in the Market for the Delivery of Video Programming," Tenth Annual Report, FCC 04–05, MB Docket No 03–172 (2004): 125–136.
5. Outdoor Life Holdings, Inc., 2004 Annual Report, Form 10-K, March 31, 2005.
6. Kagan, "TV Network Summary: Subscribers," S&P Global Market Intelligence. Accessed September 3, 2019; Comcast Holdings Corp., 2004 Annual Report, Form 10-K, March 25, 2005.
7. Comcast Corp., 2001 Annual Report, Form 10-K, March 29, 2002.
8. Tenth Annual Report.
9. "Top 50 MSOs," *Broadcasting & Cable Yearbook*, Volume 1 (New Providence, NJ: R.R. Bowker, 1996), D-78
10. National Cable and Telecommunications Association, Industry Data. www.ncta.com/industry-data/item/229. Accessed November 30, 2013.
11. Comcast Corp., 1997 Annual Report, Form 10-K, March 3, 1998.
12. Comcast Corp., 1999 Annual Report, Form 10-K, March 1, 2000; Comcast Corp., 2000 Annual Report, Form 10-K, March 2, 2001.
13. Comcast Corp., 2001 Annual Report.
14. "TV Network Summary: Subscribers."
15. "TV Network Summary: Subscribers."
16. "TV Network Summary: Subscribers."

17. Federal Communications Commission, Tennis Channel, Inc. v. Comcast Cable Communications, LLC, Hearing Designation Order and Notice of Opportunity for Hearing for Forfeiture, DA 10–1918, MB Docket No. 10–204 (2010).
18. Cable Television Consumer Protection and Competition Act of 1992, Pub. L. 102–385, 106 Stat. 1460 (1992).
19. Comcast Corp., 2010 Annual Report, Form 10-K, March 25, 2011.
20. Federal Communications Commission, Tennis Channel, Inc. v. Comcast Cable Communications, LLC, Initial Decision of Chief Administrative Law Judge Richard L. Sippel, FCC 11D-01, MC Docket No. 10–204 (2011), para. 55.
21. Tennis v. Comcast, Initial Decision, para. 55.
22. Tennis v. Comcast, Initial Decision, para. 117–121.
23. Federal Communications Commission, Tennis Channel, Inc. v. Comcast Cable Communications, LLC, Order, FCC 12–1311, MM Docket No. 10–204 (2012).
24. Comcast Cable Communications, LLC v Federal Communications Commission and Tennis Channel, Inc., No. 12–1337 (D.C. Cir. 2013).
25. Comcast v FCC and Tennis Channel, 10.
26. Tennis Channel, Inc. v. Comcast Cable Communications, LLC, 13–676 (D.C. Cir. 2013), cert. denied (US February 24, 2014); Federal Communications Commission, Tennis Channel, Inc. v. Comcast Cable Communications, LLC, Order, FCC 15–7, MB Docket No. 10–204 (2015).
27. Kagan, "Network Economics: Golf Channel," S&P Global Market Intelligence. Accessed September 3, 2019; Kagan, "Network Economics: Tennis Channel," S&P Global Market Intelligence. Accessed September 3, 2019.
28. Sinclair Broadcast Group, Inc., 2015 Annual Report, Form 10-K, February 2016,
29. Sinclair Broadcast Group, Inc., "Sinclair to Acquire Tennis Channel; Company to Hold Conference Call on January 28, 2016." Press release, January 27, 2016.
30. Sinclair Broadcast Group, Inc., 2018 Annual Report, Form 10-K, March 2019.
31. Sinclair 2018 Annual Report.
32. Football Network, General Form for Registration of Securities of Small Business Issuers, SEC Form 10SB, July 10, 2001.
33. Richard Sandomir, "A Channel Fades to Black, Swimming in Red Ink," *The New York Times*, February 19, 2004, D1.
34. Larry Eichel, "A Super Channel for Devoted Football Fans," *The Philadelphia Inquirer*, November 4, 2003, F1.
35. John Ourand, "Turning Away From Sports Tiers," *Sports Business Journal*, November 12, 2007.
36. Andy Bernstein, "Charter Communications Puts NFL Network on Digital Sports Tier – for Now," *Sports Business Journal*, January 12, 2004.
37. Comcast Corp., "Comcast to Launch NFL Network." Press release, August 16, 2004; Comcast Holdings Corp., 2004 Annual Report, Form 10-K, March 25, 2005.
38. John Ourand, "Why NFL Network Is Stick on the Sidelines," *Sports Business Journal*, January 29, 2009.
39. Kagan, "TV Network Summary: Affiliate Revenue per Avg Sub/Month," S&P Global Market Intelligence. Accessed September 3, 2019.
40. Federal Communications Commission. NFL Enterprises LLC vs Comcast Cable Communications, LLC, DA 08–2819, MB Docket No. 08–214 (2008).
41. Quoted in Brooks Boliek, "Overtime for NFL Net, Comcast," *Hollywood Reporter*, April 17, 2008.
42. 1992 Cable Act.
43. NFL v. Comcast.
44. Quoted in John Ourand and Daniel Kaplan, "NFL Net Looks to Feds for Help," *Sports Business Journal*, October 29, 2007.
45. National Football League, "NFL Expands 'Thursday Night Football Package." Press release, February 1, 2016.

46. John Ourand and John Lombardo, "NBA TV Escaping Sports Tier," *Sports Business Journal*, November 5, 2007.
47. Kagan, "TV Network Summary: Average Subscribers," S&P Global Market Intelligence. Accessed September 3, 2019; "Affiliate Revenue per Avg Sub/Month."
48. "Affiliate Revenue per Avg Sub/Month."
49. William F. Rasmussen, "E.S.P. The Entertainment and Sports Programming Television Network Proposal to the National Collegiate Athletic Association," October 11, 1978.
50. R. Vivian Acosta and Linda Jean Carpenter, "Women in Intercollegiate Sport: A Longitudinal National Study Thirty-Five Year Update," 1.
51. "Women in Intercollegiate Sport," 4.
52. John Ourand, "Comcast, CBS College Will Have an Out Clause With the Mtn.," *Sports Business Journal*, September 6, 2010.
53. Nielsen Company, "Cable University by State," *Television & Cable Factbook*, 2014.
54. John Ourand and Michael Smith, "Big Ten Could Reap $2.8B from Network Deal," *Sports Business Journal*, March 3, 2008.
55. University of Texas at Austin, IMG Communication and ESPN Inc., "License Agreement," December 24, 2010.

Further Reading

Kunz, William M. "FCC Studies of the Television Marketplace Under George W. Bush: Flawed Measurements and Invalid Conclusion." *Democratic Communique* 25, no. 2 (Fall 2012): 1–21.

LaRocca, James J. "No Trust at the NFL: League's Network Passes Rule of Reason Analysis." *UCLA Entertainment Law Review* 15, no. 1 (2008): 87–104.

Lee, Chase I. "Tennis Channel, Inc. v. FCC." *Federal Communication Law Journal* 68, no. 3 (November 2016): 433–436.

Nocera, Joe. "Power Game." *The New York Times Magazine*, November 2006, 40–41.

Rasmussen, William F. "E.S.P. The Entertainment and Sports Programming Television Network Proposal to the National Collegiate Athletic Association." Entertainment and Sports Programming Television Network, Inc. (October 1978).

Chapter Bibliography

Acosta, R. Vivian, and Linda Jean Carpenter. "Women in Intercollegiate Sport: A Longitudinal National Study Thirty-Five Year Update." www.acostacarpenter.org. Accessed December 30, 2014.

Bernstein, Andy. "Charter Communications Puts NFL Network on Digital Sports Tier – for Now." *Sports Business Journal*, January 12, 2004.

Boliek, Brooks. "Overtime for NFL Net, Comcast." *Hollywood Reporter*, April 17, 2008.

Cable Television Consumer Protection and Competition Act of 1992, Pub. L. 102–385, 106 Stat. 1460 (1992).

Comcast Cable Communications, LLC v. Federal Communications Commission and Tennis Channel, Inc. No. 12–1337 (D.C. Cir. 2013).

Comcast Corp. 1997 Annual Report, Form 10-K. March 3, 1998.

———. 1999 Annual Report, Form 10-K. March 1, 2000.

———. 2000 Annual Report, Form 10-K. March 2, 2001.

———. 2001 Annual Report, Form 10-K. March 29, 2002.

———. "Comcast to Launch NFL Network." Press release, August 16, 2004.

————. 2010 Annual Report, Form 10-K. March 25, 2011.

Comcast Holdings Corp. 2004 Annual Report, Form 10-K. March 25, 2005.

Eichel, Larry. "A Super Channel for Devoted Football Fans." *The Philadelphia Inquirer*, November 4, 2003, F1.

Federal Communications Commission. Annual Assessment of the Status of Competition in Markets for the Delivery of Video Programming, Fourth Annual Report. FCC 97-423, CS Docket No. 97-141 (1997), F11–F13.

————. Annual Assessment in the Market for the Delivery of Video Programming, Tenth Annual Report. FCC 04-05, MB Docket No 03-172 (2004).

————. NFL Enterprises LLC v. Comcast Cable Communications, LLC. DA 08-2819, MB Docket No. 08-214 (2008).

————. Tennis Channel, Inc. v. Comcast Cable Communications, LLC. Hearing Designation Order and Notice of Opportunity for Hearing for Forfeiture. DA 10-1918, MB Docket No. 10-204 (2010).

————. Tennis Channel, Inc. v. Comcast Cable Communications, LLC. Initial Decision of Chief Administrative Law Judge Richard L. Sippel. FCC 11D-01, MC Docket No. 10-204 (2011).

————. Tennis Channel, Inc. v. Comcast Cable Communications, LLC. Order. FCC 12-1311, MM Docket No. 10-204 (2012).

————. Tennis Channel, Inc. v. Comcast Cable Communications, LLC. Order. FCC 15-7, MB Docket No. 10-204 (2015).

Football Network. General Form for Registration of Securities of Small Business Issuers, Form 10SB, July 10, 2001.

Kagan. "Network Economics: Golf Channel." S&P Global Market Intelligence. Accessed September 3, 2019.

————. "TV Network Summary: Affiliate Revenue per Avg Sub/Month." S&P Global Market Intelligence. Accessed September 3, 2019.

————. "TV Network Summary: Average Subscribers." S&P Global Market Intelligence. Accessed September 3, 2019.

————. "TV Network Summary: Subscribers." S&P Global Market Intelligence. Accessed September 3, 2019.

Kunz, William M. "FCC Studies of the Television Marketplace Under George W. Bush: Flawed Measurements and Invalid Conclusions." *Democratic* Communiqué 25, no. 2 (2012), 1–21.

National Cable and Telecommunications Association, Industry Data. www.ncta.com/industry-data/item/229. Accessed November 30, 2013.

National Football League. "NFL Expands 'Thursday Night Football Package." Press release, February 1, 2016.

Nielsen Company. "Cable University by State." *Television & Cable Factbook*, 2014.

Ourand, John. "Turning Away From Sports Tiers." *Sports Business Journal*, November 12, 2007.

————. "Why NFL Network Is Stick on the Sidelines." *Sports Business Journal*, January 29, 2009.

————. "Comcast, CBS College Will Have an out Clause With the Mtn." *Sports Business Journal*, September 6, 2010.

Ourand, John, and Daniel Kaplan. "NFL Net Looks to Feds for Help." *Sports Business Journal*, October 29, 2007.

Ourand, John, and John Lombardo. "NBA TV Escaping Sports Tier." *Sports Business Journal*, November 5, 2007.

Ourand, John, and Michael Smith. "Big Ten Could Reap $2.8B From Network Deal." *Sports Business Journal*, March 3, 2008. Accessed December 29, 2014.

Outdoor Life Holdings, Inc. 2004 Annual Report, Form 10-K. March 31, 2005.

Rasmussen, William F. "E.S.P. The Entertainment and Sports Programming Television Network Proposal to the National Collegiate Athletic Association." October 11, 1978. www.espnfrontrow.com/wp-content/uploads/2011/11/ESPN-Proposal-for-Front-Row.pdf. Accessed December 20, 2014.

Sandomir, Richard. "A Channel Fades to Black, Swimming in Red Ink." *The New York Times*, February 19, 2004, D1.

Sinclair Broadcast Group, Inc. "Sinclair to Acquire Tennis Channel; Company to Hold Conference Call on January 28, 2016." Press release, January 27, 2016.

———. 2015 Annual Report, Form 10-K. February 5, 2016.

———. 2018 Annual Report, Form 10-K. March 1, 2019.

Tennis Channel, Inc. v. Comcast Cable Communications, LLC, 13–676, (D.C. Cir. 2013), cert. denied, (US February 24, 2014).

"Top 50 MSOs." *Broadcasting & Cable Yearbook*, Volume 1. New Providence, NJ: R.R. Bowker, 1996.

University of Texas at Austin, IMG Communication and ESPN Inc. "License Agreement." December 24, 2010.

5

REGIONAL SPORTS NETWORKS

The Chicago Cubs entered the waning days of the 2019 baseball season looking to do something that seemed unthinkable only a few years earlier. Long dubbed lovable losers, the Cubs exorcized 108 years of misery in 2016 when they won the World Series for the first time since 1908 with a dramatic game seven, extra inning victory over the Cleveland Indians. That title was the centerpiece of a string of playoff appearances that began in 2015 and extended through 2018, a streak that the Cubs were well positioned to extend with 12 games left in the 2019 season; two games behind the St. Louis Cardinals in the division race and a game ahead of the Milwaukee Brewers for the second National League Wild Card spot. Chicago then reverted to the Cubs of old, losing seven straight games to enter the final Wednesday of the regular season five games behind the Brewers for the final playoff spot with five games to play. Milwaukee eliminated Chicago with a 9–2 victory over the Cincinnati Reds that night, a game that ended during the final innings of what would be an eighth consecutive Cubs defeat, this one against the Pittsburgh Pirates. It was somehow fitting that many Cubs fans back in Chicago learned the team's fate during the Cubs-Pirates games on WGN, since that local independent television station had documented so much of the team's misfortune, dating all the way back to 1948. That was another streak that ended, as after 72 years, the Cubs were slated to leave WGN after the 2019 season and eliminate all local telecasts on broadcast stations in 2020.

The fate of WGN was sealed the previous February, the day after Cubs pitchers and catchers reported for spring training in Arizona, with the announcement that the rights to the team's local telecasts would move in 2020 to a new Chicago-centered regional network, Marquee Sports. That plan did not come as a surprise, since the Cubs signed only a five-year deal with WGN in 2015 that extended through the 2019 season, which coincided with the expiration of its agreement with NBC Sports Chicago. What was unknown was whether the Cubs would go out on its own or partner with a media conglomerate as the Dodgers did with Time Warner Cable in the launch of SportsNet LA in 2014. That question was answered with the revelation that the Cubs would launch the network with Sinclair Broadcast Group, owner of one of the largest local television station group in the United States. The potential value of such a partnership was made clear that fall when Sinclair reached a carriage agreement with AT&T, a deal that exchanged retransmission consent for the Sinclair-owned and/or operated stations for cash and carriage of other Sinclair properties, such as Marquee Sports. At the start of 2019, AT&T accounted for approximately 24 million video subscribers nationwide between DirecTV, AT&T U-verse, and DirecTV Now, with approximately 700,000 in the Chicago market. Securing carriage before Marquee Sports launched showed the leverage Sinclair wielded in such negotiations and was no doubt a sore point in Los Angeles, where SportsNet LA was not on DirecTV after six seasons.

The launch of Marquee Sports Network is in many respects emblematic of the issues swirling around regional sports networks (RSNs). First, it is the latest example of the migration of professional sports from free, over-the-air broadcast outlets to pay services. In 2019, the Cubs had more local telecasts on broadcast stations that any other team in the league, with 45 games on WGN and another 25 on WLS, the ABC affiliate in Chicago. Starting in 2020, as noted, all local Cubs telecasts were slated to be on Marquee Sports Network. Second, it adds fodder to the ongoing debate over the bundling of sports programming services. The business model for Marquee Sports is predicated on carriage agreements that place the service on the most widely distributed tier for each MSO rather than on a sports tier or on an à la carte basis. The objective is to generate revenue from most cable, satellite, or telco household in the Chicago market, about 2.5 million in 2019, as opposed to charging higher fees for select subscribers willing to pay extra to watch the Cubs. Third, the connection between Marquee Sports Network and Sinclair contributes to ongoing discussions around horizontal and vertical integration and media conglomerates. What is interesting in this case is that the Cubs joined the owners of the MLB White Sox, NBA Bulls, and NHL Blackhawks as well as Comcast in the 2005 launch of what is now NBC Sports Chicago. As such, network ownership is nothing new to the Cubs and the Ricketts Family that owns the team, although now it will not need to share prime viewing slots, or revenue, with other Chicago-based teams.

The Roots of Regional Networks

The potential for local sports content to be a driving force in programming services was discussed even before satellites made national cable networks viable. In the spring and summer of 1957, as the then New York Giants and Brooklyn Dodgers contemplated moves to the West Coast, Skiatron Electronics and

Television Corp. emerged as a much discussed protagonist. Skiatron had developed a system called "Subscriber-Vision" that utilized a set-top box to decode scrambled television signals. Newspapers on both coasts reported that the Giants and Dodgers had reached multi-million-dollar deals with Skiatron as negotiations continued with local governments.[1] Amid these deliberations, Congress and the FCC held hearings on "pay-as-you-see" television, with the Commission later authorizing tests of what it called "over the air subscription television systems." In hearings before a subcommittee of the House Judiciary Committee in June 1957, Dodgers owner Walter O'Malley testified that the team had reached a tentative agreement with Skiatron whether it remained in Brooklyn or moved to Los Angeles. The board of directors of the Giants approved a move to San Francisco in mid-August and announced a $2-million-a-year agreement with Skiatron in early September. O'Malley made his team's move official in early October 1957, and while a pay television agreement was not announced at that time, the Los Angeles City Council approved bids for three "toll television" systems that same month.

Winning baseball games proved easier to accomplish than developing the new television platform, however, as both the Dodgers and Giants claimed the National League pennant before their games appeared on pay TV. In 1964, Skiatron successor Subscription Television Inc. (STV) prepared to launch in Los Angeles and San Francisco under the direction of Pat Weaver, who created *The Today Show* and then served as president of NBC in the 1950s. The cable programming service focused on Los Angeles and San Francisco and offered three channels, with a mix of sports, movies, children's programming, and theatrical performances. And on July 17, 1964, a Dodgers home game against the Chicago Cubs was available to 1,500 or so homes on the west side of the city. The combination of sports and movies proved to be too much of a threat to both broadcasters and theater owners, however, with the Southern California Theater Owners Association among the most active lobbyists against STV. That November, voters in California endorsed a ballot initiative, the Free Television Act, banning subscription television, and STV suspended operations within the month. A Superior Court judge in California ruled that bill unconstitutional largely on free speech grounds in May 1965, and Weaver vowed to resume operations, but the state attorney general appealed to the Supreme Court of California. That court confirmed the lower court decision in a 6–1 vote in March 1966, but the state once again appealed.[2] When the U.S. Supreme Court refused to hear that appeal, the judicial battle was over, but Weaver no longer had the resources to move forward with STV.

The first modest foray into regional sports came in New York City in the late 1960s. The "new" Madison Square Garden opened for business in February 1968, and during the 1968–69 season, some home games of the NBA Knicks and NHL Rangers were transmitted to cable households via Sterling Manhattan Cable Television. That experiment was deemed a success, and in May 1969, the two sides signed a one-year contract to televise 125 sporting events from MSG, including all home games of the Knicks and Rangers.[3] At that time, the cable operator had just 13,000 subscribers on the island of Manhattan, providing service south of East 86th Street and West 79th[ᵗ] Street, but projected growth to 40,000 households by the spring of 1970.[4] The Manhattan Cable deal with Madison Square Garden was struck in a different era. In the 1960s and early 1970s, local television blackouts of sporting events were absolute, and even the Super Bowl was not broadcast in the market where the game was played. The same held true of the NBA Finals, which proved to be a boon for Manhattan Cable in 1970. That spring, Willis Reed and Walt Frazier led the Knicks to the title over the Los Angeles Lakers in one of the greatest battles in NBA history. The decisive game seven was contested at the Garden, so the ABC broadcast was blacked out in New York, although it was available via Manhattan Cable. When an injured Reed, not expected to play in the climactic game seven because of a severe thigh injury, limped onto the court for warm-ups, it was witnessed by a capacity crowd of 19,500 at the Garden and New Yorkers watching in homes as well as bars and restaurants. From the roots of those cable telecasts came MSG Network.

While the Knicks and the Rangers were building a new source of revenue in Manhattan, the New York Islanders of the National Hockey League and the New York Nets of the American Basketball Association were doing likewise on Long Island. In the fall of 1972, TelePrompTer Corporation and Suffolk Cablevision began offering a package of Nets and Islanders games for $50.[5] The cable landscape on Long Island changed dramatically the following year, when Charles Dolan formed Cablevision Systems Corporation. Dolan was a cable pioneer, winning the right to cable lower Manhattan in 1965 through the aforementioned Sterling Manhattan Cable, the first system in the country to lay cable underground. He was also the person who negotiated with Madison Square Garden to put the Knicks and the Rangers home games on cable television and later created Home Box Office. While Dolan was a visionary, his initial efforts in Manhattan were not a financial success and Time Inc. became a prominent investor in Sterling Communications. Time Inc. controlled 79% of the Sterling stock in September 1973 when it orchestrated a shareholder vote and assumed complete ownership of the corporation, forcing its founder out the door.

The sale of Sterling Communications to Time Inc. might have ended one chapter for Dolan, but it helped start a new one. Time Inc. elected to sell off several cable systems on Long Island and Dolan used the revenue from his 20% share of Sterling Communications to reacquire those systems.[6] That became the nucleus of Cablevision, which soon became the operator of one of the largest cable clusters in the country in the New York metropolitan area. In 1975, Cablevision signed a five-year agreement to televise the home games of the Islanders and Nets, and in 1979 it reached an agreement with both the New York Yankees and New York Mets to televise a limited number of games. In the case of the Yankees, the deal covered games that were not part of the local broadcast package of 100 games with WPIX, which carried the team from 1951 through 1998. The

Cablevision service soon became known as SportsChannel, and the balance in games between free and pay outlets soon shifted toward the latter.

While MSG and SportsChannel were taking root on the East Coast, different local models, including various pay-per-view schemes, were being explored around the country in the 1980s.[7] One of the first forays into pay TV in Los Angeles utilized the same transmission mechanism as the New York ventures, albeit with a different focus. Z Channel debuted on the systems Theta Cable in 1974 with programming befitting Hollywood: Jack Lemmon's Oscar-winning performance in *Save the Tiger* and Woody Allen in *Play It Again, Sam*. Feature films remained the focus of Z Channel for the decade that followed, although it too turned to sports in a bid for survival when it added the Dodgers and Angels to its schedule in 1988 after it became part of a joint venture between American Cablesystems, a cable systems operator in Los Angeles, and Spectacor, the parent corporation of the Philadelphia Flyers. The efforts to diversify its schedule proved to be too little too late and in 1989 the sports side of the service won out, with Z Channel becoming SportsChannel Los Angeles.

The spread of SportsChannel from New York to Los Angeles, and the integration of independent services into larger groups, is another significant pattern in the evolution of regional networks. The transformation of PRISM, and connections with both Fox Sports Net and Comcast SportsNet, is a prime example. Philadelphia Regional In-Home Sports and Movies, known by the PRISM acronym, was created in 1976 by Spectacor, the parent corporation of the NHL Philadelphia Flyers and The Spectrum, the indoor arena that opened in 1967. In 1981, that corporation launched a sister service in the Boston area, PRISM New England, that became the home for the NBA Boston Celtics. In 1983, Spectacor sold PRISM and PRISM New England to a joint venture that was owned, in part, by Cablevision, and PRISM New England became SportsChannel New England. The Philadelphia service continued to carry the PRISM name but was later joined by a sister service, PRISM: SportsChannel Philadelphia. There was an important difference between the two, as PRISM remained a premium service, charging around $12 per household per month in 1990, when SportsChannel Philadelphia debuted as a basic cable service. The other difference was that PRISM carried both movies and sports.

The creation of SportsChannel Philadelphia came at a time of growth for that brand. In June 1988, Cablevision outbid ESPN for the television rights to the National Hockey League, bidding to use that package to create a national network. In 1989 and 1990, it added five new services to the four it already owned, while also rebranding Sports Vision as SportsChannel Chicago. Six months after obtaining the rights to the NHL, Cablevision also sold 50% of its cable programming division, Rainbow Media Holdings, to NBC in a deal that also included carriage for CNBC. The expansion of SportsChannel and bid to create a national network to challenge ESPN proved to be ill-fated, and the regional sports business continued to churn through the 1990s. In 1993, Cablevision and NBC created a joint venture with Liberty Media and its regional services, Prime Networks, to share programming and sales under Prime SportsChannels America. That relationship also proved to be short lived.

The latter half of the 1990s featured two significant changes to the regional sports landscape that defines its structure two decades later. The first was the rise of Fox Sports. In May 1996, News Corp. and Tele-Communications, Inc., the largest cable MSO at the time, joined forces to create Fox/Liberty Networks, to which TCI contributed its financial interest in 15 RSNs (including seven Prime Sports networks in which it held a majority interest, and investments in three SportsChannel regional networks, as well as SportSouth in Georgia and Sunshine Network in Florida). That November, the networks were relaunched under the Fox Sports Net brand. The following year, Fox/Liberty contributed $850 million for a 40% interest in Regional Programming Partner, a venture with Rainbow Media Holdings that included Madison Square Garden Network and seven other RSNs, three of which were in top six markets (Chicago, San Francisco, and Boston). The five SportsChannel networks adopted the Fox Sports banner in January 1998, and while Madison Square Garden Network maintained the MSG moniker, it gave Fox Sports access to the largest market in the United States. Networks were added to and dropped from the Fox Sports group over time, with the most significant changes coming in February 2005, when the partnership with Rainbow Media was dissolved, and in 2008, when ownership of FSN Northwest, FSN Rocky Mountain, and FSN Pittsburgh was transferred to Liberty Media in a complicated deal that included the News Corp. interest in DirecTV. Those transactions gave News Corp. and its successor, 21st Century Fox, sole ownership of the Fox Sports regional networks.

The rise of Comcast as a force in sports television power began in its corporate hometown of Philadelphia in the mid-1990s, and the vertical links between content and distribution were evident from the beginning. Comcast was the dominant MSO in the Philadelphia area, but much of the local sports content was carried on SportsChannel Philadelphia and PRISM. The first step in establishing Comcast as a force in local programming came in March 1996 with the acquisition of a controlling interest in Spectacor, the parent corporation of the Philadelphia Flyers, and the purchase of the Philadelphia 76ers. In those transactions, Comcast gained control of the television rights to the NBA and NHL teams in the Philadelphia market. The second step came in July 1997 when it announced the creation of Comcast SportsNet Philadelphia in a joint venture with the Philadelphia Phillies. Comcast now controlled the local rights to professional baseball, basketball, and hockey franchises in the market and SportsChannel Philadelphia, and PRISM closed shop that fall at the conclusion of the baseball season.

Comcast SportsNet Philadelphia was based on a different business model than its predecessors. As discussed, PRISM debuted in 1976 as a premium service offering movies and exclusive sports programming, much of it from the Spectrum arena in Philadelphia that was controlled under the same corporate umbrella. The

76ers and Flyers remained fixtures on the service two decades later, with subscribers charged $12 to $15 per month.[8] SportsChannel Philadelphia launched in 1990 as a basic cable service, as opposed to a premium service, and a half decade later charged between 25 and 35 cents per household per month.[9] With common control of a significant share of local cable households and the three sports franchises, Comcast SportsNet launched on October 1, 1997, as a basic service but one demanding much higher carriage fees than SportsChannel Philadelphia ever imagined. Local cable operators said that the initial carriage fee set for SportsNet Philadelphia was $1.50 per household per month, although Comcast claimed the cost range was between $1.20 and $1.35.[10] In either case, SportsNet Philadelphia became one of the most expensive basic cable services and shifted the cost of the service from sports fan willing to subscribe to a premium service to almost all subscribers.

Comcast chose not to adopt the premium business model of PRISM, but it did utilize its distribution system. When SportsNet Philadelphia launched, it did so, at least in part, through the microwave infrastructure that PRISM had in place.[11] The use of microwave and fiber optic facilities to distribute SportsNet Philadelphia allowed Comcast to circumvent a provision of the 1992 Cable Act that mandated that cable operators make services in which they hold a financial interest available to competitors. When SportsNet Philadelphia launched, it was not made available to DirecTV and other direct-broadcast-satellite services that competed with Comcast in the Philadelphia marketplace. Section 628(b) of the act addressed "unfair methods of competition" that were designed "to hinder significantly or to prevent any multichannel video programming distributor from providing satellite cable programming or satellite broadcast programming to subscribers."[12] The FCC, however, cited the inclusion of "satellite" in the description of programming services to exclude services distributed through "terrestrial" mechanisms.[13] The Commission did not close the "terrestrial loophole" until 2010 when Comcast was focused on its proposed acquisition of NBCUniversal.

The control of live content through joint ventures with professional teams became the blueprint for the creation of SportsNet services. In 2004, Comcast SportsNet Chicago launched as a joint venture between Comcast and the owners of the MLB Cubs and White Sox, NBA Bulls, and NHL Blackhawks, with each gaining a financial interest of 20%. In 2007, Comcast gained a 60% interest in Fox Sports Net Bay Area in a joint venture with News Corp. and then brought the San Francisco Giants into the ownership group a few months later. The service was rebranded Comcast SportsNet Bay Area in time for the 2008 baseball season. In 2011, it announced the creation of Comcast SportsNet Houston, a joint venture with the MLB Astros and NBA Rockets that debuted prior to the 2012–13 basketball season. Comcast was the largest multichannel distributor in the market, but it could not reach carriage agreements with the other large distributors, including DirecTV, Dish, and AT&T U-verse. Comcast recorded a $249 million reduction in the value of the network in 2013 and CSN Houston filed for Chapter 11 bankruptcy protection in September of that year. In time, it became an AT&T SportsNet outlet.

There have been various ebbs and flows in the regional sports marketplace since the mid-1990s, but the basic ownership structure remained in place until December 2017 when Disney announced its intention to acquire entertainment assets for 21st Century Fox for $67 billion. Comcast, which was in discussions with Fox before the initial agreement was struck, made another bid the following June, but Disney increased its offer to $71.3 billion and the deal was done. While Fox opted to retain most of its news and sports assets, including the Fox network as well as Fox Sports 1, Fox Sports 2, and its interest in the Big Ten Network, the deal did include its 21 regional sports networks and its 80% financial interest in YES Network. Disney believed that the combination of ESPN and the RSNs could create synergies in local markets, but the Department of Justice was concerned with the leverage the combination would create in negotiations with MSOs. The government argued that this would "eliminate substantial head-to-head competition" and would "likely result in higher prices for cable sports programming" in the markets with Fox regional networks.[14] It is a testament to the importance of sports programming that the government focused on the combination of ESPN and regional sports networks rather than the merging of the Disney and Fox film studios in its assessment of the deal.

The proposed final judgment between Disney and the Justice Department was submitted to the U.S. District Court for the Southern District of New York on June 27, 2018. That agreement required the divestment of all assets related to the Fox RSNs within 90 days of the closing of the deal between Disney and 21st Century Fox. After fielding various offers, Disney sold the 21 regional networks it acquired outright and Fox College Sports to Sinclair Broadcast Group for $10.6 billion. Those assets were placed in an indirect wholly owned subsidiary, Diamond Sports Group LLC, but the connection to Sinclair was undeniable. The YES Network was not included in that deal, since its original agreement with 21st Century Fox gave the Yankees the right to reclaim ownership in the event the network was sold. Sinclair joined Amazon and other private investors to acquire a financial interest in YES Network as well, with Sinclair taking the lead in carriage negotiations with MSOs. It is worth noting that the retransmission agreement between Sinclair and AT&T that was mentioned earlier also included carriage for the Fox RSNs and YES Network.

Regional Sports Networks in the 2010s

The $71.3 billion sale of 21st Century Fox assets to The Walt Disney Co. could become a watershed moment for regional sports networks. The settlement reached with the Department of Justice that resulted in sale of the Fox regional networks was a substantial power shift in the marketplace, one that propelled Sinclair Broadcast Group to an even more prominent position and bound together one of the largest local broadcast station groups with the largest collection of regional networks. What was also important was that sports television, and the rising cost of such services, was the focus of a major merger review. The attention paid to the price tag for ESPN was nothing new, as the four-letter network has been a focal point for many debates in Congress. What was different, however, was the attention paid to the fees for regional sports networks. The high price for such services is not new, but the deal between Disney and Fox transformed what is often a local concern into a national issue. Most debates over regional sports networks, such as the creation of Marquee Sports, center on a single market and/or single team. And the local conditions can be quite different. While New York and Los Angeles were home to four RSNs with rights to professional baseball, basketball, and hockey teams in October 2019, the fourth and fifth ranked markets, Philadelphia and Dallas-Ft. Worth, had only one each: NBC Sports Philadelphia and Fox Sports Southwest, respectively. That does not diminish the importance of such discussions, but it changes the parameters of the debate.

Siphoning of Sorts From Free Platforms to Pay Platforms

The establishment of baseball as the national pastime is intertwined with the evolution of broadcast radio and television in the United States. From the first radio broadcast of the Pirates and Phillies on KDKA in Pittsburgh in 1921 to the first television broadcast of the World Series between the New York Yankees and then Brooklyn Dodgers in 1947, the expansion and growth of the game was linked with the parallel development of broadcast radio and television. While broadcast radio remains an important part of the game, pay television services have largely replaced free-to-air outlets at the local level, a migration that was most evident in the final days of the 2014 season. The introduction of a second Wild Card team in each league in 2012 meant that more teams were in playoff contention as the season reached Labor Day weekend. That contributed to a banner month of baseball, with three teams – Detroit, St. Louis, and Oakland – claiming playoff berths on the final day of the season. Few of those games, however, were on local broadcast stations outside of national telecasts on FOX. By the 2014 season, all of the local telecasts for 19 of 29 US-based team had moved to pay services, with only two teams carrying 30 or more local telecasts on free-to-air stations. The percentage of pay-only teams was even higher among those that reached the playoffs, as seven of ten had migrated totally to cable, although the Los Angeles Dodgers did air their final six games on KDOC-TV when SportsNet LA could not reach agreements with cable and satellite operators. Of the other three teams – Baltimore, San Francisco, and Washington – only 1 out of 74 games under team control was on a local broadcast station in the month of September.

The migration of local television rights for Major League Baseball teams since 1980 is documented in Table 5.1. The rapid decline of broadcast-only teams through the 1980s is noteworthy, but the rise of cable only teams since 2000

TABLE 5.1 Siphoning of local baseball rights from broadcast to cable, 1980–2019

	1980	1985	1990	1995	2000	2005	2010	2015	2019
Total U.S.-Based Teams	24	24	24	26	28	29	29	29	29
Broadcast Only Teams	22	11	8	4	0	0	0	0	0
Broadcast and Cable Teams	2	13	16	22	26	23	17	9[1]	8
Cable Only Teams	0	0	0	0	1	6	12	20	21

Source: Team media guides and schedules and team and television outlet press releases.

1 Total for 2015 includes the Philadelphia Phillies and Texas Rangers. In that year, the Phillies placed a single game, Opening Day, on the NBC affiliate, WCAU, while the Rangers telecast two games on an independent station, KTXA, to accommodate college football conflicts on Fox Sports Southwest.

is most dramatic. At that time, the Cincinnati Reds were the lone team with a pay-only television deal, a group that increased to 21 of 29 in 2019. Among the other eight teams, only two teams, the Chicago Cubs and Chicago White Sox, allocated more than 25 games to local broadcast stations, with a total of 70 and 55, respectively, while the New York Mets and New York Yankees televised 25 and 21 games, respectively, on WPIX, the CW affiliate in New York. The Cleveland Indians were at the other end of the group, allocating four local telecasts to WKYC. The story with the Philadelphia Phillies and San Francisco Giants was more complicated. Most Giants games were carried on NBC Sports Bay Area, with the same true for the Phillies and NBC Sports Philadelphia. In each case, however, a small number of games were carried on the NBC affiliate in those markets, KNTV and WCAU. Both of those were NBC-owned and operated stations in markets where Comcast's share of multichannel video subscribers was over 50%. In other words, a dozen or so games might not have been on the NBC Sports regional networks, but those games remained under the Comcast corporate umbrella.

The final team with local telecasts on broadcast stations in 2019 is an important case to consider. As discussed earlier, the Los Angeles Dodgers signed a 25-year, $8.35-billion deal with Time Warner Cable in 2013 to create SportsNet LA. That service launched prior to the start of the 2014 season, but struggled to gain carriage as MSOs in the Los Angeles market balked at what some considered to be exorbitant carriage fees. Time Warner Cable merged with Charter Communications in 2015, but that did little to change negotiations. At the start of the 2019 season, DirecTV and Dish Network, as well as Cox Communications, still did not carry SportsNet LA, which meant that it was missing from around 2 million of the 3.6 million multichannel video households in the Los Angeles market. In February 2019, an agreement was announced that allowed ten Dodgers games between April and mid-June to be simulcast on a local broadcast station, KTLA, and SportsNet LA. In early August, with the Dodgers en route to a seventh straight National League West title, five more simulcasts were added on the last five Saturdays of the season. The Dodgers and SportsNet LA had done this in previous years, but 10 to 15 games did little to placate fans who were unable to watch most of the games over the course of the season.

There is another dimension of the migration from free-to-air to pay platforms that is significant. The completion of Orioles Park at Camden Yards in 1992 ushered in a golden age of baseball-only stadiums, one former Commissioner Bud Selig said "led to all these wonderful stadiums and allowed us to finally market our sport to its potential."[15] Those stadiums came at a cost, however; oftentimes a burden that fell upon local taxpayers. Between 1999 and 2012, 15 of 30 major league baseball teams moved into new stadiums, with an average cost of $456 million. That average was more than $400 million per stadium, even when the $1.1 billion price tag for Yankee Stadium is removed from the group. With 10 of those 15 stadiums, public financing covered 50% or more of the total cost, with Nationals Park in Washington, DC, and Great American Ballpark in Cincinnati the highest at 100% and 96%, respectively. While the teams were open to public funding of their stadiums, they demanded that taxpayers pay to see the teams pay on television, as eight of the ten teams were exclusively on pay platforms in the local market. Cincinnati is an interesting case, as voters in Hamilton County approved an increase of one-half of 1% in the local sales tax to build and maintain two new riverfront stadiums, one for football and one for baseball. The Reds broadcast some of their games on local broadcast station WSTR in the mid-1990s, but it moved all its local telecasts to Fox Sports Ohio in 2000, four seasons after voters approved the tax increase and three seasons before Great American Ballpark opened.

Big Money Deals

The Dodgers deal to create SportsNet LA was the third seismic shift to hit the Los Angeles television market in less than 24 months. In February 2011, the Los Angeles Lakers signed a $3-billion, 20-year agreement with Time Warner Cable to create not one but two regional sports networks – one in English and one in Spanish – that would feature the NBA franchise: TWC SportsNet and TWC Deportes, starting in 2012–13. That moved the Lakers off the Fox-owned Prime Ticket, the regional network then team owner Dr. Jerry Buss helped launch in 1985. The deal also eliminated local Laker telecasts on broadcast stations. The second mega deal was struck before the end of 2011. That December, the Los Angeles Angels reached a new carriage agreement with Fox Sports West for similar terms, $3 billion over 20 years. The $150 million per season average was a significant increase over its previous ten-year, $500-million deal with Fox Sports. With that contract in place, it was clear that the Dodgers would reap even greater riches and that came to fruition in January 2013 with the 25-year, $8.35-billion agreement to launch the new network. In less than 24 months, two new English language regional sports networks were added in the Los Angeles market, deals totaling close to $15 billion were signed between teams and sports services, and the multichannel video bills for Angelenos were altered forever.

The total value of such deals is difficult to calculate. In the mid-1990s, Major League Baseball instituted various mechanisms to address the revenue disparity and competitive imbalance that existed in the game at that time. The league's 1996 Collective Bargaining Agreement (CBA) with the players' association introduced limited revenue sharing and payroll taxes, but in the eyes of the commissioner's Blue Ribbon Panel on Baseball Economics, those provisions "produced neither the intended moderating of payroll disparities nor improved competitive imbalance."[16] The most damning conclusion of that panel's work was the fact that in the five years prior to issuing its report in 2000, the teams in the third and fourth quartiles based on payrolls did not win a single game in the Divisional Series or League Championship Series, and the teams from the second, third, and fourth quartiles did not win a single game in the World Series. That panel recommended far greater sharing of local revenues and an increase in payroll taxes, and MLB followed suit in the two decades since then, with the CBA that covers 2017 through 2021 sharing 48% of local revenues equally among the 30 clubs in the league. The rights fees that teams receive from regional sports networks is subject to revenue sharing. That part of the financial equation is clear. What complicates matters is that the profit or loss related to RSN ownership is not, based on the fact that such revenue is not guaranteed.

That distinction has fueled the movement toward what some have called "individual RSNs" and/or team ownership interest in such networks.[17] The New York Yankees, for example, received an annual rights fee estimated at $85 million from the YES Network for the 2012 season, but it generated additional revenue through its majority interest in the service. In November of that year, News Corp. acquired a 49% interest in YES Network at the same time the Yankees agreed to a 20-year extension in their rights deal with the service, taking it through the 2042 season.[18] That agreement was reported to include escalators in the rights fee of 4% to 7% a year, taking the fee the Yankees receive from $85 million in 2012 to over $350 million in 2042.[19] The Yankees retained a 20% interest in the network when 21st Century Fox, one part of the divided News Corp., increased its ownership to 80% in 2014. That was significant given the fact that YES Network was the largest and most profitable regional network in the nation in 2013 with operating income estimated at more than $250 million.[20] As noted earlier, the San Francisco Giants acquired an estimated 30% equity interest in what is now NBC Sports Bay Area when it signed a 25-year deal with the service in December 2007, sharing ownership at the time with Comcast and News Corp.[21] The Giants also received a percentage of advertising revenue from the network. Such deals make it difficult to estimate the total revenue local television generates for some professional teams.

What is clear in the examination of local television contracts and regional sports networks is that the game has changed over the last decade. Prior to 2010, the Yankees were the unquestioned leader in this regard among baseball teams, both in terms of their annual rights fee and revenue from their interest in the

YES Network. It was the local television deals signed between 2010 and 2014 that made headlines and transformed the sports and television marketplaces. The first prominent deal came in September 2010 when the Texas Rangers agreed to a 20-year extension with Fox Sports Southwest with rights fees estimated at the time to be worth $1.6 billion, starting with the 2015 season.[22] At the other end of that period, the Philadelphia Phillies signed a 25-year, $2.5-billion deal to remain on NBC Sports Philadelphia in January 2014, which included a 25% ownership interest in the service. The aforementioned deals with the Angels and Dodgers in Los Angeles and changes in the ownership structure for the YES Network in New York fell in between. The Seattle Mariners signed an extension with ROOT Sports Northwest in 2013 that included an annual rights fee in excess of $100 million and a majority ownership interest in the service. What was significant about the period between 2010 and 2014 is that the largesse extended well outside Top 10 or 15 markets. The San Diego Padres signed a $1.4 billion deal with News Corp. in 2012 that was built around the launch of a new network, Fox Sports San Diego, in which the team also received a 20% equity interest.[23] At that time, San Diego was ranked 28th among local television markets in the United States.

The link between staggering new regional television agreements and team player acquisitions and contracts is clear to see. The cause and effect between such deals and household cable and satellite rates is much harder to determine. One trend that is clear is that cable and satellite rates were more or less immune from the global recession that took hold in 2008. The average monthly price for expanded basic cable service increased 5.9% in the 12 months ending January 1, 2009, to $52.37, compared to an increase of 0.1% for the Consumer Price Index.[24] That same pattern was evident in the two years that followed, with an increase of 3.7% in the 12 months ending January 1, 2010, and an increase of 5.4% for the 12 months ending January 1, 2011.[25] In both cases, the annual increase in cable rates outpaced increases in the Consumer Price Index. The increases in the average price for expanded basic service slowed somewhat in the five-year period prior to January 1, 2016, averaging 4.4%, but that was still well ahead of the average CPI, an average of 1.5%.[26] There is no disputing the fact that regional sports networks contributed to these increases. Kagan estimated that affiliate-fee revenue from all regional sports networks increased 44% over a five-year period, from $3.2 billion in 2007 to $4.6 billion in 2011.[27] The average annual rate increase for regional sports networks was more than 12% in 2007 and 2008 and averaged 8.7% per annum in 2009, 2010, and 2011.[28] In 2011, regional sports networks charged an average of $2.30 per household per month, more than double the highest priced non-all-sports cable or satellite service on the expanded basic tier.

The rise in affiliate fees, and the high stakes involved, was most evident in Southern California in the summer of 2012. Time Warner Cable entered the programming marketplace seeking a reported $3.95 per month per household in Los Angeles for the English- and Spanish-language networks to feature the Lakers.[29]

A little more than 100 miles south, Time Warner Cable endured a season-long impasse with Fox Sports San Diego over a reported carriage fee of $5 for the new network featuring the Padres.[30] Such prices would rank the networks among the most expensive regional networks at the end of 2011, including YES Network, Fox Sports Detroit, and New England Sports Network. Relative to other markets, Fox Sports Detroit was something of a bargain as it held the local rights for three major professional packages in the city, the MLB Tigers, NBA Pistons, and NHL Red Wings. The other two controlled the rights to two of the three in their markets, the MLB Yankees and NBA Nets with YES Network in New York City, and the MLB Red Sox and NHL Bruins with New England Sports Network in Boston.

The fragmentation of the marketplace and proliferation of regional sports networks is a significant contributor to rising cable rates. The financial impact of the doubling of RSNs in Los Angeles and New York is evident in Table 5.2. Through the first half of 2012, the Los Angeles market was home to two News Corp.-owned networks that held the non-broadcast rights for all six local professional sports teams, Fox Sports West and Prime Ticket. Kagan estimated the average affiliate fee for Fox Sports West was $2.30 per household per month while Prime Ticket collected an additional $2.27 a month in 2009, increasing 20 cents over the next two years to averages of $2.50 and $2.47, respectively, in 2011. The cost for local sports changed in 2012 with the creation of the TWC SportsNet featuring the Lakers. TWC SportsNet debuted with an estimated per household cost of $3.10 per month, but the total price for the same collection of professional teams increased from around $4.97 per month in 2011 with two networks to $7.61 per month with three in 2012. That increase, moreover, was before the addition of

TABLE 5.2 Estimated average revenue per average subscriber per month for New York City and Los Angeles regional sports networks, 2000–2018

	2000	2003	2006	2009	2012	2015	2018
MSG Network	$1.95	$1.72	$1.54	$2.00	$2.77	$3.55	$4.42
MSGPlus (f.k.a. FSN New York)	$1.20	$1.15	$1.26	$1.71	$2.43	$2.64	$3.17
SportsNet New York			$1.38	$1.58	$2.05	$2.65	$2.96
YES Network		$2.25	$2.94	$3.20	$4.00	$5.94	$6.47
NEW YORK TOTALS	$3.15	$5.12	$7.12	$8.49	$11.25	$14.78	$17.02
Fox Sports West	$0.87	$1.81	$1.93	$2.30	$1.95	$2.39	$3.12
Prime Ticket (f.k.a. FSN West 2)	$0.60	$1.05	$1.70	$2.27	$2.56	$1.34	$2.13
Spectrum SportsNet	–	–	–	–	$3.10	$3.63	$4.42
Spectrum SportsNet LA	–	–	–	–	–	$3.87	$4.98
LOS ANGELES TOTALS	$1.47	$2.86	$3.63	$4.57	$7.61	$11.23	$14.65

Source: Kagan, a media research group within S&P Global Market Intelligence, accessed October 1, 2019.

SportsNet LA, which launched in 2014 with an estimated price of just under $4 per household per month. The total cost for the four Los Angeles services was estimated at $11.23 per month in 2015, although all four were not carried in many cable and satellite households in the market.

The multichannel landscape that confronted Los Angeles had already played out in New York City. Like its West Coast counterpart, New York long supported two regional sports networks, Madison Square Garden Network and SportsChannel. The tide turned in 2002 when the Yankees moved from MSG to YES Network and again in 2006 when the Mets moved from Fox Sports Net New York, the successor of SportsChannel, to SportsNet New York (SNY). In 2012, Kagan estimated that the four networks collected estimated affiliate fees that topped $11 combined per month. YES Network was the most expensive at $4 per month, but it was also the service with the most complete programming schedule, with the MLB Yankees in the spring/summer/fall and the NBA Nets in the in the fall/winter/spring. MSG and MSG Plus collected just over five dollars per month combined ($5.20), but the slate on those services was much more limited, with no professional baseball and a significant dose of hockey. What is most significant is that the fee for YES Network increased 77.8% from 2003 to 2012, a rise of $1.75 per household per month. Between 2012 and 2018, YES Network increased from $4 to $6.47 per month, an increase of 61.8%. SportsNet New York experienced a more modest rise between 2012 and 2018, as its fee increased from an estimated $2.05 to $2.96, an increase of 44.4% over three years.

The economic model for regional sports networks is important to remember. When YES Network launched in 2002, it did so without carriage in close to three million Cablevision households in the region. Cablevision offered to distribute YES Network as part of a premium package or as a standalone channel, but the Yankees and their financial backers filed a federal lawsuit seeking carriage on the expanded basic tier.[31] Two years later, an arbitration panel mandated that Cablevision carry YES Network on the expanded basic tier for a period of six years.[32] When that decision was announced, Cablevision said it would add 95 cents a month to the price of its expanded basic service, called Family Choice, while stating that it was "absorbing most of the cost of carrying YES" on that tier.[33] The financial impact of such a decision is massive. In 2005, the YES Network cost an estimated $2.73 per household per month and with an estimated 8.9 million subscribers, it generated over $24 million a month in subscriber fees alone.[34] By 2018, it cost an estimated $6.47 per household per month, and while the average number of subscribers had dropped to 8.2 million, it generated just over $53 million per month.[35]

Prominent Ownership Groups

There are regional sports networks that stand on their own, outside of the dominant ownership groups, but such networks are rare and have one thing in common, with ownership resting in the hands of professional sports teams. In 1984, the Boston Red Sox and Boston Bruins created New England Sports Network (NESN) as a premium service, converting it to a basic service in 2001. Three decades after its launch, Fenway Sports Group, the parent corporation of the Red Sox, and Delaware North, the parent corporation of the Bruins, owned the network. Around the same time that NESN moved to the expanded basic tier, the Yankees created YES Network outside the major media conglomerates with financial backing from Goldman Sachs. Not all such endeavors were successful, however. The Minnesota Twins followed the Yankees model and tried to launch a network in Minneapolis-St. Paul prior to the 2004 season, but local cable operators and satellite services balked at the reported $2.20 per household per month charge.[36] Victory One folded a month into the season and Twins games returned to Fox Sports North.

The dominance of the Fox Sports group was evident at the end of the 2019 baseball season and the start of the 2019–20 basketball and hockey seasons. While Fox Sports was still the brand used, ownership and control resided in the hands of Sinclair Broadcast Group. No matter the name, various measures spoke to the prominence of the Sinclair-owned group. As of October 2019, it owned and operated 21 regional sports networks, with an additional investment in YES Network. As noted earlier, the scheduled launch of Marquee Sports in 2020 would bring that total to 23. It is also important to note the number of teams with which Fox Sports had local rights. That group reached its apex at the dawn of the new century, when it held the rights to 22 of 28 U.S.-based MLB teams (78.6%) in 2001 and 24 of 28 NBA teams (85.7%) in 2001–02. The rights for MLB, NBA, and NHL teams attributable to the three largest RSN groups as of October 2019 are listed in Table 5.3. The prominence of the Fox RSN group was most evident with the NBA, in which it held the local rights of 17 of 29 teams located in the United States (58.6%). The Fox RSN share was a little lower than the other two, 51.7% (15 out of 29) with the U.S.-based MLB teams and 50% (12 out of 24) with the U.S.-based NHL teams.

There were various departures that somewhat diluted the dominance of the Fox group, but the most significant change was the transfer of three regional sports networks to Liberty Media in 2006. Each of those networks, Fox Sports Northwest, Fox Sports Pittsburgh, and Fox Sports Rocky Mountains, held the rights to an MLB team, with Northwest and Rocky Mountains also the rights holders to two NBA teams each at one point in time. The deal for those services was announced in December 2006, but it was triggered two years earlier when John Malone acquired an 18% interest in News Corp. through Liberty Media, which led Rupert Murdoch and his board to implement a "poison pill" provision to fend off a hostile takeover. After months of deliberations, Murdoch exchanged his controlling interest in DirecTV, the three regional sports networks, and $550 million in cash for Malone's interest in News Corp. The FCC approved the transaction in 2008. Those three services became part of DirecTV Sports Networks

TABLE 5.3 Dominant U.S.-based regional sports network groups with MLB contracts at the end of the 2019 season and NBA and NHL contracts at the start of 2019–20 season

Network Group	Parent Corporation	Regional Sports Networks	MLB Teams Under Contract	NBA Teams Under Contract	NHL Teams Under Contract
Fox Sports Net	Sinclair Broadcast Group, Inc.	22[1]	15	17	12
NBC Sports Regional Networks	Comcast Corp.	8[2]	6	7	4
AT&T SportsNet	AT&T Inc.	4[3]	4	2	2
Totals[4]	–		25 of 29	26 of 29	18 of 24

Source: Sinclair Broadcast Group, Inc. (2019); Comcast Corp. (2019); and AT&T Inc. (2019).

1 Includes Sinclair Broadcast Group minority interest in YES Network.
2 Includes the Comcast interest in SportsNet New York and that RSN's rights to the New York Mets.
3 In corporate documents, AT&T states that it has three wholly owned regional networks in the Rocky Mountains (Denver, Las Vegas. And Salt Lake City), Southwest (Houston), and Pittsburgh, as well as one network in Seattle (Northwest) in which it holds a non-controlling interest.
4 Totals are for U.S.-based teams and do not include the one MLB team, one NBA team, and seven NHL teams in Canada.

and were rebranded as ROOT Sports in 2011. ROOT Sports Southwest became the fourth in that group in late 2014 after a court approved reorganization and transfer of ownership from Comcast SportsNet Houston. In 2017, two years after AT&T completed the acquisition of DirecTV, the Houston, Pittsburgh, and Rocky Mountain services assumed the AT&T SportsNet brand, while ROOT Sports Northwest, in which AT&T holds a minority interest, retained that name.

The rise of Comcast as a major player in the regional sports marketplace followed a different pattern. The control of cable households long made Comcast a force in the launch of programming services, but it became more significant in January 2011 when it acquired 51% of NBCUniversal from General Electric in a deal valued at $7.5 billion. NBC did not have holdings in regional sports networks at the time, having long before divested its interest in the Cablevision controlled Rainbow Media, but it did possess a broadcast sports division and the combination created a multi-tiered sports group that encompasses broadcast and cable as well as national, regional, and local. The Comcast approach to the ownership of regional sports networks becomes evident in the examination of the markets in which the cable operator had large clusters of subscribers. The cable giant surpassed 500,000 video customers in 16 of the 25 largest television markets in the United States in 2019. All seven of its owned and operated regional services were in one of those markets, with two in the San Francisco-Oakland-San Jose designated market area, CSN Bay Area and CSN California, and one, CSN Mid-Atlantic, covering both Washington, DC, and Baltimore. Six of those networks, in fact, were in one of the ten largest local television markets in the nation based on 2019–20 Nielsen rankings, with Chicago (3rd), Philadelphia (4th), and Boston (9th) joining the one RSN in Washington, DC (7th), and the two in San Francisco-Oakland-San Jose (6th). Comcast also held a minority interest in SportsNet New York, located in the largest marketplace, in a joint venture with the New York Mets and Charter Communications.

There were RSNs owned and operated outside of the Sinclair, Comcast, and AT&T triumvirate with major professional sports rights in the fourth quarter of 2019, most of which represented some form of vertical integration. The most common form of integration is shared ownership between teams and RSNs, arrangements that oftentimes contribute to the proliferation of services in a market, as documented with New York and Los Angeles. As discussed earlier, the Boston Red Sox and Boston Bruins share ownership of New England Sports Network (NESN), while NBC Sports Boston holds the rights to the Boston Celtics. A similar situation exists in Denver, where Stan Kroenke launched Altitude Sports in 2004 to carry the games of the two teams he owned, the NBA Nuggets and NHL Avalanche, while the MLB Rockies remained on what is now AT&T SportsNet Rocky Mountains. MSG Network shared ownership with the NBA Knicks and NHL Rangers in New York, and for decades, the vertical structure extended to Cablevision Systems Corp., the largest MSO in the market. As noted previously, there was a time when MSG outlets also carried both the Yankees and the Mets, but both broke away to launch networks of their own. Cablevision was sold to European telecom conglomerate Altice in June 2016, but the connection between MSG Networks and the Knicks and Rangers remains.

Mid-Atlantic Sports Network provides another, albeit more complicated, example. When Major League Baseball was exploring new homes for the Montreal Expos after the league took ownership of the team in 2002, Washington, DC, was deemed to be the "prime candidate" for the franchise.[37] Orioles majority owner Peter Angelos, however, stood in the way of such a move, since the nation's capital was just 40 miles from Baltimore and well within the his team's assigned broadcast territory. At the time, the Orioles were exploring the idea of launching their own regional sports network after their contract with Comcast SportsNet Mid-Atlantic expired after the 2006 season, and that network became the linchpin in negotiations between Angelos and the league. In April 2005, the two parties announced the launch of the Mid-Atlantic Sports Network (MASN), which would be home to both the Orioles and the Washington Nationals, the relocated Expos. The Orioles started with a 90% ownership interest in the service, with the league holding the other 10%, a share that would increase one percentage point per year until it reached 33%. Comcast tried to block the launch of the network in court in 2005 but was unsuccessful, while the FCC later gave MASN the right to demand arbitration in its negotiations for carriage on Comcast systems in the area when it approved an unrelated merger. That was the television terrain that Ted Lerner inherited when he became majority owner of the team in June 2006. That was not the end of the legal issues, however, as there have been ongoing battles between the Nationals and MASN, with a New York Supreme Court judge settling one dispute over the rights fee the network paid the team in 2015.[38]

Summary

The analysis of regional sports networks reveals undeniable patterns. First, there has been a clear migration of local television rights from free-to-air to pay platforms over the last 20 years in professional baseball, basketball, and hockey. Second, this shift has resulted in a dramatic increase in the revenue these teams generate for their local television rights, and, in turn, a significant rise in what television households pay for regional sports networks, which are almost always bundled and sold with expanded basic services. Third, ownership of these networks is concentrated in the three large conglomerates, including Sinclair Broadcast Group (Fox Sports), Comcast (NBC Sports Regional Networks), and AT&T (AT&T SportsNet). The end result of these patterns is that ever more resources are ending up in fewer and fewer hands and television households are paying more and more for these services.

Notes

1. Philip Benjamin, "Closed TV Linked to Baseball Shift," *The New York Times*, June 1, 1957.
2. Weaver v. Jordan, 64 C. 2d 235 (1966); Weaver v. Jordan, 385 US 844 (1966).
3. Gerald Eskenazi, "Garden, Cable TV Sign 1-Year Pact," *The New York Times*, May 21, 1969, 52.
4. "Garden, Cable TV."
5. "First Pay TV on L.I. Offers Basketball and Hockey," *The New York Times*, October 24, 1972, 86.
6. Tony Schwartz, "Cable TV Pioneer Still Takes Risks," *The New York Times*, August 3, 1981, D1.
7. Robert V. Bellamy, Jr., "Impact of the Television Marketplace on the Structure of Major League Baseball," *Journal of Broadcasting & Electronic Media* 32, no. 1 (1988): 73–87.
8. Michael L. Rozansky, "Cable Giant Comcast Pushes Out Local Philadelphia Sports Channel," *The Philadelphia Inquirer*, July 27, 1997.
9. "Cable Giant Comcast."
10. Michael L. Rozansky, "Regional Sports Channel Hits Snags," *The Philadelphia Inquirer*, September 8, 1997.
11. Comcast had also created a local cable service, CN8, in 1996 that was transmitted to operators in the region through a fiber optic system. This gave Comcast another path to reach local systems.
12. Cable Television Consumer Protection and Competition Act of 1992 S. 12 102nd Congress.
13. Federal Communications Commission, DirecTV Inc v Comcast Corp., Report and Order, 13 FCC Rcd 21822 (1988).

14. United States of America v. the Walt Disney Company and Twenty-First Century Fox, Inc., Complaint, 18 Civ. 5800 (S.D.N.Y. 2018).
15. Peter Schmuck, "Camden Yards, the Stadium that Changed Baseball and Baltimore, Turns 20," *The Baltimore Sun*, March 31, 2012.
16. Richard C. Levin, George J. Mitchell, Paul A. Volker, and George F. Will, "The Report of the Independent Members of the Commissioner's Blue Ribbon Panel on Baseball Economics," *Major League Baseball*, July 2000.
17. Stephen Dixon, "A Channel Worth Changing? The Individual Regional Sports Network: Proliferation, Profits, Parity, and the Potential Administrative and Antitrust Issues That Could Follow," *Journal of the National Association of Administrative Law Judiciary* 33, no. 1 (2013).
18. Richard Sandomir, "Ownership Change Unlikely to Alter YES's Formula," *The New York Times*, November 12, 2012.
19. "Ownership Change Unlikely to Alter YES's Formula."
20. Mike Ozanian, "Murdoch Buys Control of New York Yankees Channel for $3.9 Billion," *Forbes*, January 24, 2014.
21. John Dempsey, "Giants Play Ball With Cabler," *Daily Variety*, December 11, 2007.
22. David Baron, "Rangers, Fox Sports Southwest Agree to $11.6 Billion Deal," *Houston Chronicle*, September 27, 2010. chron.com.
23. Christina Settimi, "MLB's Most Valuable Television Deals," *Forbes*, March 16, 2014. www.forbes.com/pictures/mlh45egkd/kyle-blanks-everth-cabrera/#1c0a5676245f
24. Federal Communications Commission, Report on Cable Industry Prices, DA 11–284, MM Docket No. 92–266 (2011).
25. Federal Communications Commission, Report on Cable Industry Prices, DA 12–1322, MM Docket No. 92–266 (2012); Federal Communications Commission, Tennis Channel Inc. v. Comcast Cable Communications, L.L.C., Memorandum Opinion and Order, FCC 12–78, MB Docket No. 10–204 (2012).
26. Federal Communications Commission, Report on Cable Industry Prices, 18–128, MM Docket No. 92–266 (2018).
27. Mike Farrell, "WILD PITCH: RSN Fee Increases Outpace Cable," *Multichannel News*, March 12, 2012, 16.
28. "WILD PITCH."
29. Joe Flint, "Time Warner Cable Warily Enters Sports Programming Game," *Los Angeles Times*, September 12, 2012.
30. "Time Warner Cable Warily Enters Sports Programming Game."
31. Yankees Entertainment and Sports Network, LLC v. Cablevision Systems Corporation and CSC Holdings Inc., 224 F. Supp. 2d 657 (S.D.N.Y. 2002).
32. Cablevision Systems Corp., "Cablevision Reaction to Yes Network Arbitration Ruling," Media release, March 24, 2004. cablevision.com.
33. "Cablevision Reaction."
34. Kagan, "Network Economics: YES Network," S&P Global Market Intelligence. Accessed October 1, 2019.
35. "Network Economics: YES Network."
36. Aron Kahn, "Waiting Game Is Costly," St. Paul Pioneer Press, April 25, 2004.
37. Craig Timber and Steve Fainaru, "In the Game for Baseball, With the Score Uncertain," *The Washington Post*, March 23, 2003.
38. James Wagner, "New York Judge Sides With Orioles in TV Rights Dispute With the Nationals," *The Washington Post*, November 5, 2015.

Further Reading

Bellamy, Jr., Robert V. "Impact of the Television Marketplace on the Structure of Major League Baseball." *Journal of Broadcasting & Electronic Media* 32, no. 1 (1988): 73–87.

Caves, Kevin W., Chris C. Holt, and Hal J. Singer. "Vertical Integration in Multichannel Television Markets." *Review of Network Economics* 12, no. 1 (2013): 61–92.

Dixon, Stephen. "A Channel Worth Changing? The Individual Regional Sports Networks: Proliferation, Profits, Parity, and the Potential Administrative and Antitrust Issues That Could Follow." *Journal of the National Association of Administrative Law Judiciary* 35, no. 1 (2013): 302–340.

Gunzerath, David. "'Darn That Pay TV!': STV's Challenge to American Television's Dominant Economic Model." *Journal of Broadcasting & Electronic Media* 44, no. 4 (2000): 655–673.

Snyder, Adam. "Facing off Over Regional Sports." *Channels*, January 1990, 62–66.

Steffy, Loren. "Squeeze Play." *Texas Monthly*, April 10, 2014, 48–50. www.texasmonthly.com/politics/squeeze-play/

Chapter Bibliography

Baron, David. "Rangers, Fox Sports Southwest Agree to $11.6 Billion Deal." *Houston Chronicle*, September 27, 2010. Chron.com.

Bellamy, Jr., Robert V. "Impact of the Television Marketplace on the Structure of Major League Baseball." *Journal of Broadcasting & Electronic Media* 32, no. 1 (1988): 73–87.

Benjamin, Philip. "Closed TV Linked to Baseball Shift." *The New York Times*, June 1, 1957, 1.

Cable Television Consumer Protection and Competition Act of 1992 S. 12 102nd Congress, Cablevision Systems Corp. "Cablevision Reaction to Yes Network Arbitration Ruling." Media release. 2004. Cablevision.com.

Caves, Kevin W., Chris C. Holt, and Hal J. Singer. "Vertical Integration in Multichannel Television Markets." *Review of Network Economics* 12, no. 1 (2013): 61–92.

Dempsey, John. "Giants Play Ball With Cabler." *Daily Variety*, December 11, 2007.

Dixon, Stephen. "A Channel Worth Changing? The Individual Regional Sports Networks: Proliferation, Profits, Parity, and the Potential Administrative and Antitrust Issues That Could Follow." *Journal of the National Association of Administrative Law Judiciary* 35, no. 1 (2013): 302–340.

Eskenazi, Gerald. "Garden, Cable TV Sign 1-Year Pact." *The New York Times*, May 21, 1969, 52.

Farrell, Mike. "WILD PITCH: RSN Fee Increases Outpace Cable." *Multichannel News* 33, no. 11 (2012).

Federal Communications Commission. DirecTV Inc v. Comcast Corporation, Report and Order. 13 FCC Rcd 21822 (1998).

———. Report on Cable Industry Prices. DA 11–284, MM Docket No. 92–266 (2011).

———. Report on Cable Industry Prices. DA 12–1322, MM Docket No. 92–266 (2012).

———. Tennis Channel Inc. vs. Comcast Cable Communications, L.L.C., Memorandum Opinion and Order. FCC 12–78, MB Docket No. 10–204 (2012).

———. Report on Cable Industry Prices. DA 18–128, MM Docket No. 92–266 (2018).

"First Pay TV on L.I. Offers Basketball and Hockey." *The New York Times*, October 24, 1972, 86.

Flint, Joe. "Time Warner Cable Warily Enters Sports Programming Game." *Los Angeles Times*, September 12, 2012. latimes.com

Gunzerath, David. "'Darn That Pay TV!': STV's Challenge to American Television's Dominant Economic Model." *Journal of Broadcasting & Electronic Media* 44, no. 4 (2000): 655–673.

Kagan. "Network Economics: YES Network." S&P Global Market Intelligence. Accessed October 1, 2019.

Kahn, Aron. "Waiting Game Is Costly." St. Paul Pioneer Press, April 25, 2004. nexisuni.

Levin, Richard C., George J. Mitchell, Paul A. Volker, and George F. Will. "The Report of the Independent Members of the Commissioner's Blue Ribbon Panel on Baseball Economics." *Major League Baseball*, July 2000.

Moss, Diana. "Regional Sports Networks, Competition and the Consumer." *Loyola Consumer Law Review* 21, no. 1 (2008): 56–74.

Ozanian, Mike. "Murdoch Buys Control of New York Yankees Channel for $3.9 Billion." *Forbes*, January 24, 2014. forbes.com

Rozansky, Michael L. "Local TV Sports Fans to See a Change, In Cost." *The Philadelphia Inquirer*, July 27, 1997, A1.

———. "Regional Sports Channel Hits Snags." *The Philadelphia Inquirer*, September 8, 1997, E1.

Sandomir, Richard. "Ownership Change Unlikely to Alter YES's Formula." *The New York Times*, November 12, 2012. newyorktimes.com

Schmuck, Peter. "Camden Yards, the Stadium that Changed Baseball and Baltimore, Turns 20." *The Baltimore Sun*, March 31, 2012.

Schwartz, Tony. "Cable TV Pioneer Still Takes Risks." *The New York Times*, August 3, 1981, D1.

Settimi, Christina. "MLB's Most Valuable Television Deals." *Forbes*, March 16, 2014. www.forbes.com/pictures/mlh45egkd/kyle-blanks-everth-cabrera/#1c0a5676245f

Snyder, Adam. "Facing Off Over Regional Sports." *Channels*, January 1990, 62–66.

Steffy, Loren. "Squeeze Play." *Texas Monthly*, April 10, 2014, 48–50. www.texasmonthly.com/politics/squeeze-play/

Timber, Craig, and Steve Fainaru. "In the Game for Baseball, With the Score Uncertain." *The Washington Post*, March 23, 2003, C7.

United States of America v. The Walt Disney Company and Twenty-First Century Fox, Inc., Complaint, 18 Civ. 5800 (S.D.N.Y. 2018).

Wagner, James. "Ruling Gives O's Victory Over Nats." *The Washington Post*, November 5, 2015, D1.

Weaver v. Jordan. 64 C. 2d 235 (1966).

———. 385 US 844 (1966).

Yankees Entertainment and Sports Network, LLC v. Cablevision Systems Corporation and CSC Holdings Inc., US District Court for the Southern District of New York, 224 F. Supp. 2d 657 (2002).

6

STREAMING AND OUT-OF-MARKET SERVICES

The role that digital platforms might assume in the future of sports television was a topic of great debate but one with few definitive answers as the 2010s moved toward a close. Many industry analysts expected some members of the so-called FANG group – Facebook, Amazon, Netflix, and Google – to be major players in February 2018 when bidding for English Premier League rights in the United Kingdom opened for seven packages of matches starting with the 2019–20 season. Incumbent rights holders Sky and BT claimed five of seven sets in that first round of bidding, with the other two going unclaimed, and the U.S.-based new media titans remained on the sidelines. At the other end of 2018, reports that Amazon even explored a first-round bid for the regional sports networks Disney acquired from Fox was enough to make headlines.[1] Those stories, in turn, fueled a wave of speculation on the reasons Amazon would consider buying the regional networks.[2] Another topic of discussion in the opening round was confusion over what rights the RSNs controlled. Major League Baseball Commissioner Rob Manfred entered the process, asking the bankers in charge of the auction to inform potential buyers that digital rights were not included and that all the RSNs being bid on controlled were linear television rights.

There were significant developments in regard to sports streaming between those headline-grabbing moments. In March 2018, Facebook reached a deal with Major League Baseball for exclusive rights to 25 mid-week afternoon games, an agreement that pulled content from regional networks. In April, Disney launched a subscription streaming service within ESPN (ESPN+) and Time Warner did likewise within Turner Sports (B/R Live). In May, global streaming service DAZN announced its intent to start a U.S. service later in the year. Then in June, Amazon acquired one of the remaining Premier League packages for the U.K. in a second round of bidding, two single-day fixtures concentrated in the month of December.

There were, however, also headlines in that timespan that advocates for the migration of sports from broadcast and cable platforms to streaming services wanted to ignore. In Australia, Optus Sport held exclusive rights to 39 of the 64 matches of the FIFA World Cup in June and July, but after serious technical issues during the opening weekend of the tournament, the subscription streaming service was made available for free and all matches were simulcast on broadcast outlet SBS. In the United States, Turner Sports experienced difficulties with the pay-wall for a much publicized head-to-head golf match between Tiger Woods and Phil Mickelson in November, forcing AT&T to make the pay-per-view match available for free and refunding fees to customers who purchased the feed through B/R Live or DirecTV.

The question unanswered was when the rights to marquee events in the United States would migrate from broadcast or cable television to streaming services. The Facebook experiment with Major League Baseball made headlines, but it was also the focus of scorn from fans who were accustomed to seeing all games on national, regional, or local outlets. The package, moreover, included midweek, mid-afternoon games, about as far from marquee as one could get on the baseball schedule. One television executive was quoted as sayings that Facebook "only got the scraps" in the deal.[3] The NFL had dalliances with streaming starting in 2015 when Yahoo! paid a reported $15 million for exclusive rights to a single game outside the home markets of the teams involved.[4] What made that unique was that the match-up between the Buffalo Bills and Jacksonville Jaguars was from London at 9:30 am Eastern Time and fell outside the usual Sunday television windows for the league. That stream attracted 15.2 million unique viewers, with a third of the audience outside the United States.[5] The NFL signed a $10-million deal with Twitter for worldwide streaming rights to ten *Thursday Night Football* games in 2016, with that package moving to Amazon Prime in 2017, which renewed that deal for 2018 and 2019 with 11 games in each of those seasons. All of those games, however, were also part of national broadcasts on CBS and NBC in 2016 and 2017 and FOX in 2018 and 2019.

While major marquee events had not migrated to streaming services at the close of the 2010s, it is worth remembering that there was nothing to stop such deals. As discussed earlier, some nations in Europe and others around the world adopted lists of protected events that must remain on free-to-air broadcast stations so as not to deprive a portion of the public of the right to watch sporting events that were of importance to society. There were no such safeguards in place in the United States, evident with the migration of events to cable services such as ESPN. As discussed earlier, the Federal Communication Commission implemented rules to stop the siphoning of sports from free-to-air to pay platforms in the 1970s, but those limitations were struck down in court. The question, then, was a financial one: what were the business models that would make such a migration viable, in terms of the fees leagues, conferences, and organizations collect, the potential profit for the media conglomerates when weighed against the possible risks, and the ultimate cost to the viewing audience?

Consistent with evolving platforms, streaming video services have created a language of their own, one that requires clear definitions. Over-the-top, or OTT, is often used to describe film and television content that is delivered outside of broadcast television or traditional multichannel video programming distributors via the Internet. What is important to note is that the focus with OTT is on the method of delivery and the disruption of linear television and often involves the transmission of programming available on broadcast or cable outlets through the Internet, such as the streaming of *Thursday Night Football* games. There are important distinctions between that and so-called direct-to-consumer or DTC services. Those are predicated on a different economic framework, one in which streaming is more than a supplement and offers programming on an exclusive basis to streaming services. Those two models are often integrated into a single service. That is most evident with CBS All Access, which includes CBS primetime programs to allow viewers to circumvent linear television, but also features original programming like *Star Trek: Discovery* and *The Good Fight*. Hulu and Netflix feature a similar mix.

The examination of sports-related services in the latter part of the 2010s reveals elements of both approaches. That analysis, moreover, makes clear that there is no single model being pursued among the major media conglomerates, unlike linear television where the sports divisions of Comcast, Disney, Fox, and ViacomCBS, at a minimum, show common patterns. The divergent paths are evident in the degree of investment in streaming services among the group as well as the approaches among those most active in that sector. The difference between Disney and Comcast provides clear examples, from services such as ESPN+ that are built on a low subscription cost and large subscriber base, to those such as NBC Sports Gold that offer more targeted content at a higher price. The focus in streaming to date, for the most part, has been on content that does not fit on linear television networks and content from outside of primary markets, whether that is non-national NBA games outside of the cities of the teams involved or the Premier League and other European football matches in the United States. The rise of combat sports such as boxing and mixed martial arts on such platforms reveals a very different pattern, one with far more exclusive content, and, perhaps, a glimpse of the future.

Different Streaming Strategies

The creation of original content such as Hulu's *The Handmaid's Tale* and Netflix's *The Crown* revolutionized television and made streaming services a must-have for many viewers, but the transformation of the sports marketplace has been much more muted. To be certain, there was a concerted effort to get programming to would-be viewers on the desired platforms and devices, and a determination to monetize those feeds, but the focus for marquee properties remained on the commercial broadcast and cable networks. That was most evident with the Olympic

Games, which were locked up until 2032 with NBC Sports at the dawn of the 2020s. The $1.22 billion in rights fees NBC paid to the International Olympic Committee in 2016 gave it access to more than 7,000 hours of live television produced by the Olympic Broadcasting Services (OBS), only a fraction of which were broadcast on NBC, a total of 260.5 hours.[6] NBCUniversal presented a total of 2,084 hours on 11 linear networks, but even that was less than half of 4,500 streaming hours on NBCOlympics.com. Those hours were available to authenticated cable and satellite television subscribers without an additional fee, but there were limited options for cord cutters. And while digital sales were 33% above the 2012 Olympic Games, there was no question that the bulk of the record $1.2 billion in national advertising sales were directed at the primetime broadcasts on NBC.[7] The question was when streaming would become the primary feed for a marquee property.

The major conglomerates pursued divergent paths regarding packaging and pricing of streaming properties. CBS was the lone member of the big four broadcast networks that was not an early investor in Hulu, with NBCUniversal and News Corp. holding equity interests when it launched in 2008, and Disney making an investment in 2009. CBS went in a different direction, launching its own over-the-top service, CBS All Access, in 2014, one that cost $5.99 a month or $9.99 a month commercial-free at the start of 2019. That service features the CBS primetime programs produced within CBS Television Studios, but it also streams sports programming from the CBS network, including two major golf tournaments, The Masters and PGA Championships, and in-market NFL games. That service also includes CBS Sports HQ, which launched in 2018 with sports news, scores, and highlights. FOX and ABC followed different paths, albeit for different reasons. News and sports were the centerpieces of Fox Corp. after it completed the sale of its entertainment assets to Disney in March 2019, but Fox Sports was not aggressive in the streaming marketplace under 21st Century Fox. Programming from the FOX network, FS1, and BTN were available to authenticated pay television subscribers through the Fox Sports Go website and app as well as through DirecTV Now, YouTube TV, PlayStation Vue, and other streaming services based on local agreements on a market-by-market basis. ABC took a similar approach with the ABC Go website and app and its limited sports inventory, such as the NBA Finals, but with the shuttering of ABC Sports in 2006, all such content was integrated into ESPN platforms.

NBC took a more diversified approach to streaming than its broadcast network brethren. Much like ABC and FOX, live content on the NBC network was available via the network websites and apps, including nbc.com/live. Comcast and NBC Sports, however, were also early adopters of subscription streaming services for sports. In 2014, NBC Sports launched *Tour de France Live*, selling single-day web access for $4.99 and the entire race for $29.99, while the Android and iPhone apps for the tour cost $14.99. That business model expanded in 2016 when it launched NBC Sports Gold, offering a collection of streaming packages, many for niche sports. Streaming is well suited for niche sports that cannot generate large enough television audiences for commercial supported business models but can attract devoted fans willing to purchase content at a certain price point. At the end of 2018, NBC offered ten different streaming passes ranging from about $20 to about $75 for a season, with more on the way. The sport specific passes covered international sports, including track and field ($74.99), figure skating ($59.99), alpine and nordic skiing and biathlon ($69.99), cycling ($49.99), speed skating ($19.99), IndyCar ($54.99), and supercross ($74.99), as well as the PGA Tour ($64.99), Premier League ($49.99), and European rugby ($69.99). Many of these packages connect to NBC's ongoing relationship with the International Olympic Committee and international sports federations, while others are an outgrowth of its rights deals and relationships with the PGA Tour and other organizations.

The divergent approaches are also evident with two of the most aggressive conglomerates in this area, Disney and AT&T. As discussed, ESPN launched a multisport, direct-to-consumer subscription streaming service, ESPN+, in April 2018. That integrated service cost $4.99 a month or $49.99 for a year and offered a variety of sports, with "hundreds" of MLB, NHL, and MLS games and "thousands" of college sports events as well as Top Rank Boxing and Grand Slam tennis, heralded in the press release that announced its launch.[8] Tennis provides an interesting example of what streaming contributes to the sports television ecosystem. ESPN acquired exclusive rights to Wimbledon starting in 2012 and did likewise with the U.S. Open starting in 2015, ending long runs on NBC (43 years) and CBS (47 years), respectively. While the marquee matches are carried on ESPN and ESPN2, both tournaments provided television coverage of all competition courts for the first time in 2018, 18 courts for Wimbledon and 16 courts for the U.S. Open. All that content, more than 500 matches, was available on ESPN+. Disney also acquired additional new programming that was targeted for ESPN+, including the UFC and European football. In March 2019, ESPN+ touted that it would stream 1,530 live events and 115 original programs for "just $4.99 a month."[9]

Turner Sports pursued different strategies before the AT&T merger with Time Warner was completed and WarnerMedia underwent significant restructuring in March 2019. Turner had long combined traditional rights packages with hosting web and streaming services, reaching an agreement with the PGA of America to operate PGA.com in 2003 before acquiring programming, marketing, and technical operations of NBA TV and NBA.com when those operations moved to Atlanta prior to the start of the 2008–09 season as part of a new eight-year deal for the *NBA on TNT*. Turner assumed a similar role with the NCAA after joining forces with CBS in a 14-year, $10.8 billion deal for the NCAA Men's Basketball Tournament that was announced in April 2010. Five months later, Turner acquired the digital rights to 88 NCAA championships across all divisions in all sports, outside of the Bowl Championship Series in football, including streaming rights to 63 championships.

The NBA and NCAA rights became cornerstones of the Bleacher Report Live streaming service that Turner launched in April 2018 just days prior to the debut of ESPN+. That service, often shortened to B/R Live, was built on the brand name of the Bleacher Report, a sports-oriented website that launched in 2008 and Turner acquired in 2012. The offerings on B/R Live were far more limited when it launched than those on ESPN+, with the National Lacrosse League, World Wrestling League, and Red Bull Global Rallycross among the properties mentioned in a press release announcing its launch, although the lattermost ceased operations before its scheduled first round that May.[10] Far more important from a Turner perspective was the integration of *NBA League Pass* into the service and the introduction of a pricing system that allowed viewers to purchase a single game and even join live NBA games in progress for a reduced price. While a single game cost $6.99 in the 2018–19 season, the cost went down after the first, second, and third quarters. NBA Commissioner Adam Silver said, "Let's sell the fan what it is they want."[11]

That à la carte model was central to the B/R Live business plan and a point of demarcation from ESPN+. One of the driving forces for launching the service was the acquisition of rights to the Union of European Football Associations starting in 2018, including the UEFA Champions League and Europa League. Turner offered different pricing options for the slate of games that extended from the summer of 2018 through the spring of 2019, including an annual subscription to the B/R Live Soccer Pass for $79.99 as well as a monthly rate of $9.99 and per match price of $2.99.[12] The passes also included the Scottish Premiership and other content, but the UEFA matches were the most significant. And while TNT telecast 47 matches from the Champions League across the 2018–19 campaign, the bulk of the programming was on B/R Live. Turner used the same pricing system for a much lower profile property, the National Lacrosse League, where fans could purchase a 2018–19 season pass for $39.99, a monthly pass for $7.99, or a single game, live or replay, for $2.99. There was also programming on B/R Live that was free of charge, such as ONE Championship, a mixed martial arts competition out of Singapore.

There were other multi-national conglomerates that established a beachhead in the U.S. sports streaming market in 2018. Perhaps the least well known was Access Industries, the parent corporation of Warner Music Group and Perform Group, with the lattermost the home of the DAZN streaming services. In one sense, Access Industries represented a throwback to the age of industrial diversification once prominent around Hollywood, with motion picture studios owned at different times by Coca-Cola Co. (Tri-Star), General Electric Co. (Universal), Gulf+Western (Paramount), Kinney National (Warner Bros.), and Matsushita Electric Industries (Universal). In another sense, Access was a modern phenomenon as it was the investment arm of Soviet-born, U.S.-educated, Britain-based billionaire Leonard Blavatnik, with holdings in four primary sectors: natural resources and chemicals, media and telecommunications, venture capital/technology, and real estate.

The DAZN streaming service first gained a foothold in Europe and Asia in 2016 when it launched direct-to-consumer services in Austria, Germany, and Switzerland on August 10 before starting a service in Japan on August 23. In July 2017, it expanded into North America with the debut of DAZN Canada. The biggest news at the launch of the Canadian service resulted from a five-year contract with the National Football League that gave the service exclusive rights to *NFL Sunday Ticket, NFL RedZone*, and *NFL Game Pass*. The headlines continued into the season, however, as the NFL streams suffered from a litany of problems, with a representative of the league apologizing for "inadequate service" before the first week of games was even over.[13] Under a headline that read "Still not clear what the NFL thought it was getting itself into with DAZN," a columnist for the *National Post* in Canada outlined some of the issues, including "viewers reporting error codes, audio problems, delayed feeds, fuzzy pictures and more skipping than a schoolyard" among the issues.[14] The DAZN Canada struggles highlighted some of the challenges of streaming live sports, a clear difference from on demand entertainment programming. Prior to the start of the 2018 season, DAZN and the NFL made the *Sunday Ticket* portion of its package available through cable and satellite services across Canada, releasing some of the exclusive rights it had held.

The arrival of DAZN in the United States occurred in two steps. On May 8, 2018, former ESPN President John Skipper was named the executive chairman of the Perform Group. Skipper had stepped down from his ESPN position five months earlier, later admitting to substance abuse problems and a blackmail attempt from a former dealer. Two days after Skipper was named executive chairman, Perform Group announced an eight-year, $1-billion joint venture with British sports promoter Matchroom Sport to create Matchroom Boxing USA.[15] That venture was scheduled to stage 16 fight cards a year in the United States, with a new DAZN streaming service as the exclusive domestic live and on demand home for those bouts. DAZN also gained access to 16 fight cards in the U.K. that were featured on the Sky satellite service. The streaming service launched in September 2018 in time for a heavyweight bout between WBA, IBF, and WBO title holder Anthony Joshua and challenger Alexander Povetkin from Wembley Stadium in London.[16] The impact of Skipper's arrival at Perform Group was evident in November 2018 when DAZN completed a three-year, $300-million digital rights partnership with Major League Baseball that included the creation of a weeknight whip around and live look-in show co-produced by DAZN and MLB, modeled after *NFL RedZone*, as well as on-demand MLB content.[17] That was a natural extension for the two parties, since DAZN carried MLB games on its services in Japan as well as Austria, Germany, and Switzerland.[18] The deal with DAZN in the United States was also one of many endeavors for Major League Baseball on digital platforms.

Professional League Services

The precursor to streaming for professional sports leagues was *NFL Sunday Ticket*, the DirecTV satellite service that gives subscribers access to all out-of-market games in the non-national television windows. The NFL launched *Sunday Ticket* for C and Ku band satellite systems in 1994, with DirecTV offering the last five weekends of the regular season for $49.95 after reaching a distribution agreement with the league in mid-October. Twenty years later, in 2014, DirecTV extended its exclusive rights to *NFL Sunday Ticket* for eight years through 2022 at $1.5 billion a season. That contract allowed for limited streaming options, with households unable to receive DirecTV for one reason or another able to subscribe to NFLSUNDAYTICKET.TV for $293.94 for the season in 2019; $395.94 with the addition of *NFL RedZone* and *Fantasy Zone*. The combined services were also available to students enrolled in post-secondary educational institutions for $99.96 for the season. In 2018, the NFL allowed AT&T to offer *Sunday Ticket* through the DirecTV Now streaming service in seven markets: Boston, Hartford, Los Angeles, Louisville, Philadelphia, Phoenix, and San Antonio. That led to speculation that the NFL might exercise an option and terminate its deal with DirecTV after the 2019 season and pursue a global streaming and satellite deal for *Sunday Ticket*, but that did not occur.[19]

The distribution of out-of-market games for professional baseball, basketball, and hockey had similar roots but evolved in a different manner. DirecTV and other satellite distributors started offering *NBA League Pass* and *NHL Center Ice* during the 1994–95 season, with *MLB Extra Innings* starting shortly thereafter, but satellite distribution did not remain the exclusive domain of those services. iNDEMAND, a service owned by prominent cable operators, started offering the NBA and NHL out-of-market services in the 1999–2000 season and added the MLB out-of-market service in 2001. Those leagues were far more aggressive than the NFL in pursuing streaming, although the revenue generated was far less than the $1.5 billion a season DirecTV paid for professional football. The streaming options available in the 2019 season for MLB and NFL and the 2019–20 seasons for NBA and NHL are detailed in Table 6.1. Major League Soccer offered its own streaming service, *MLS Live*, until April 2018 when that programming became part of ESPN+.

There are both similarities and differences among those streaming packages. The leagues that share the most in common are Major League Baseball and the National Hockey League, which focus on services that include all teams or a single team, both for the entire season. Those similarities are to be expected. In 2015, the two leagues announced a unique six-year arrangement, with MLB Advanced Media (MLBAM) acquiring the rights to distribute live out-of-market NHL games for $100 million per season through BAM Tech, which was spun-off from MLBAM.[20] The NHL also acquired an equity interest in BAM Tech as part of that

TABLE 6.1 Streaming and out-of-market packages for the 2019 seasons for Major League Baseball and National Football League and 2019–20 seasons for the National Basketball Association and National Hockey League

League	Product	Price
Major League Baseball (MLB)	MLB.TV Single Team	$91.99/year
	MLB.TV Premium	$118.99/year
National Basketball Association (NBA)	NBA League Pass Single Game	$5.99/game
	NBA Team Pass	$17.99/month or $119.99/year
	NBA League Pass	$28.99/month or $199.99/year
	NBA League Pass Premium[1]	$39.99/month or $249.99/year
National Football League (NFL)	NFL Sunday Ticket	$293.94/full season
	NFL Sunday Ticket Max[2]	$395.94/full season
National Hockey League (NHL)	NHL.TV Single Team Pass	$115.99/year
	NHL.TV All Access	$24.99/month or $144.99/year

1 NBA League Pass Premium is commercial-free, covering breaks with live in-arena cameras.
2 *NFL Sunday Ticket Max* includes various premium features including the *NFL RedZone* and DirecTV *Fantasy Zone* and additional streaming options on computers, consoles, and mobile devices.

agreement. The roots to that deal were planted in 2000 when MLB clubs committed to investing $1 million per year for four years, $120 million total, to create back-end infrastructure for MLB.com. Rather than creating a single website, that venture launched a media company that supported the creation of non-baseball services, with HBO working with MLBAM in 2015 to launch its stand-alone streaming service. The Walt Disney Co. acquired a 33% interest in BAMTech for $1 billion in 2016, a deal that included the right to acquire a majority interest over a number of years, a right it exercised in 2017 when it paid $1.58 billion for an additional 42% stake, bringing it ownership interest to 75%.[21] BAMTech provided the infrastructure for the launch of ESPN+ in 2018 and Disney+ in 2019.

Major League Baseball and the National Hockey League are linked in another regard. In 2012, two class action lawsuits were filed against the leagues, various regional sports networks, and two multichannel video programming distributors, Comcast and DirecTV. The consolidated lawsuits claimed that the leagues and their teams entered into collective "agreements to eliminate competition in the distribution of [baseball and hockey] games over the Internet and television [by] divid[ing] the live-game video presentation into exclusive territories" in violation of the Sherman Antitrust Act.[22] A focal point of those claims was that the defendants protected distribution systems through anticompetitive "blackouts" and colluded to "sell 'out of market' packages only through the League [which] exploit[s]

[its] illegal monopoly by charging supra competitive prices."[23] In a subsequent ruling in the case, the court discussed a New York Yankees fan who lived in Iowa and had to purchase an "out-of-market package" that included all teams "instead of simply buying the YES Network" either over the Internet or through a cable or satellite distributor.[24] Even with the purchase of the league-wide out-of-market package, the feeds from the regional sports networks of the two teams involved were blacked out in their home territories.

Streaming assumed an important role in that dispute and in the ultimate settlement. In a 2015 decision, the court refused to certify the case as a class action in regard to the damages claim, arguing that the plaintiffs could not prove the "damages cases on a class-wide basis" but did allow the case to move forward in an attempt to force the leagues to change the way they sold games.[25] That trial was scheduled to start on January 19, 2016, but the parties reached an agreement on a tentative settlement days before and the trial was averted. Under that deal, Major League Baseball agreed to offer a single-team television-streaming package starting in 2016 for $84.99, a 35% reduction from the most commonly purchased version of MLB.TV. The cost of the league-wide package was also reduced $20 to $109.99 yearly. The league-wide service included a "Follow Your Team" option, which for an additional $10 allowed subscribers to watch the games of one out-of-market team even when playing an in-market team. One condition of that option was that it also required individuals to be MVPD subscribers with a participating local regional sports network. For the 2019 season, the league-wide, yearlong subscription was $118.99, and the single-team option was $91.99. There was an additional incentive for MLB to promote streaming, since it was unable to raise the cost of the league-wide bundle unless it reached an agreement with Comcast, DirecTV, and Fox regional networks to allow in-market streaming for authenticated subscribers.

The NBA was the most creative in squeezing revenue from the streaming of regular season games and it was not the result of litigation. That service was part of the league's agreement with Turner Broadcasting in which the AT&T unit was responsible for the production and distribution of NBA TV and NBA.com. In 2018–19, consistent with the MLB and NHL services, subscribers could subscribe to the games of a single team with an *NBA Team Pass* for $119.99 for the season or all out-of-market games for all teams with an *NBA League Pass* for $199.99 for the season. For an extra $50, $249.99 total, *NBA League Pass Premium* offered all games for all teams commercial free, with the in-arena feed streamed during timeouts and halftime. There were prorated rates for those services when purchased at later points in the season. Fans that did not want to commit to an entire season could purchase a single game for $6.99, with prorated rates for partial games, such as $2.99 starting in the third quarter and $1.99 starting in the fourth quarter. There were also VR options with a limited selection of games. And those services were available on a wide range of platforms. The NBA replicated those options in 2019–20, with the single game price reduced to $5.99.

It is not surprising that the NBA was the most aggressive in exploring streaming opportunities. First, the average television viewer for professional basketball in the United States is much younger than that for the other major team sports. In one analysis of Nielsen viewership data, the NBA audience in 2016 averaged 42 years of age, compared with 57 for Major League Baseball, 50 for the National Football League, and 49 for the National Hockey League.[26] The NBA, moreover, was aging at a slower rate than the other leagues, with the median age increasing just two years between 2000 and 2016, from 40 to 42, compared to five years for MLB, six years for the NFL, and 16 years for the NHL (33 to 49) over the same period.[27] Second, the NBA was far more liberal in sharing highlights on social media than the other professional sports leagues through the mid-2010s. In one interview published in 2018, Commissioner Adam Silver used the difference between a meal and a snack to summarize the league's strategy:

> If we provide those snacks to our fans on a free basis, they're still going to want to eat meals – which are our games. There is no substitute for the live game experience. We believe that greater fan engagement through social media helps drive television ratings.[28]

The NBA extracts value from its social media presence, with one Nielsen analysis of the 2017–18 season tallying 1.5 billion fan interactions across Facebook, Twitter, Instagram, and YouTube, and estimated that the media value generated via social media for sponsors was $490 million.[29]

That openness to social media and streaming platforms extends to markets outside the United States as well. That is most evident in China, one reason for consternation with a tweet from Houston Rockets General Manager Daryl Morey about protests in Hong Kong in October 2019. The All-Star Game in February 1987 was the first-ever NBA broadcast in China and state-run Chinese Central Television (CCTV) retained the linear television rights to the league three decades later. What is more significant are the inroads of the league on non-traditional platforms. In 2015, the NBA announced a five-year expansion of its agreement with Tencent Holdings Limited, an investment and Internet-services conglomerate that ranks as one of the world's largest and most recognized outside the United States.[30] That agreement included the launch of NBA League Pass in China for the first time in 2016–17, which included packages that included all games for $164 a season (RMB 1,080) and a single game for $2.20 (RMB 15), as well as a Team Pass for $55 a season (RMB 360) and covered both personal computers and mobile devices.[31] The deal with Tencent also included content for various social media platforms, including Weixin, the version of WeChat used in mainland China, and QQ.com, an instant messenger service. In 2019, the league announced a deal with another Chinese giant, Alibaba, to create an "NBA Section" on various shopping outlets as well as bringing game highlights and other programming to nearly 700 million people on various platforms.[32] Alibaba banned the sale of products related to the Houston Rockets in October 2019 in response to the tweet from the team's general manager.

NFL experiences with streaming and social media were altogether different from those of the NBA. As noted, exclusivity for *NFL Sunday Ticket* was a cornerstone of the NFL deal with DirecTV and the impetus for the $1.5 billion annual price tag, and AT&T platforms remained the lone outlets for out-of-market games at the close of the 2010s. The NFL signed a new agreement with Verizon in the midst of the 2017 season that expanded its rights deal and included streaming of in-market and national games to smartphones through Yahoo! Sports, which it acquired earlier that year, and NFL Mobile from Verizon. It could also stream national games to tablets. While that deal did not give Verizon access to out-of-market games, the rights to in-market and national games, including the Super Bowl, were valuable in an era of cord cutting. NFL rights holders, CBS, FOX, NBC, and ESPN obtained the rights to stream their games through in-house services, but those platforms required either authentication through cable, satellite, or telco providers or a subscription to an over-the-top service such as CBS All Access. As such, Verizon provided a route for NFL fans without MVPD service, or without an antenna, to stream local or national games. Those rights cost Verizon more than $450 million per season and more than $2.25 billion over five seasons.

While the billions in revenue generated each year through media rights makes the NFL the envy of the professional sports league in the United States, it has struggled to find its footing on social media. A defining characteristic of the NFL contracts is that the rights to all regular season games are part of the national television deals, a stark contrast to baseball and basketball, in particular, where local television rights create wide disparities between big market and small market teams. The NFL approach to media rights places significant power in the league office and centralized control is also a component of the NFL social media policy. In October 2016, in the midst of the presidential election and a decline in television ratings, the NFL instituted a new social media policy that limited the ability of teams to share videos, animated GIFs, or livestreams of games and prohibited them from shooting their own video within the stadium while games were in progress. The prohibition included posting highlights from television coverage on social media. Those policies were attached to fines that reached $100,000 per violation.[33] Those rules only lasted a matter of weeks, as the league office relaxed the social media policy before the end of the regular season.

"A Fiery, Paywalled Hell"

The banner headline in world football at the start of 2019 was the Liverpool Football Club and its pursuit of its first league title since 1989–90, three seasons before the Premier League was even called the Premier League.[34] At the dawn of the new year, the Reds were unbeaten and held a seven-point lead over the defending champions, Manchester City. Liverpool lost 2–1 to Manchester City in the first week of January to tighten the standings, but its fans in the United States had another concern. As Liverpool navigated three different competitions – Premier League, UEFA Champions League, an annual competition among the top clubs from leagues across Europe, and the FA Cup, open to teams from ten levels of English football – the team's games were on three different streaming platforms. Four of its six group stage matches in the UEFA Champions League were streamed on the Turner-owned B/R Live, with the other two featured on TNT. Days after it lost to Manchester City, Liverpool was knocked out of the FA Cup by Wolverhampton in a match streamed on ESPN+. While it remained atop the table, its Premier League match at end of the month against Leicester City was available in the United States only through *Premier League Pass*. That prompted *Sports Illustrated* writer Grant Wahl to address a tweet to NBC Sports with a link to an earlier podcast that pleaded with television executives not to put matches behind "additional" paywalls, arguing that the sport had not "grown nearly enough in the US to shut out new fans with barriers to watching games."[35] Wahl acknowledged the irony that the Planet Futbol podcast was also behind a paywall at SI.tv.

The rising prominence and long-term impact of streaming on sports is per-haps most evident in the United States in the coverage of European football. The 20-team Premier League is arguably the preeminent domestic club league in the world, and it commands the most extensive television coverage in the United States. In an agreement reached in August 2015, NBC Sports extended its hold on the Premier League through 2021–22, with the total cost for six additional seasons reaching $1 billion. That package is a cornerstone of programming on NBC Sports Network, with additional matches featured on NBC and CNBC. And when the Premier League wrapped the 2018–19 season on May 12 with ten simultaneous matches on "Championship Sunday," NBCUniversal carried one on the NBC broadcast network, seven on national cable services, and one on regional sports networks, with just one match relegated to NBCSports.com and the NBC Sports app. The Premier League receives the most coverage on television plat-forms, but the various means NBC Sports utilizes to monetize that investment connects to the assessment of the sport on American television, which a *Deadspin* headline in 2018 proclaimed was "Going Straight to a Fiery, Paywalled Hell."[36]

NBC Sports made a commitment to televise all Premier League matches as part of its current rights deal and streaming assumes an important role in that promise. In 2016–17, the first year of the new deal, matches that did not air on NBC-owned broadcast and cable outlets were available to most authenticated cable and satellite subscribers via the NBC Sports streaming site, *Premier League Extra Time*. That changed with the 2017–18 season when NBC created an over-the-top service, *Premier League Pass*, as part of NBC Sports Gold, a direct-to-consumer live streaming platform. *Premier League Pass*, which cost $49.99 per season, gave subscribers access to 130 matches in 2017–18 and guaranteed 150 exclusive matches in 2018–19, including at least four per team. That meant that

U.S.-based fans of even the most prominent Premier League clubs needed to access *Premier League Pass* to see all their team's games. That exclusivity was the selling point in the press release NBC Sports issued on the eve of the new Premier League season in the summer of 2018.[37]

The Premier League offerings on NBC Sports Gold evolved further in 2019–20. The Sky satellite service built its subscriber base on Premier League rights in the 1990s and remained the dominant rights holder in the U.K. at the end of the 2010s. Comcast acquired complete ownership of Sky in November 2018 and the value of that deal was evident two months later. In January 2019, NBC Sports Network simulcast a six-hour Sky Sports News program, *Premier League Transfer Day Special.* That special was billed as the first major sports collaboration since Comcast acquired Sky, but it was by no means the last. For the 2019–20 season, NBC Sports offered two streaming options for the Premier League: *Matchday Pass* for $39.99 and *Premier League Pass* for $64.99. *Matchday Pass* included streaming of all live matches, including exclusive access to a minimum of four matches per team. *Premier League Pass* offered the same access to live contests but added on-demand access to all 380 matches and other shoulder programming, including match analysis from Sky Sports.

The exclusive coverage of some Premier League matches on the NBC Sports Gold platform generates the most headlines in the United States, but the balance between broadcast/cable services and streaming platforms still favors the former with most fixtures. That is not the case with the other prominent European professional club leagues in France, Germany, Italy, and Spain. The U.S. rights for the five most prominent leagues and the UEFA Champions League and Europa League are detailed in Table 6.2. The Fox investment in the sport is most evident with its deal with FIFA for the World Cup, which started with a $400 million deal for the 2018 and 2022 tournaments and was extended to include 2026, but European football was once a staple of the Fox empire and the featured attraction on the now defunct Fox Soccer Channel. The five-year deal between Fox Sports and the Bundesliga dates to 2015–16 with a pledge that all matches would be carried on some platform and linear services. FS1 and FS2 assumed a prominent role in the Fox coverage, with some matches on *Fox Soccer Plus*, a premium service. The arrival of the Bundesliga in 2015 coincided with the launch of a new streaming service, *Fox Soccer Go*, which was renamed *Fox Soccer Match Pass* in 2017. That service streamed all Bundesliga matches, but it was not a part of the 2018 World Cup, as streaming for that tournament was available to authenticated cable, satellite, and telco subscribers through the Fox Sports Go app.

While coverage of the Bundesliga on FS1 and FS2 gave the league a presence in the United States beyond streaming, that is becoming less true of the Spanish La Liga and French Ligue 1. Both those leagues are carried on beIN Sports, part of the global network of sports channels that are part of the Qatar-based, Al Jazeera-controlled beIN Media Group. beIN Sports launched English and Spanish language channels in the United States in 2012 and acquired the rights to La

TABLE 6.2 Broadcast, cable, and streaming outlets for European Football Leagues and UEFA tournaments, 2019–20 season

Country	League	Games per Season	U.S. Rights Holder	Broadcast and Cable Outlets	Streaming Service	Cost
England	Premier League	380	NBC Sports	NBC, NBCSN, and CNBC[1]	Match Day Pass Premier League Pass	$39.99/ season $64.99/ season
France	Ligue 1	380	beIN Sports	beIN Sports	beIN Sports Connect	$10/month $60/year[2]
Germany	Bundesliga	306	Fox Sports	FS1, FS2, and Fox Soccer Plus	Fox Soccer Match Pass	$19.99/ month $139.99/ annual
Italy	Serie A	380	ESPN	ESPN and ESPN2	ESPN+	$4.99/ month
Spain	La Liga	380	beIN Sports	beIN Sports	beIN Sports Connect	$10/month $60/year
Pan-European	UEFA Champions League	125	Warner Media	TNT	B/R Live	$9.99/ month
Pan-European	UEFA Europa Cup	205	Warner Media	TNT	B/R Live	$9.99/ month

1 NBC Sports Group uses additional channels on occasion, but NBC, NBCSN, and CNBC are the regular outlets.
2 beIN Sports Connect price is based on the cost for the World Sports package on Sling TV as of November 2019.

Liga and Ligue 1 in 2012–13 and extended those rights with new deals starting in 2015–16. Lionel Messi with Barcelona and Neymar with Paris Saint-German are big names in the Spanish and French leagues, respectively, while the Spanish league was also home to Cristiano Ronaldo before his 2018 transfer from Real Madrid to Juventas in the Italian league. In spite of that, beIN Sports has struggled to gain carriage in the United States. It suffered significant setbacks in 2018 when Comcast and AT&T dropped the channel from its distribution systems, with the Federal Communications Commission refusing to intercede in its initial filing against Comcast.[38] The end result was that the linear beIN Sports service was in fewer than 17 million households at the start of 2019. That left beIN Sports Connect, the streaming service with all La Liga and Ligue 1 matches, as the only English-language options for most U.S. based fans of teams in those leagues.

The Italian Serie A was also carried on beIN Sports in the United States until the 2018–19 season when it moved to ESPN+. There was very little pretense to the ESPN approach to Serie A, as it became a cornerstone of the new streaming service. In the 2018–19 season, ESPN+ offered exclusive coverage of 342 matches, with a mere 38 also carried on one of the ESPN linear networks in a sponsored Serie A Match of the Week. The commitment to the streaming service was evident the first weekend of the season, when ESPN+ had exclusive coverage of Ronaldo's debut with Juventas, while Torino versus Roma was the Match of the Week on ESPNews. The acquisition of Serie A was not the lone rights deal to bolster ESPN+. As noted earlier, ESPN also obtained the rights to the FA Cup starting with the 2018–19 tournament. What was unique about the ESPN approach to the FA Cup was that all 79 matches, including the final at Wembley Stadium in London, were streamed exclusively on ESPN+. In September 2019, ESPN and Bundesliga announced a six-year deal starting with the 2020–21 season. While some matches will appear on its linear networks, the ESPN announcement made clear the focus of deal: "ESPN+ to Be the US Home For Bundesliga, Beginning August 2020."[39]

That business model is now prominent with the marquee European football leagues as well as pan-European tournaments through the Union of European Football Associations (UEFA). As noted earlier, Turner acquired the multiplatform rights to the UEFA Champions League and UEFA Europa League for three years starting with the 2018–19 season. The Champions League is an annual tournament that features the winners from the first-division club leagues in each member country from the previous season as well as additional teams based on performance in previous tournaments, including the top four teams from the four highest-ranked associations, Spain, England, Italy, and Germany, in 2018–19 and 2019–20. In general, the next tier of teams from each league is drawn into the Europa League. The group stages for both tournaments are contested in the fall, with 16 matches for each two-day round in the Champions League and 24 matches for each two-day round in the Europa League. The sheer volume of matches, coupled with fragmented audience loyalties in the United States, makes the tournaments a challenge for linear networks and an opportunity for streaming services.

Fox Sports held the rights to the UEFA tournaments through the 2017–18 season and spread matches across FS1, FS2, and *Fox Soccer Plus* and even the Fox regional sports networks, with the Champions League final in 2018 between Real Madrid and Liverpool on the FOX Network. Fox Sports showed 146 matches from the Champions League on television each year and more than 200 for the Europa League.[40] Those totals were reduced to a dramatic degree under the new contract. Turner Sports used the signing of the deal with UEFA in August 2017 to announce the launch of a new premier streaming platform, what became B/R Live. In the first year under the new deal, Turner planned to televise 46 matches on TNT from the Champions League and just one from the Europa League, with the final match between Premier League teams Chelsea and Arsenal from Baku, Azerbaijan, carried on TNT and B/R Live. Univision, which acquired the Spanish-language rights starting in 2018–19, did televise more than twice as many Champions League matches in the first year, with 97 matches total.

There was a time when European football was a novelty on television in the United States. In 1961, the FA Cup Final between Tottenham and Leicester became the first overseas event ever shown on ABC's *Wide World of Sports*. Tottenham won 2–0, but the match was best remembered for Leicester City's Len Chalmers, who suffered a broken leg 20 minutes into the match but continued playing until the end, with "poor old Chalmers" becoming a recurring refrain in the coverage. Over time, the explosion of sports programming services transformed European football from exotic to familiar, but there is a growing cost. The migration of prominent leagues and tournaments to streaming services are important taken on their own, but the significance is far greater when considered together. The annual cost for the four prominent streaming services alone would total $330. An article in *The New York Times* outlined the fate of a British football fan and estimated the total cost to follow their side, including cable or satellite service, at $750 a year.[41] Following European football is no longer a "lonely, frustrating pursuit," as Kevin Draper argued, but a "Balkanized landscape of channels and streaming services can make keeping your eye on your favorite team harder than ever."[42] Harder and also more expensive.

A New Ring for Combat Sports

The state of sports streaming provided an interesting subtext to the World Boxing Association middleweight title fight between Ryota Murata and Rob Brant in Las Vegas, Nevada, in October 2018, at least for those who could read Japanese. Twelve months earlier, Murata claimed the WBA belt with a victory over Hassan N'Dam in Tokyo. In that title bout, Murata's trunks were emblazoned with the DAZN logo, even though the bout was broadcast live nationwide on one of the Japanese networks, FUJI TV. The connection to DAZN was an important one, however, as the streaming service committed $1 billion to the sport of boxing as it expanded into markets around the world, with Murata signing a promotional agreement to become a DAZN "Ambassador" days before that bout. That connection proved problematic for the title fight in Las Vegas, since that bout was streamed live in the United States on ESPN+ and in Japan on DAZN. When the two met in the ring, Murata's trunks once again featured the DAZN name, albeit this time "Da Zone" was translated and written in katakana, part of the Japanese writing system that is used for words of foreign origin.

The Murata-Brant bout was part of a series of deals between ESPN and Top Rank, Inc., and Bob Arum, one of the most prominent promoters in the fight game who traces his roots to Muhammad Ali in the 1960s. In August 2017, ESPN and Top Rank signed a four-year, multi-platform agreement that promised 18 main events in the first year. What was most significant about that deal was that it included what was then an unnamed, multi-sport, direct-to-consumer service that Disney had announced earlier that month. The streaming service would receive only "select main events" but it would feature all undercards, re-airs of all ESPN and pay-per-view events, and Top Rank archival fights.[43] ESPN and Top Rank expanded that deal in April 2018, the same month ESPN+ launched, and the direct-to-consumer service was a focal point of the new agreement, with the service adding 12 exclusive "Top Rank on ESPN" cards per year as well as six live international events.[44] The ink was barely dry on that contract when the two parties announced a new seven-year contract in August 2018 that extended through 2025. That deal, called "the most comprehensive, exclusive rights agreement in the history of boxing," included 54 live events a year, including 12 exclusive primetime events and 24 premium international events on ESPN+.[45] That service, moreover, streamed the undercard for all 54 events, including the 18 events that concluded with bouts on ESPN.

The relationship between Disney and Top Rank guaranteed that ESPN+ would receive exclusive coverage to some main events, like earlier deals that utilized more established platforms, basic cable, and pay-per-view, with a direct-to-consumer service. That was not the case with the liaison between DAZN and Matchroom Boxing. The latter was a division of Matchroom Sport, which formed in the early 1980s in the U.K. to promote snooker before turning its attention to boxing in 1987 with the Frank Bruno-Joe Bugner bout at White Hart Lane, the famous grounds of the Tottenham Hotspurs. From those origins, the London-based Matchroom evolved into one of the most prominent boxing promoters in the world, with its fight cards on Sky Sports in the U.K. a mainstay of the sport. In May 2018, the parent corporation of DAZN, Perform Group, and Matchroom Boxing signed what was promoted as boxing's first "billion dollar deal" to create a joint venture, Matchroom Boxing USA.[46] With that $1 billion investment over eight years, DAZN was to receive 16 fight cards a year from venues across the United States as well as Matchroom's 16 fight cards a year from the U.K. Five months later, DAZN signed a five-year deal with Oscar De La Hoya and Golden Boy Promotions for exclusive rights to ten fight nights a year.[47] There were two aspects of that agreement that were most significant. The multi-million dollar deal included $365 million for 11 bouts for Mexican superstar Canelo Alvarez, regarded as one of the best pound-for-pound fighters in the world.[48] And DAZN received worldwide rights to all of those bouts, which supported its streaming services in Canada, Japan, and various countries in Europe as well as the United States.

It is not surprising that boxing would take center stage, or center ring, in the battle between ESPN+ and DAZN. The sport was at the forefront with different television business models. In 1951, when former heavyweight champion Joe Louis faced Lee Savold at the Polo Grounds in New York, an estimated 22,000 paid up to $1.30 to watch the bout from outside New York in eight movie theaters in six cities, one of the starting points of what was known as theater television.[49] Headlines in *The New York Times* said "Free Home TV Challenged" prior to the fight, but hailed it as a "Sports Boon."[50] In 1971, an estimated 300 million watched the first fight between Muhammad Ali and Joe Frazier around the world, but the only live coverage outside of Madison Square Garden in the United States and Canada was in about 350 theaters, with an average ticket price being between $11 and $12.[51] In a preview of that bout, Jerry Perenchio, one of the promoters, said the live gate at the Garden was "not the primary factor. The closed-circuit tv network is."[52] In time, closed-circuit television gave way to pay-per-view as cable systems introduced new technology, and the Evander Holyfield–George Foreman bout in 1991 reached 1.4 million households and became the first bout to generate over $50 million in revenue through pay-per-view. That fight was the first that Time Warner distributed through TKVO, the distribution unit that worked in concert with HBO for pay-per-view events and was renamed HBO PPV in 2001.

Boxing long garnered the most prominent pay-per-view headlines, with the 2015 bout between Floyd Mayweather and Manny Pacquiao making the biggest news, with 4.4 million buys and $400 million in revenue from the U.S. pay-per-view market alone. While mixed martial arts could not challenge those numbers, the Ultimate Fighting Championship (UFC) did make serious inroads over the last half of the decade. In 2016, for example, the five pay-per-view events with over a million total buys were all from the UFC fight cards, with the top three all involving Conor McGregor.[53] Boxing held the top three spots in 2017, with the Mayweather-McGregor fight taking top honors with 4.3 million buys and over $400 million in revenue, but UFC still claimed 10 of the top 15 in terms of revenue.[54] And just like boxing, fans of mixed martial arts were accustomed to paying for the product, since pay-per-view was a critical source of revenue since its debut in 1993 with UFC 1: The Beginning, and most the "numbered" events remain on PPV platforms.

Pay-per-view events were critical to the evolution of mixed martial arts in the United States, but the future might be tied to the direct-to-consumer marketplace. In May 2018, Disney and William Morris Endeavor Entertainment announced a five-year deal to make ESPN and ESPN+ the exclusive home of UFC starting in January 2019, covering a total of 42 events. That deal includes 20 events per year that are featured on ESPN+ with the service also streaming the prelims for ten additional events that conclude with featured bouts on ESPN. The remaining 12 are pay-per-view events with preliminary bouts on the ESPN linear network.[55] In the first main event under the new deal, a *UFC Fight Night on ESPN+* on January 19, Henry Cejudo defended his flyweight title against TJ Dillashaw in a bout that lasted just 32 seconds. While the length of the bout made headlines, there were other numbers that were also quite significant, as ESPN+ added 525,000 new subscribers on that day alone and 568,000 over a two day period.[56] ESPN+ had exclusive coverage of the main event and the early prelims, but some of the other prelim matches for the 13-fight card were shown on the ESPN and ESPN Deportes linear networks and generated a 1.4 rating, the same as an NBA doubleheader days earlier that featured the Boston Celtics and Toronto

Raptors in the first game and the Golden State Warriors and New Orleans Pelicans in the second game.[57]

Mixed martial arts also became a focal point of DAZN following its launch in September 2018. The previous June, a month after the launch of DAZN US was first announced, the service reached a five-year deal with another combat sports franchise, Viacom-owned Ballator MMA. That deal included seven exclusive fight cards on the streaming services as well as 15 more that were simulcast on Paramount Network Television, which Viacom also owned.[58] As noted, the first big event on DAZN US was a boxing card that featured Anthony Joshua's successful defense of his WBA, WBO, and IBF heavyweight titles against Alexander Povetkin from Wembley Stadium in London, but the stream of Bellator 206 just seven days later previewed the prominence that franchise would have on DAZN. What was perhaps most significant about that deal from a business standpoint was that the rights to the Bellator fights were once again worldwide, including the DAZN services in Canada and Japan as well as Austria, Germany, Italy, and Switzerland in Europe. The move of Bellator to DAZN did raise concerns similar to those with European football, with an opinion piece on a MMA news website asking, "Will Bellator's move to DAZN take things one streaming service too far?"[59]

Summary

It is difficult to generalize about the impact and direction for the streaming of sporting events in the United States at the end of the 2010s. One can conclude without equivocation that major events had not migrated to streaming platforms, but there is little else that was definitive. For example, while Comcast used NBC-Sports.com and NBC Sports Gold to stream excess content from rights deals for which NBC and NBC Sports Network were the main outlets, such as the Premier League, Disney was far more aggressive in obtaining content for which ESPN+ was the driver, including the Bundesliga in Germany and Serie A in Italy. Such out-of-market content, moreover, was the focal point in the streaming market over the later part of the decade, with the NBA among the professional leagues to pursue ancillary revenue through such services, both in the United States and around the world. Where streaming of significant events is most evident is in sports with long histories of alternative content delivery, such as boxing and mixed martial arts. Many observers predicted a migration of sports programming to streaming platforms that mirrors the rise of fictional television on services such as Netflix, Hulu, and Amazon, but it was unclear when that would happen in earnest and what the financial model might be for success in that area.

Notes

1. David Faber, "Amazon Bids for Disney's 22 Regional Sports Networks, Including YES Network, sources say," *CNBC*, November 20, 2018. cnbc.com.

2. Marisa Guthrie, "Amazon Bid for Fox Networks May Escalate Sports Rights Arms Race," *The Hollywood Reporter.com,* December 7, 2018.

3. Quoted in John Ourand and Michael Smith, "Facebook About to Get Serious?" *Sports Business Journal,* March 19, 2018. sportsbusinessjournal.com.

4. John Ourand, "What Experts Hope to Learn from Yahoo's Stream NFL Game," *Sports Business Journal,* October 19, 2015. sportsbusinessjournal.com.

5. Richard Sandomir, "Streaming Experiment a Success, for What It Is," *The New York Times,* October 27, 2015, F5.

6. NBC Sports Press Box, "NBCUniversal to Present Unprecedented 6,755 Hours of Rio Olympic Programming." Press release, June 28, 2016. nbcsportsgrouppressbox.com/

7. Jeanine Poggi, "Thanks, Zika: NBC Hits Record $1.2 Billion in Ad Sales for Olympics," *AdAge,* August 4, 2016. https://adage.com/print/305335

8. Kristie Adler, "ESPN+ to Launch April 12, Bringing Sports Fans More Live Sports, Exclusive Originals and On-Demand Library – All for $4.99 Per Month," ESPN Media Zone, April 2, 2018. espnpressroom.com/press-releases/.

9. Kevin Ota, "ESPN+ March: More Than 1,530 Live Events, 115 Original Programs," *ESPNMediaZone.* Press release, March 1, 2019. espnpressroom.com/press-releases/.

10. Turner Sports, "Turner to Launch New 'Bleacher Report Live' Sports Streaming Service." Press release, March 27, 2018.

11. Quoted in Jacob Bogage, "Bleacher Report Introduces A la Carte Live Sports Streaming in New App," *The Washington Post,* March 27, 2018.

12. Turner Sports, "B/R Live to Provide Direct Access to More Than 340 Live UEFA Champions League & UEFA Europa League Matches." Press release, July 31, 2018. www.warnermediagroup.com/newsroom/press-releases/

13. Quoted in Charean Williams, "NFL Releases Statement After Continued Problems With Canadian Streaming Effort," *ProFootballTalk,* September 11, 2017.

14. Scott Stinson, "Still Not Clear What the NFL Thought It Was Getting Itself Into with DAZN," *National Post,* September 15, 2017, para. 3.

15. Perform Group, "Matchroom Boxing and Perform Group Seal Boxing's First Billion Dollar Deal." Press release, May 10, 2018. performgroup.com.

16. DAZN, "DAZN Kicks Off Stacked Fall Lineup of Boxing and MMA With Heavyweight Title Fight: Anthony Joshua vs. Alexander Povetkin." Press release, July 17, 2018. https://media.dazn.com/en-us/press-releases-us/

17. Eric Fisher, "MLB Gets in DAZN with Digital Rights," *Variety,* November 19, 2018.

18. DAZN, "Major League Baseball and DAZN Announce Three-year Live Digital Rights Deal in United States." Press release, November 15, 2018. https://media.dazn.com/en-us/press-releases-us/

19. Mike Florio, "NFL Could Soon Pull Plug on DirecTV Deal," *ProFootballTalk,* September 30, 2018. https://profootballtalk.nbcsports.com/2018/09/30/nfl-could-soon-pull-plug-on-directv-deal/

20. Maury Brown, "How the NHL Deal With MLB Advanced Media Is Just the Beginning for 'BAM Tech' Spin-Off," *Forbes,* August 5, 2015.

21. The Walt Disney Co., "The Walt Disney Company to Acquire Majority Ownership of BAMTech." Press release. August 8, 2017.

22. Laumann v. NHL, 907 F. Supp. 2d at 471 (S.D.N.Y. 2012).

23. 907 F. Supp. 2d at 471.

24. Laumann v. NHL, 105 F. Supp. 3d 384 (S.D.N.Y. 2015).

25. 105 F. Supp. 3d, 384.

26. John Lombardo and David Broughton, "Going Gray Sports TV Viewers Skew Older," *Sports Business Journal,* June 5, 2017.

27. "Going Gray."

28. Quoted in Christopher Vollmer and Daniel Gross, "NBA Commissioner Adam Silver Has a Game Plan," *Strategy-Business*, no. 91 (Summer 2018): para. 11.

29. Nielsen Co., "NBA Teams Score a Slam Dunk With Social Media," *Nielsen Insights*, November 5, 2018. www.nielsen.com/en/insights/news/2018/nba-score-a-slam-dunk-with-social-media.print.html

30. NBA Communications, "NBA, Tencent Announce China Digital Partnership: Deal Includes Launch of NBA League Pass, NBA Game Time App." Press release, January 29, 2015. nba.com.

31. SVG Staff, "NBA China, Tencent Launch NBA League Pass in China," *Sports Video Group News*, October 18, 2016. www.sportsvideo.org/2016/10/18/nba-china-tencent-launch-nba-league-pass-in-china/

32. NBA Communications, "NBA and Alibaba Expand China Partnership." Press release, March 6, 2019. nba.com.

33. Darren Rovell, "NFL Team Can Be Fined for Posting Video Under New Social Media Policy," *ESPN.com*, October 9, 2016.

34. Prior to 1992–93, the Premier League was called the Football League First Division, a name dating back to the nineteenth century.

35. Grant Wahl, "To NBC Sports for Putting Today's Liverpool Game Behind a 2nd Pay-wall in the United States," January 30, 2019. https://twitter.com/GrantWahl.

36. Billy Haisley, "Soccer on American TV Is Going Straight to a Fiery, Paywalled Hell," *Deadspin*, August 7, 2018. https://deadspin.com/soccer-on-american-tv-is-going-to-a-fiery-pay-1828176306.

37. NBC Sports, "NBC Sports Gold's 'Premier League Pass' Returns for 2018–19 Season with 150 Exclusive Games & At Least 4 Matches Per Club – Fans Can Buy Now." Press release, July 16, 2018. nbcsportspressbox.com/press/

38. Federal Communications Commission, "beIN Sports, LLC vs Comcast Cable Communications, LLC and Comcast Corporation, Memorandum Opinion and Order," August 2, 2018.

39. Mac Nwulu, "ESPN+ to Be the US Home for Bundesliga, Beginning August 2020," *ESPN Press Room*, September 30, 2019. espnpressroom.com/us/press-releases/

40. Sam Carp, "Turner Goes OTT With Majority of Champions League Coverage," *SportsProMedia*, August 2, 2018. www.sportspromedia.com/champions-league-us-coverage-turner-ott-platform-europa-league

41. Kevin Draper, "How to Watch European Leagues (and What You'll Pay)," *The New York Times*, August 11, 2018, D3.

42. "How to Watch European Leagues (and What You'll Pay)."

43. Top Rank, Inc., "ESPN and Top Rank Announce Mega Comprehensive Multi-Year Agreement for New Fight Series." Press release, August 26, 2017. www.toprank.com/news/.

44. Top Rank, Inc., "ESPN+ Announces New Exclusive Boxing Programming Headlined by Crawford vs. Horn on June 9." Press release, April 9, 2018. www.toprank.com/news/.

45. Top Rank, Inc., "ESPN and Top Rank Announce Historic Agreement." Press release, August 2, 2018. www.toprank.com/news/.

46. DAZN, "Matchroom Boxing and Perform Group Seal Boxing's First Billion Dollar Deal." Press release, May 10, 2018. https://media.dazn.com/en-us/press-releases-us/

47. DAZN, "DAZN & Golden Boy Promotions Sign Historic Five-Year Global TV Streaming Partnership." Press release, October 17, 2018. https://media.dazn.com/en-us/press-releases-us/

48. Scooby Axson, "Canelo Alvarez Signs 5-Year, $365 Million Fight Deal With DAZN," *Sports Illustrated*, October 17, 2018. www.si.com/boxing/2018/10/17/canelo-alvarez-signs-365-million-deal-dazn

49. The Associated Press, "22,000 at 8 Movie Theatres in 6 Cities Hail First 'Closed' Television of Major Fight," *The New York Times*, June 16, 1951.

50. Jack Gould, "Free Home TV Challenged: Only Theaters to Get Bout," *The New York Times*, June 6, 1951, 1; James P. Dawson, "Video in Theatres Seen Sports Boon," *The New York Times*, June 17, 1951.

51. William N. Wallace, "Worldwide Televising of Fight Is the Biggest Item in a $25-Million Gamble," *The New York Times*, March 7, 1971.

52. Dave Anderson, "Ali and Frazier Make It Official: They Sign for Title Fight Here March 8," *The New York Times*, December 31, 1970.

53. Deana Myers, "PPV in 2016 Slows but 2017 Could Pick Up Again," *Economics of TV & Film*, S&P Global Market Intelligence, July 14, 2017.

54. Deana Myers, "Yo-yo Trend Likely for PPV After Big 2017," *Economics of TV & Film*, S&P Global Market Intelligence, August 1, 2018.

55. Ardi Dwornik, "ESPN and ESPN+ to Become Exclusive Media Home of UFC in the US," *ESPN Press Room*, May 23, 2018.

56. Michael Sharka, "*Debut UFC Fight Night on ESPN+ Is a Record-Setting Night*," *ESPN Press Room*, January 20, 2019, para. 1.

57. "Debut UFC Fight Night on ESPN+ Is a Record-Setting Night," para. 2.

58. Bellator MMA, "Bellator & DAZN Sign Nine-Figure, Multi-Years Distribution Deal." Press release, June 26, 2018. ballator.com/articles/.

59. Ben Fowlkes, "Will Bellator's Move to DANZ Take Things Just One Streaming Service Too Far," *MMAJunkie.com*, September 30, 2018. https://mmajunkie.usatoday.com/2018/09/will-bellator-move-to-dazn-take-things-one-streaming-service-too-far.

Further Reading

Galily, Yair. "When the Medium Becomes 'Well Done': Sport, Television, and Technology in the Twenty-First Century." *Television & New Media* 15, no. 8 (2014): 717–724.

Grow, Nathanial. "End the Blackouts." *The Hardball Times*, January 14, 2015. https://tht.fangraphs.com/end-the-blackouts/

Hutchins, Brett. "Sport on the Move: The Unfolding Impact of Mobile Communications on the Media Sport Content Economy." *Journal of Sport and Social Issues* 38, no. 6: 509–527.

Hutchins, Brett, Bo Li, and David Rowe. "Over-the Top Sport: Live Streaming Services, Changing Coverage Rights Markets and the Growth of Media Sport Portals." *Media, Culture & Society* 41, no. 7: 975–994.

Weiner, Jonah. "Stream of Rivals." *The New York Times Magazine*, July 14, 2019.

Chapter Bibliography

Adler, Kristie. "ESPN+ to Launch April 12, Bringing Sports Fans More Live Sports, Exclusive Originals and On-Demand Library – All for $4.99 Per Month." *ESPN Media Zone* April 2, 2018.

Anderson, Dave. "Ali and Frazier Make It Official: They Sign for Title Fight Here March 8." *The New York Times*, December 31, 1970, 31.

Associated Press. "22,000 at 8 Movie Theatres in 6 Cities Hail First 'Closed' Television of Major Fight." *The New York Times*, June 16, 1951, 10.

Axson, Scooby. "Canelo Alvarez Signs 5-Year, $365 Million Fight Deal With DAZN." *Sports Illustrated*, October 17, 2018. www.si.com/boxing/2018/10/17/canelo-alvarez-signs-365-million-deal-dazn

Bellator MMA. "Bellator & DAZN Sign Nine-Figure, Multi-Years Distribution Deal." Press release, June 26, 2018.

Bogage, Jacob. "Bleacher Report Introduces A la Carte Live Sports Streaming in New App." *The Washington Post*, March 27, 2018. Washingtonpost.com

Brown, Maury. "How the NHL Deal With MLB Advanced Media Is Just the Beginning for 'BAM Tech' Spin-Off." *Forbes*, August 5, 2015.

Carp, Sam. "Turner Goes OTT with Majority of Champions League Coverage." *SportsProMedia*, August 2, 2018. www.sportspromedia.com/champions-league-us-coverage-turner-ott-platform-europa-league. Accessed February 15, 2019.

Dawson, James P. "Video in Theatres Seen Sports Boon." *The New York Times*, June 17, 1951.

DAZN. "Matchroom Boxing and Perform Group Seal Boxing's First Billion Dollar Deal." Press release, May 10, 2018. https://media.dazn.com/en-us/press-releases-us/.

———. "DAZN Kicks Off Stacked Fall Lineup of Boxing and MMA With Heavyweight Title Fight: Anthony Joshua vs. Alexander Povetkin." Press release, July 17, 2018. https://media.dazn.com/en-us/press-releases-us/.

———. "DAZN & Golden Boy Promotions Sign Historic Five-Year Global TV Streaming Partnership." Press release, October 17, 2018. https://media.dazn.com/en-us/press-releases-us/.

———. "Major League Baseball and DAZN Announce Three-Year Live Digital Rights Deal in United States." Press release, November 15, 2018. https://media.dazn.com/en-us/press-releases-us/.

Draper, Kevin. "How to Watch European Leagues (and What You'll Pay)." *The New York Times*, August 11, 2018, D3.

Dwornik, Ardi. "ESPN and ESPN+ to Become Exclusive Media Home of UFC in the US." *ESPN Press Room*. Press release, May 23, 2018.

Faber, David. "Amazon Bids for Disney's 22 Regional Sports Networks, Including YES Network, Sources Say." *CNBC*, November 20, 2018. www.cnbc.com/2018/11/20/amazon-bids-for-disneys-22-regional-sports-networks-including-yes-network-sources-say.html.

Federal Communications Commission. beIN Sports, LLC vs Comcast Cable Communications, LLC and Comcast Corporation. Memorandum Opinion and Order, August 2, 2018.

Fisher, Eric. "MLB Gets in DAZN with Digital Rights." *Variety*, 19 November 2018.

Florio, Mike. "NFL Could Soon Pull Plug on DirecTV Deal." *ProFootballTalk*, September 30, 2018. https://profootballtalk.nbcsports.com/2018/09/30/nfl-could-soon-pull-plug-on-directv-deal/

Fowlkes, Ben. "Will Bellator's Move to DANZ Take Things Just One Streaming Service Too Far." *MMAJunkie.com*, September 30, 2018. Accessed April 5, 2019.

Gould, Jack. "Free Home TV Challenged: Only Theaters to Get Bout." *The New York Times*, June 6, 1951, 1.

Guthrie, Marisa. "Amazon Bid for Fox Networks May Escalate Sports Rights Arms Race." *The Hollywood Reporter.com*, December 7, 2018.

Haisley, Billy. "Soccer on American TV Is Going Straight to a Fiery, Paywalled Hell." *Deadspin*, August 7, 2018. https://deadspin.com/soccer-on-american-tv-is-going-to-a-fiery-pay-1828176306.

Laumann v. NHL. 907 F. Supp. 2d 465 (S.D.N.Y. 2012).

———. 105 F. Supp. 3d 384 (S.D.N.Y. 2015).

Lombardo, John, and David Broughton. "Going Gray Sports TV Viewers Skew Older." *Sports Business Journal*, June 5, 2017.

Myers, Deana. "PPV in 2016 Slows but 2017 Could Pick Up Again." Economics of TV & Film, S&P Global Market Intelligence, July 14, 2017.
———. "Yo-yo Trend Likely for PPV After Big 2017." Economics of TV & Film, S&P Global Market Intelligence, August 1, 2018.
NBA Communications. "NBA, Tencent Announce China Digital Partnership: Deal Includes Launch of NBA League Pass, NBA Game Time App." Press release, January 29, 2015. www.nba.com/2015/news/01/29/nba-tencent-announce-china-digital-partnership/
———. "NBA and Alibaba Expand China Partnership." Press release, March 6, 2019. https://pr.nba.com/nba-alibaba-china-partnership/
NBC Sports. "NBCUniversal to Present Unprecedented 6,755 hours of Rio Olympic Programming." Press release, June 28, 2016. nbcsportsgrouppressbox.com/
———. "NBC Sports Gold's 'Premier League Pass' Returns for 2018–19 Season With 150 Exclusive Games & At Least 4 Matches Per Club – Fans Can Buy Now." Press release, July 16, 2018. nbcsportspressbox.com/press/
Nielsen Co. "NBA Teams Score a Slam Dunk With Social Media." *Nielsen Insights*, November 5, 2018. www.nielsen.com/en/insights/news/2018/nba-score-a-slam-dunk-with-social-media.print.html
Nwulu, Mac. "ESPN+ To Be the US Home for Bundesliga, Beginning August 2020." *ESPN Press Room*, September 30, 2019. https://espnpressroom.com/us/
Ota, Kevin. "ESPN+ March: More than 1,530 Live Events, 115 Original Programs." *ESPNMediaZone*. Press release, March 1, 2019. https://espnpressroom.com/us/
Ourand, John, and Michael Smith. "Facebook About to Get Serious?" *Sports Business Journal*, March 19, 2018. sportsbusinessjournal.com.
———. "What Experts Hope to Learn from Yahoo's Stream NFL Game." *Sports Business Journal*, October 19, 2015. sportsbusinessjournal.com.
Perform Group. "Matchroom Boxing and Perform Group Seal Boxing's First Billion Dollar Deal." Press release, 10 May 2018. www.performgroup.com/news-and-insights/matchroom-boxing-perform-group-seal-boxings-first-billion-dollar-deal-2/
Poggi, Jeanine. "Thanks, Zika: NBC Hits Record $1.2 Billion in Ad Sales for Olympics." *AdAge*, August 4, 2016. https://adage.com/print/305335
Rovell, Darren. "NFL Tyeam Can Be Fined for Posting Video Under New Social Media Policy." *ESPN.com*, October 9, 2016.
Sandomir, Richard. "Streaming Experiment a Success, for What It Is." *The New York Times*, October 27, 2015, F5.
Sharka, Michael. "Debut *UFC Fight Night* on ESPN+ Is a Record-Setting Night." *ESPN Press Room*, January 20, 2019.
Stinson, Scott. "Still Not Clear What the NFL Thought It Was Getting Itself Into With DAZN." *National Post*, September 15, 2017. https://nationalpost.com/sports/football/nfl/still-not-clear-what-the-nfl-thought-it-was-getting-itself-into-with-dazn
"SVG Staff, NBA China, Tencent Launch NBA League Pass in China." *Sports Video Group News*, October 18, 2016. www.sportsvideo.org/2016/10/18/nba-china-tencent-launch-nba-league-pass-in-china/
Top Rank, Inc. "ESPN and Top Rank Announce Mega Comprehensive Multi-Year Agreement for New Fight Series." Press release, August 26, 2017. www.toprank.com/news/.
———. "ESPN+ Announces New Exclusive Boxing Programming Headlined by Crawford vs. Horn on June 9." Press release, April 9, 2018. www.toprank.com/news/
———. "ESPN and Top Rank Announce Historic Agreement." Press release, August 2, 2018. www.toprank.com/news/

Turner Sports. "Turner to Launch New 'Bleacher Report Live' Sports Streaming Service." Press release, March 27, 2018. www.warnermediagroup.com/newsroom/press-releases/

———. "B/R Live to Provide Direct Access to More Than 340 Live UEFA Champions League & UEFA Europa League Matches." Press release, July 31, 2018. www.warner mediagroup.com/newsroom/press-releases/

Vollmer, Christopher, and Daniel Gross. "NBA Commissioner Adam Silver Has a Game Plan." *Strategy-Business* 91 (2018).

Wahl, Grant. "To NBC Sports for Putting Today's Liverpool Game Behind a 2nd Paywall in the United States." January 30, 2019. https://twitter.com/GrantWahl.

Wallace, William N. "Worldwide Televising of Fight Is the Biggest Item in a $25-Million Gamble." *The New York Times*, March 7, 1971, S2.

Walt Disney Co. "The Walt Disney Company to Acquire Majority Ownership of BAMTech." Press release, August 8, 2017. https://www.thewaltdisneycompany.com/walt-disney-company-acquire-majority-ownership-bamtech/

Williams, Charean. "NFL Releases Statement After Continued Problems With Canadian Streaming Effort." *ProFootballTallk*, September 11, 2017.

7

CONCLUSION

The distribution of e-mail invitations to an Apple special event scheduled for March 25, 2019, in the Steve Jobs Theater on its Cupertino, California, campus, triggered two weeks of speculation about what would be revealed. Industry insiders predicted that the tech giant would announce the creation of a new streaming service for Apple TV and new bundled content for Apple News. Sports leagues, conferences, and organizations dreamed that this would be the moment that Apple, and its deep pockets, dove into the marketplace for live sports programming. As the event drew near, however, those hopes were dashed for the most part. In an article on SI.com the week prior to the event that explored how Apple curates content for its Apple TV interface and app, Senior Vice President for Internet Software and Services Eddy Cue was asked how much he was thinking about competing for exclusive rights to sporting events. His answer was concise: "Not a lot, honestly."[1] The Apple event held true to form, with the announcement of a new streaming service with exclusive original shows, a subscription news service that included *The Wall Street Journal*, new video game platforms, and even an Apple credit card. And while sports television was not expected to be a focal point, how little it was discussed was noted, with John Ourand of *Sports Business Journal* estimating that it amounted to just 15 seconds, total.[2]

The reticence of Apple to venture into the sports media rights marketplace was understandable. After all, other members of the first family of new media – Facebook, Amazon, Netflix, and Google – took small steps into the sports arena in the latter half of the 2010s, but there was not a game-changing venture. What was more telling was the lack of conviction that hovered over the multi-billion-dollar deal between the National Football League and DirecTV for *NFL Sunday Ticket*. As discussed in Chapter 6, the AT&T satellite service held exclusive rights to deliver out-of-market games as part of an eight-year, $12-billion deal with the league that extends through 2022. There was, however, a window during which the NFL could exercise an opt-out clause and terminate the contract after the 2019 season. The league expressed an interest in expanding the platforms on which the service was delivered and, of course, increasing the revenue it generated. Streaming was at the top of that list of options, and there were reports that Amazon, DANZ, and ESPN+ were among the parties that discussed the package with the league.[3] There were no announcements before the 2019 season started in September, however, and the opt-out window appeared to close. As a result, the NFL settled for the $1.5 billion a year guaranteed through the end of the contract with AT&T for its out-of-market package. That also meant that the migration of major sports packages to online delivery remained somewhere in the future.

The oft-predicted exodus of major sporting events from broadcast and cable to streaming platforms may not have materialized, but the first half of the 2020s will hold intrigue in the marketplace for whether or not such a shift occurs. As discussed in Chapter 3, the CBS, FOX, and NBC contracts for the National Football League expire after the 2022 season, while the current ESPN deal for *Monday Night Football* runs out a year earlier. While the NFL is the most implausible candidate to migrate to digital platforms, with even an increase in games on basic cable improbable, most of the contracts for Major League Baseball and the National Hockey League expire in 2021, while those for the National Basketball Association end in 2025. That does not mean that deals will not be locked into place well before those dates, as Fox Sports extended its MLB contract (which includes exclusive rights to the World Series) through 2028 in November 2018, three years before it was set to expire. The one thing that was established as the 2010s closed was that for 12 years to follow, through 2032, NBC would remain home to the Olympic Games, and CBS and WarnerMedia would share the NCAA Men's Basketball Championships. The future television home for most other major sporting events was up in the air.

The Fox Sports deal for the World Series, All-Star Game, and other MLB rights was significant for another reason. That deal was signed as 21st Century Fox was finalizing the sale of 20th Century Fox Film Corp. and other entertainment assets to Disney. That deal was a tacit acknowledgment that Fox could not compete in the streaming wars with Netflix, Disney, and others, but it also came with a pledge that the "new" Fox Corp. would redouble its commitment to live news and sports. The decision to tack seven years onto its MLB contract three years before it expired, with an increased number of games on the FOX broadcast network starting in 2022, was evidence that Fox Corp. would indeed be a major force in the sports marketplace moving forward. While that deal might have eliminated any lingering doubts in one instance, the completion of the merger of AT&T Inc. and Time Warner Inc. and the announcement that Viacom Inc. and CBS Corp. would recombine, no doubt, raised others. AT&T changed little within WarnerMedia after it took control in June 2018, for example, but it made significant structural changes soon after the U.S. Court of Appeals for the

DC Circuit rejected the final Justice Department attempt to stop the merger in February 2019. That included a reorganization around content areas, with Turner Sports becoming part of WarnerMedia News & Sports. It remained to be seen how the merger of Viacom and CBS could impact on CBS Sports after that deal closed in December 2019.

What was undeniable was the power of conglomeration in sports television. At the dawn of the 2020s, there were four corporations that contained a broadcast television network and at least one cable service dedicated to sports: Comcast, Disney, Fox, and ViacomCBS. While the relationships between the different outlets within their respective corporations varied, what was most important were the combinations that corresponded to the four above: NBC and NBC Sports Network, ABC and ESPN, FOX and Fox Sports 1, and CBS and CBS Sports Network, respectively. There were other important connections within some, from the link to cable households through Comcast to the stand-alone sports streaming service within Disney, but the basic requirements for membership in the group existed in all four. Even with the NFL, where the rights to games were tied to the broadcast network in the cases of CBS, FOX, and NBC, those contracts granted access to footage that supported studio and shoulder programming on various cable outlets within the same corporations. In most other cases, agreements were between a league and a corporation, and the content was allocated to both broadcast and cable outlets. That was true of MLB on FOX and Fox Sports 1, the NBA on ABC and ESPN, and the NHL on NBC and NBCSN. Similar distribution patterns were evident with national events, such as the U.S. Open Golf Championships on FOX and Fox Sports 1, and international events, such as the Olympic Games on NBC, NBCSN, and a collection of NBCUniversal services, including Spanish-language Telemundo.

What is also significant is that these sports television platforms, for the most part, are embedded in vast media conglomerates. There was a time when the combination of a broadcast network and major motion picture studio under the same corporate umbrella did not make sense following the imposition of the Financial Interest and Syndication Rules in 1970. Those rules prohibited the networks from holding ownership or syndication rights in programs on their primetime schedule, with the Federal Communications Commission arguing that "the public interest requires limitation on network control and an increase in the opportunity for development of truly independent sources of prime time programming" and "diversity of program ideas."[4] The final remnants of those rules were allowed to expire in 1995, and soon after, in four-year increments, Walt Disney Pictures and ABC were brought under the same corporate umbrella in 1996, with Paramount Pictures and CBS and Universal Pictures and NBC following suit in 2000 and 2004, respectively. One of the arguments for the termination of the fin/syn rules was the rise of cable television and the multiplicity of outlets, but the collection of those assets within a small collection of conglomerates undermined any hopes of true diversity of ownership and/or program ideas. In the mid to late 2000s, in fact, the majority of fictional programs on the primetime schedules of the broadcast networks as well as the original programming on basic and premium cable services were owned by one of six media conglomerates.[5] Five of those six were tied to both a major motion picture studio and a broadcast network, with Sony Corp. the one outlier in that group without ownership of broadcast properties.

Those connections are even more significant now. Many of the mergers and acquisitions discussed earlier were designed to strengthen the conglomerates for the streaming wars that have begun in earnest or to surrender in the face of even larger opponents. Some of the fusions were vertical, such as the mergers of Comcast and NBCUniversal and AT&T and Time Warner, combining content producers with corporations that control the pipes that send that content to television, tablets, smartphones, and other devices through cable, satellite, and telco services. Those mergers have received more scrutiny, although the federal government allowed the combination of Comcast and NBCUniversal with only behavioral remedies and failed in its bid to stop the melding of AT&T and Time Warner. There are other mergers that were horizontal, combining multiple content producers, which have received limited state scrutiny. The transfer of entertainment assets from 21st Century Fox to Disney is a case in point, as the sole objection from the U.S. government was over the combination of ESPN and the Fox regional sports networks. The debut of Disney+ in November 2019 was hailed as the biggest shot across the bow of Netflix, in part because of the libraries of film and television content that Disney acquired from Fox, such as *The Simpsons* and the first six *Star Wars* films, in addition to those it controlled within Disney. The recombination of Viacom Inc. and CBS Corp. was designed to position ViacomCBS to be competitive in this space as well.

The premiere of Disney+ was one in a series of debuts in the streaming marketplace planned for 2019 and 2020, which included the launch of Apple TV earlier in the month. NBCUniversal was scheduled to reach the market with its own OTT service in April 2020 called Peacock, while WarnerMedia was expected to follow suit a month later with HBO Max. There was also no doubt that the arrival of ViacomCBS would bring new content libraries to CBS All Access. How sports were intertwined in these services remained to be seen. In a July 2019 earnings call, AT&T Chairman and CEO Randall Stephenson said that the company planned to offer live sports on HBO Max, mentioning the NBA, MLB, and NCAA basketball and stating "those are going to be really, really important elements for HBO Max."[6] That discussion fell a little more than a year after Turner launched B/R Live to coincide with the arrival of the UEFA Champions League and Europa League for the 2018–19 tournaments. While some matches were available on the Turner linear networks, about half of the Champions League and all but one of the Europa League matches were exclusive to B/R Live. The idea of building a streaming service with European football as a cornerstone arose again in November 2019, when CBS Corp. CEO Joe Ianniello confirmed on an earnings call that his corporation had won those same UEFA rights starting in

2021. This, once again, was a deal that fed different platforms in a conglomerate, with limited matches expected to air on CBS and CBS Sports Network. The focus, however, was on the CBS All Access, as that service was expected to stream all matches, most on an exclusive basis, with Ianniello trumpeting the fact that the deal brought "exclusive, live, marquee sports" to All Access for the first time.[7]

That pattern of conglomeration connects to core concepts that form the foundation for the critical political economy of the media. As discussed in Chapter 1, Peter Golding and Graham Murdock focused on four historical processes that are critical to understand, three of which were the "growth of the media; extension of corporate reach" and "commodification."[8] There is little doubt that the sports television marketplace in the United States represents each of these patterns. The available outlets for sports programing have multiplied exponentially since the 1980s, so the growth of the media is clear, but so too is the extension of corporate reach. There are sports-related services that started as brash new ideas and launched as entrepreneurial gambles, with ESPN just one example, but the ownership of most of those same services can be traced to a handful of corporations. That pattern from differentiation to concentration mirrors what Ben Bagdikian argued in *The Media Monopoly* and *The New Media Monopoly*, that while 50 companies dominated the newspaper, television, publishing, and film industries in 1983, there were as few as five companies two decades later.[9] The prominence of sports content on commercial networks also connects to commodification and long-standing debates on the audience commodity within critical political economy among Dallas Smythe and others.[10] Much of the growth of services in the late 2010s, moreover, focused on new streaming platforms that enable conglomerates to monetize media rights, which connects with another aspect of the process of commodification.

The fourth and final process that Golding and Murdock outline, the "changing role of state and government interaction," is also important to consider. There are Congressional acts that have dealt with sports television in a direct manner, such as the Sports Broadcasting Act of 1961, as well as court decisions that did likewise, such as *NCAA v. Board of Regents of the University of Oklahoma*. The impact of the broader ethos of deregulation is just as significant, with the demise of the Financial Interest and Syndication Rules discussed earlier being just one example. The changes in the broadcast ownership rules since the 1980s allowed for the building of much larger station groups, and some of the dominant sports conglomerates took advantage of that largesse, CBS Corp. and Fox Corp., in particular. When many reacted in a negative manner to the FCC decision to raise the national audience reach cap from 35% to 45% of television households nationwide in 2003, Congress and the White House compromised on 39%, since that was the lowest level that would not require the CBS and FOX groups to sell stations. The value of those stations, and the connection to sports rights, is most evident in the collection of stations Fox Corp. owns in markets with National Football Conference teams, which was expected to grow in 2020 with the completion of a deal with

Nexstar Media Group to acquire FOX affiliates in Seattle and Milwaukee, albeit with a sale of the FOX affiliate in Charlotte. The parallel pattern is seen with CBS Corp. and cities with American Football Conference teams. There are also cases of government inaction that accelerated these processes, with the unwillingness to implement à la carte pricing for content services in the face of lobbying from The Walt Disney Co. being one prime example.

The question that must be asked is whether corporate connections determined the winners and losers in the evolution of sports television and the extent to which all three branches of the U.S. government – legislative, executive, and judicial – influenced outcomes in what is supposed to be a "free" market. That story is perhaps most captivating in the analysis of cable programming services across different sectors of the industry, considering both national networks and regional networks, and both general sports networks and specialized sports networks. The executives of such networks would no doubt pin the success of those services, measured in terms of both augmented carriage fees and increased household penetration, on the decisions that were made, and there would be some truth in such claims. The Outdoor Life Network, for example, acquired the rights to the Tour de France in 2001 and introduced live daily coverage in the United States, replacing taped telecasts on ABC and ESPN. When the Tour debuted on OLN, its service reached an estimated 36 million households, a number that grew to around 64 million in time for the race in 2005. That stretch was significant for American cycling, since those years corresponded to the third through seventh Tour titles for Lance Armstrong. In 2012, the International Cycling Union stripped Armstrong of those titles for his part in what the U.S. Anti-Doping Agency described as the "most sophisticated, professionalized and successful doping program that sport has ever seen."[11] While Armstrong no longer holds those titles, at least in the record books, OLN did not lose the households gained over that string of victories.

There is little doubt that the acquisition of the Tour de France was a gamble for OLN founder and CEO Roger Werner. The deal was announced days after Armstrong won his first Tour in 1999, returning to the sport after surviving testicular cancer. Werner convinced the owner of the *L'Équipe* newspaper and the famous bike race, Amaury Sport Organisation, to forego the 75 million households that ESPN reached to sign with an upstart that reached about 20 million at the time, although an increase in the annual rights fees from $400,000 to $750,000 no doubt helped ease those concerns. It would be romantic to view the rise of OLN around the bet on live coverage of the Tour de France that Werner made, but it's more complicated than that. As discussed earlier, cable operators Comcast, Cox, and MediaOne were initial investors in OLN, and there was a link to the households of Tele-Communications Inc. for about 12 months after Fox/Liberty Networks acquired a one-third interest in 1998. That stake transferred to News Corp. when Fox/Liberty was dissolved in 1999, but the more significant transaction came in October 2001 when Comcast acquired the 83.2% of OLN it did not own in a complicated deal with News Corp. That was two months before

Comcast announced the merger with AT&T Broadband in December 2001, which gave the combined operator 22 million subscribers when it was completed 11 months later. That series of transactions made Outdoor Life Network an owned and operated service of the largest MSO in the United States, so its growth must be viewed through that lens as well.

The pattern of vertical integration that Comcast and Outdoor Life Network represents is one of the ways in which conglomeration matters in the battle for expanded carriage and higher fees for programming services. In the 1980s, it was not uncommon for cable operators to negotiate an ownership interest in such services in exchange for carriage. There were also cases when MSOs invested in a programmer in financial distress, most notably a $550-million infusion into Turner Broadcasting in 1987 after some of Ted Turner's acquisitions plunged his corporation deep into debt. The result of such negotiations was evident in the Fifth Annual Report on competition in the video programming marketplace that the FCC released on December 23, 1998.[12] In that study, the Commission listed 50 national programming services in which Tele-Communications Inc., the largest MSO at that time, held a financial interest. That collection, moreover, did not include another 18 national services in which TCI held limited influence through a 10% financial interest in Time Warner Inc. The list of regional services in that report included another 21 regional sports networks in which TCI held a financial interest. Tele-Communications Inc. was soon after split in two, with the cable systems sold to AT&T Inc., while the content services were placed under the Liberty Media mantle, but the importance of vertical integration in the 1980s and 1990s, and the link to sports programming services such as the Golf Channel and the predecessors of both Fox Sports 1 and NBC Sports Network, is important to remember.

The value of vertical integration, and the associated concerns it raises, has not changed over time. In the assessment of sports television across the 2010s, the connections between Comcast's cable systems and the NBC broadcast network and owned-and-operated stations, as well as its national and regional sports networks, were a recurring theme. The decade began with the transfer of control of NBCUniversal from General Electric to Comcast Corp. under federal review and ended in the aftermath of a failed attempt by the federal government to block the merger of AT&T Inc. and Time Warner Inc. That, too, focused on vertical connections and the impact the combination would have in the marketplace, with the sports content on TBS and TNT figuring prominently in the argument that the Department of Justice advanced in court. The delivery mechanisms were different, with a shift from cable in the case of Comcast and NBCUniversal to satellite and telco in the case of AT&T and Time Warner, but the issues remained the same. The government, moreover, argued that the behavioral conditions agreed upon in the approval of the Comcast acquisition of NBCUniversal had not done enough and that divestiture of assets, either Turner Broadcasting or DirecTV, was needed before the deal would be approved. The fact that the Justice Department was unsuccessful in that case does not mean the concerns were unwarranted.

Vertical integration remains important, but horizontal connections are now, perhaps, even more significant in sports television, and Congressional intervention in the marketplace assumes a prominent role. The Cable Television Consumer Protection and Competition Act of 1992 was enacted in response to the dramatic rise in cable rates following deregulation in the 1980s. The 1992 Cable Act was also supposed to address concerns over vertical and horizontal integration, although the writing of the bill and subsequent implementation empowered another form of horizontal combinations. A recurring theme in the debate over the act focused on the future of broadcast television in the face of competition from cable programming services. The anecdote was a requirement that a "multichannel video programming distributor" could not retransmit the signal of a local broadcast station except "(A) with express authority of the originating station" unless the station elected the so-called "must carry" provision.[13] Representative Jack Fields (R., Texas), who later assumed a prominent role in the drafting of the Telecommunications Act of 1996 as chair of the House subcommittee on Telecommunications and Finance, argued that without what become known as retransmission consent, there was a "real fear over-the-air TV could go the way of the dinosaur."[14] CBS Chairman Laurence Tisch estimated that retransmission would be worth $1 billion a year for local stations, but even before the bill passed, John Malone and Tele-Communications, Inc. made clear that multiple-system operators did not intend to pay for retransmission of local broadcast stations.

Tisch sold CBS to Westinghouse in 1995 and passed away in 2003, so he did not see the day when local stations generated significant retransmission revenue, but in time, that day did arrive. As Malone predicted, MSOs did not exchange cash to retransmit broadcast signals that were free-to-air, at least not for many, many years. Kagan estimated that total broadcast retransmission revenue was at $214.6 million in 2006, did not reach $500 million until 2008, and topped $1 billion for the first time in 2010.[15] Even those increases impacted the bottom line of the large station groups. CBS Corp., for example, which owned 30 local television stations at the start of 2008, reported $26.4 million in retransmission revenue in that year, a figure that increased to $118.0 million in 2010.[16] The value of those agreements accelerated over the decade that followed, surpassing $10 billion combined in 2018.[17] In that year, Kagan estimated that all four major network groups – ABC, CBS, FOX, and NBC – generated in excess of $1 billion in such fees. That second revenue stream in addition to advertising is changing the market for sports rights, making it more viable for broadcast networks to match cable programming services such as ESPN that have long benefited from two significant revenue streams, advertising and carriage fees.

There was a second part of Malone's response to the 1992 Cable Act and retransmission consent that proved to be prescient. Congress did not set parameters for such negotiations, and the FCC did nothing to limit what was on the table, only mandating that broadcasters must negotiate rights to their entire signal rather than to individual programs. In a speech in 1993, after the bill was signed into law, Malone stated, "I don't intend to pay any money. I will scratch backs."[18] The pattern that emerged in retransmission negotiations in the 1990s was that most of those agreements were tied to the carriage of cable programming services under the same corporate umbrella as the broadcast station groups. In other words, broadcast licensees that were mandated to serve the public interest, convenience, and necessity in the Communications Act of 1934 were able to extend their corporate reach and pad their bottom lines through retransmission consent. Five of the most successful launches in the 1990s – ESPN2, FX, MSNBC, HGTV, and Food Network – were dubbed "retransmission networks" because of the link to large local station groups. ESPN2, in fact, was linked to two such groups, Capital Cities/ABC and Hearst Corp., when it launched in October 1993.

The bundling of broadcast and cable programming became a hallmark of The Walt Disney Co. in retransmission negotiations. In 1997, Disney signed a widespread, ten-year deal with Tele-Communications, Inc., that covered ESPN, ESPN2, and ESPNews, which was struggling to gain carriage, as well as the Disney Channel, A&E, the History Channel, and Lifetime in exchange for transmission of the ABC-owned and operated stations. Disney claimed that there were individual agreements for each service, but TCI President Leo Hindery described the deal as "one all-encompassing agreement" with the Disney organization.[19] The peril of such disputes became clear a few years later when Time Warner Cable dropped the ABC affiliates from its systems in seven markets, including New York, Los Angeles, and Philadelphia, at 12:01 am on May 1, 2000, after a months-long dispute. At that time, Disney blamed the MSO, stating that it had given Time Warner Cable permission to continue carrying the stations while negotiations continued, but the distributor said it could not legally carry the signals without a long-term agreement. The network went dark on the Time Warner systems for 39 hours, held hostage in a bigger battle. The list of Disney demands included the conversion of the Disney Channel from a premium, à la carte service to the basic tier, carriage of SoapNet and ToonDisney, and increased carriage for ESPN2, ESPN Classic, and ESPNews. Disney turned to the FCC for relief, arguing that the cable operator violated rules banning removal of local stations during a Nielsen sweeps period, and the Commission ruled against Time Warner Cable. Before the month was over, the two parties signed a new, long-term agreement that included all the Disney desires, including a commitment to bring ESPN2 distribution in line with ESPN, a pledge to grow ESPN Classic to more than nine million Time Warner households, and a promise to add ESPNews to all its systems.

The leverage granted to the parent corporations of large station groups through retransmission consent is one of the consequences of the 1992 Cable Act. The power gained in the carriage of cable programming services is most evident when looking across different segments of sports television over the course of the 2010s. The Tennis Channel struggled with carriage after its launch in 2003, so much so that it pursued legal action against Comcast through the FCC and in the courts. As discussed in Chapter 4, the fortunes of that service changed when it was acquired by Sinclair Broadcast Group in 2016 and was included in retransmission negotiations for its collection of local stations, which numbered 163 in 79 markets at the end of 2015. What was remarkable in that case was that Sinclair announced additional carriage for the Tennis Channel before its acquisition was even completed, stating in its annual report that it had "been successful in negotiating significant increases in carriage with MVPDs, with more penetration expected."[20] That pattern was repeated with regional sports networks, with both Marquee Sports Network, the service that launched in February 2020 for the first spring training game for the Chicago Cubs, and with the Fox regional sports networks Sinclair acquired from The Walt Disney Co. The carriage agreement announced in July 2019 between Sinclair and Charter Communications, the second largest cable multi-system operator, included coverage of the Tennis Channel, Marquee Sports Network, and the Fox regional sports networks, as well as other assets, in exchange for carriage of Sinclair stations on Charter systems, even though the government had not yet approved the sale of the RSNs. The agreement between Sinclair and DirecTV signed in October 2019 was even more significant, since that deal included carriage of Marquee Sports Network on the satellite system from its launch. That was most telling given the fact that the RSN that carries the Los Angeles Dodgers, SportsNet LA, remained off DirecTV six seasons after its launch.

Looking across sectors of sports television points to other issues, with the combined cost of such services perhaps the most prominent. The late John McCain sponsored multiple Congressional acts to promote à la carte pricing on multi-channel video programming systems in the U.S. Senate, all of which failed in the face of lobbying from Disney and other conglomerates. The end result is that most of the sports programming services discussed in this analysis were bundled and sold as part of expanded basic or equivalent service tiers rather than as a premium service or as part of a sports tier in the 2010s. The carriage fees for the major multichannel services – ESPN, ESPN2, FS1, and NBCSN – might not seem excessive to some when addressed in isolation, costing around $10 a month in 2019. That conversation becomes more complicated, however, with the inclusion of single sports services such as the Golf Channel, single league or conference services such as NFL Network, and other national services. The total cost spirals even higher with the inclusion of regional sports networks, in particular in markets such as New York City and Los Angeles with multiple RSNs. In 2019, the Spectrum Select packages in representative New York and Los Angeles systems included ten sports services, six national and four regional, and those alone averaged between $27 and $29 per household per month, respectively. Comcast systems in Chicago were lower, given the fact that there was only one major regional network, NBC Sports Chicago, but those eight channels still averaged close to $17 a month, with an expected spike in 2020 with the launch of a second RSN, Marquee Sports. The cost of the regional services was so high that MVPDs in many markets add a "Regional Sports Fee" to monthly bills. Kagan reported that those surcharges reached $8.25 on Comcast systems and $8 on Cox systems in 2019.[21]

The transfer of wealth from cable, satellite, and telco households to sports leagues, conferences, and associations via a handful of media conglomerates does not end with the price of programming services. As discussed, the 1992 Cable Act introduced retransmission consent to the television landscape, but for the better part of two decades, the focus in such agreements was on the increased distribution and/or carriage fees of programming services under the same corporate umbrella as the large broadcast station group. In time, the focus turned to cold, hard cash, and there is no question that the value of sports content, whether it be the NFL or the Olympic Games, assumes a prominent role in those negotiations. In the 2010s, retransmission and virtual multichannel carriage fees saw double-digit percentage growth each year, starting with 63% in 2010, 43% in 2011, 36% in 2012, and 50% in 2013. As discussed earlier, those fees surpassed $10 billion in 2018. Once again, there was a direct cost of subscribers, with many MVPDs adding a "Broadcast TV Fee" or other such charge to monthly bills. In 2019, that surcharge alone was $11 a month for Charter's Spectrum TV and $10 a month on both Comcast and Cox systems.[22]

That is the dichotomy for multi-system operators. The ability to watch live sporting events on broadcast and cable channels remains one of the strongest inducements for subscriptions to traditional multichannel video services. In a PricewaterhouseCoopers report in 2017, for example, 81% of those surveyed who self-identified as sports fans subscribed to pay TV, compared to 73% overall.[23] Just as significant was that 82% of those in the sports fan group said they would trim or cut the cord if it were not for sports. The challenge for MSOs is clear: the sports content that slows cord cutting accounts for a disproportionate share of monthly bills. In its 2018 report on cable industry prices, the FCC found that the average charge for expanded basic service was $71.37 a month with a mean of 167.9 channels as of January 1, 2016.[24] That works out to an average cost of 47 cents per channel per month, and while there were prominent sports services at or below that amount at that time, such as the Golf Channel ($0.40) and NBCSN ($0.33), most of the national and regional services were far beyond that price point. That same report found that the expanded basic service includes an average of 3.9 channels dedicated to regional sports networks, so while the price for RSNs in New York and Los Angeles might be higher than most, the number of channels is consistent with the mean. The average prices in the FCC report, moreover, do not include the regional sports and broadcast television fees that some operators add to bills to address the high price of sports programming.

The question that remains is what changes the dawn of a new decade will bring to the sports television marketplace. As discussed earlier, while the rights to the Olympic Games, NCAA Final Four, and World Series are under contract until 2028 or beyond, there are a series of packages that will expire between 2021 and

2025, including the NFL, NHL, and NBA. The outcome of those negotiations could provide a template for what is to come, although there is also conjecture that leagues are looking for one more big contract with broadcast networks and cable services before they confront the future. In November 2019, Kevin Mayer, chair of the Direct-to-Consumer & International segment of Disney, said in an interview at a CodeMedia event that he could envision a point in time when ESPN was offered on an over-the-top basis rather than bundled with other programming services but also said, "I don't think we're really very close to that point."[25] What becomes clear is that the role television assumes will not diminish moving forward. NBA Commissioner Adam Silver has long expressed a willingness to explore fundamental changes to the league schedule, and there were widespread reports in November 2019 that the NBA and NBA Players Association were in serious discussions about sweeping changes to the schedule in time for the league's 75th anniversary season in 2021–22. These included reseeding of the four conference finalists based on regular records, an in-season tournament similar to those in European football, and play-in games prior to the playoffs.[26] The proposals were focused on changes that would not just stem the decline in ratings in the regular season and post season but could also generate television and sponsorship revenue in a fragmented marketplace.[27] The next month, Silver expanded on some of those concerns at a sports conference, calling the pay television "broken" while focusing on the degree to which "young viewers" were "turning out cable, traditional cable."[28]

Therein lie the opportunities and the challenges that the future holds for sports television. The question remains how sports leagues, conferences, and organizations will attempt to further monetize their television rights in a changing media landscape and how media conglomerates will respond to those opportunities. In January 2019, DC United, the Major League Soccer team based in Washington, DC, announced a four-year agreement to move its local telecasts to a subscription-based streaming service operated through FloSports, an OTT service based in Austin, Texas. The press release from the service heralded a "Historic" agreement and promised original programming and exclusive content on FloFC.com, including behind-the-scenes access.[29] DC United Senior Vice President Sam Porter said, "When you look at all the cord-cutting that is going on, it's really not as radical as it would have been a couple of years ago."[30] Major League Soccer would appear to be an ideal candidate for such a service, with the average age of its fans the lowest among the professional sports leagues in the United States.[31] While the demographic of the fan base might have been conducive to a streaming service, there were a range of technical challenges from the outset, with the first few minutes of United's season debut from New York in March missed even at the team's official watch party at a local DC sports bar. Three days before the regular season finale in October, DC United said that its final game would be streamed, free of charge, on the team's website and that it would "no longer be distributing our match telecasts" through FloSports.[32]

The struggles of DC United did not stop others from venturing down the same road, as the Colonial Athletic Conference signed an agreement with Flo-Sports that May, making it the first collegiate conference to sign with a direct-to-consumer service as its primary media partner. A *Forbes* headline called that deal a "Blueprint" for other conferences to follow.[33] The issues DC United encountered with FloSports, moreover, could prove to be a precursor for further concentration and consolidation in the sports marketplace. As discussed earlier, Major League Soccer shuttered the *MLS Live* streaming service in 2018 and moved the out-of-market package to ESPN+. The 23 teams in the league retained their local television rights, and the non-national DC United matches carried on ESPN+ were blacked out in the Washington, DC, market. Another MLS team, the Chicago Fire, followed a different path with its local rights. The month before the ESPN over-the-top service launched in April 2018, the Fire signed a three-year agreement with that gave ESPN+ exclusive rights to the 27 Chicago matches that were not carried on national television networks, moving those matches from a regional network, NBC Sports Chicago. While Fire supporters were required to subscribe to the service to see the matches, which cost $4.99 a month, it did give them access to other MLS games and additional content. That decision also put the Fire matches on streaming services with the financial backing and technical expertise of The Walt Disney Co., neither of which FloSports could match.

Therein lies a possible forecast for the future. While one could see a path for a multi-billion-dollar behemoth such as Amazon, Apple, Facebook, Google, or Netflix venturing into the sports television marketplace, it is hard to picture anyone else challenging the media oligarchs who are guarding the gates. The embrace of neoliberalism and widespread deregulation that emerged in the 1980s during the Reagan administration fueled the government-sanctioned horizontal and vertical integration that paved the road to where we were at the end of the 2010s. Four of the largest media conglomerates in the world, Comcast, Disney, Fox, and ViacomCBS, dominated the marketplace, combining broadcast networks and cable services in sports media groups. The lone interlopers in the group, AT&T and Sinclair, brought their own advantages to the market: vertical links between DirecTV/U-verse and WarnerMedia within AT&T and horizontal connections between the regional sports networks/Tennis Channel and local broadcast stations within Sinclair. There are others that have taken tentative steps into the fray and some on the fringe could pull back, with pressure from activist shareholders within AT&T to unload DirecTV to reduce debt being a glimpse into one possible scenario. The sports television landscape, however, was stable at the end of the 2010s, and it was undisputed that the quartet of Comcast, Disney, Fox, and ViacomCBS had every intention of continuing and extending their dominance in the 2020s.

Notes

1. Quoted in Jacob Feldman, "Inside Apple's Sports Surveillance Room That Could Change the Way We Watch Live Events," *SI.com*, March 19, 2019, para. 6.
2. John Ourand, "SBJ Media: Sports Not a Big Part of Apple's Streaming Plans," *SBJ Media with John Ourand*, Newsletter, March 25, 2019.
3. John Ourand and Ben Fischer, "NFL Takes a Long View on 'Sunday Ticket'," *Sports Business Journal*, June 12, 2019.
4. Federal Communications Commission, "In the Matter of Amendment of Part 73 of the Commission's Rules and Regulations With Respect to Competition and Responsibility of Network Television Broadcasting," 23 FCC 2nd 382 (1970).
5. William M. Kunz, "Prime-Time Television Program Ownership in a Post-Fin/Syn World," *Journal of Broadcasting & Electronic Media* 53, no. 4 (2009): 636–651.
6. Randall L. Stephenson, "Q2 2019 AT&T Inc. Earnings Call," July 24, 2019.
7. Joseph Ianniello, "Q3 2019 CBS Corporation Earnings Conference Call," *CBS Corp.*, November 12, 2019.
8. Peter Golding and Graham Murdoch, "Culture, Communication and Political Economy," in *Mass Media & Society*, 3rd ed., ed. James Curran and Michael Gurevitch (New York: Oxford University Press, 2000), 72–74.
9. Ben H. Bagdikian, *The Media Monopoly* (Boston, MA: Beacon Press, 1983); Ben H. Bagdikian, *The New Media Monopoly* (Boston, MA: Beacon Press, 2004).
10. See Dallas W. Smythe, "Communications: Blindspot of Western Marxism," *Canadian Journal of Political and Social Theory* 1, no. 3 (1977): 1–27; Graham Murdock, "Blindspots About Western Marxism: A Reply to Dallas Smythe," *Canadian Journal of Political and Social Theory* 2, no. 2 (1978): 109–119; Eileen Meehan, "Understanding How the Popular Becomes Popular: The Role of Political Economy in the Study of Popular Communication," *Popular Communication* 5, no. 3 (2007): 161–170.
11. Travis T. Tygart, "Statement from USADA CEO Travis T. Tygart Regarding the US Postal Service Pro Cycling Team Doping Conspiracy," October 10, 2012. cyclinginvestication.usada.org.
12. Federal Communications Commission, "Annual Assessment of the Status of Competition in Markets for the Delivery of Video Programming, Fifth Annual Report," December 23, 1998.
13. Retransmission consent, 47 CFR § 76.64.
14. Quoted in Robert Naylor, Jr., "Legislation Would Force Cable to Negotiate With Broadcasters Over Signal," *Associated Press*, September 24, 1991.
15. Atif Zubair, "Economics of Broadcast TV Retransmission Revenue 2019," S&P Global Market Intelligence, September 10, 2019. Accessed November 17, 2019.
16. Tony Lenoir, "Retrans for Public Station Groups Grows 31.4% in '11, Reaches 14.2% of Total TV revs," S&P Global Market Intelligence, March 22, 2012. Accessed November 17, 2019.
17. "Economics of Broadcast TV Retransmission Revenue 2019."
18. Quoted in Wayne Walley, "Malone: Stations Must Give Extras to Get Fees," *Electronic Media*, February 22, 1993, 22.
19. Linda Moss, "TCI Locks Up Disney, ESPN in 10-Year Deal," *Multichannel News* 15, no. 18 (1997): 1.
20. Sinclair Broadcast Group, Inc., 2015 Annual Report, Form 10-K, February 26, 2016, 13.
21. Adam Gajo, John Fletcher, Scott Dobson, and Brian Bacon, "Economics of Networks: The 2019 Sports Report," S&P Global Market Intelligence, April 4, 2019.
22. "Economics of Networks: The 2019 Sports Report."
23. Pricewaterhouse Coopers, "Consumer Intelligence Series: I Stream, You Stream" (2017).

24. Federal Communications Commission, "Report on Cable Industry Prices," MM Docket No. 92–266, February 8, 2018, 13–14.
25. Quoted in John Ourand, "SBJ Media: A Direct-to-Consumer Future for ESPN," Street & Smith's SBJ Media with John Ourand, newsletter, November 20, 2019.
26. Adrian Wojnarowski and Zach Lowe, "Source: NBA Considering Reseeding Conference Finalists, Postseason Play-in," *ESPN.com*, November 23, 2019.
27. "Source: NBA Considering Reseeding Conference Finalists."
28. Quoted in John Ourand, "Adam Silver Skeptical of Pay TV System," *Street & Smith's SBK Media with John Ourand*, newsletter, December 4, 2019.
29. FloSports, "FloSports and D.C. United Reach Historic Multiyear Broadcast Partnership." Press release, January 7, 2019.
30. Quoted in Steven Goff, "United Cuts the Cord and Opts for Pay Service," *The Washington Post*, January 8, 2019, D3.
31. John Lombardo and David Boughton, "Going Gray: Sports TV Viewers Skew Older," *Sports Business Journal*, June 5, 2017.
32. DC United, "D.C. United Club Statement." Press release, October 3, 2019.
33. J.P. Pelzman, "How the CAA's Streaming Deal with FloSports Could Be a Blueprint for Other College Conference," *Forbes*, August 29, 2019.

Chapter Bibliography

Bagdikian, Ben H. *The Media Monopoly*. Boston, MA: Beacon Press, 1983.
———. *The New Media Monopoly*. Boston, MA: Beacon Press, 2004.
DC United. "D.C. United Club Statement." Press release, October 3, 2019.
Federal Communications Commission. Amendment of Part 73 of the Commission's Rules and Regulations with Respect to Competition and Responsibility of Network Television Broadcasting. 23 FCC 2nd 382 (1970).
———. Annual Assessment of the Status of Competition in Markets for the Delivery of Video Programming, Fifth Annual Report, December 23, 1998.
———. Report on Cable Industry Prices. DA 12–128, February 8, 2018.
Feldman, Jacob. "Inside Apple's Sports Surveillance Room That Could Change the Way We Watch Live Events." *SI.com*, March 19, 2019.
FloSports, Inc. "FloSports and D.C. United Reach Historic Multiyear Broadcast Partnership." Press release, January 7, 2019.
Goff, Steven. "United Cuts the Cord and Opts for Pay Service." *The Washington Post*, January 8, 2019, D3.
Gojo, Adam, John Fletcher, Scott Dobson, and Brian Bacon. "The 2019 Sports Report." Economics of Networks, S&P Global Market Intelligence, April 4, 2019.
Golding, Peter, and Graham Murdoch. "Culture, Communication and Political Economy." In *Mass Media & Society*, 3rd ed., ed. James Curran and Michael Gurevitch, 70–92. New York: Oxford University Press, 2000.
Ianniello, Joseph. "Q3 2019 CBS Corporation Earnings Conference Call." *CBS Corp.*, November 12, 2019.
Kunz, William M. "Prime-Time Television Program Ownership in a Post-Fin/Syn World." *Journal of Broadcasting & Electronic Media* 53, no. 4 (2009): 636–651.
Lenoir, Tony. "Retrans for Public Station Groups Grows 31.4% in '11, Reaches 14.2% of Total TV revs." S&P Global Market Intelligence, March 22, 2012.
Lombardo, John, and David Boughton. "Going Gray: Sports TV Viewers Skew Older." *Sports Business Journal*, June 5, 2017.

Meehan, Eileen. "Understanding How the Popular Becomes Popular: The Role of Political Economy in the Study of Popular Communication." *Popular Communication* 5, no. 3 (2007): 161–170.

Moss, Linda. "TCI Locks Up Disney, ESPN in 10-Year Deal." *Multichannel News* 15, no. 18 (1997): 1.

Murdock, Graham. "Blindspots About Western Marxism: A Reply to Dallas Smythe." *Canadian Journal of Political and Social Theory* 2, no. 2 (1978): 109–119.

Naylor, Jr., Robert. "Legislation Would Force Cable to Negotiate With Broadcasters Over Signal." *Associated Press*, September 24, 1991.

Ourand, John. "CBS Confirms Its Commitment to Sports Following Departure of Moonves." *Sports Business Journal*, September 24, 2018.

————. "SBJ Media: Sports Not a Big Part of Apple's Streaming Plans." *Street & Smith's SBJ Media with John Ourand*. Newsletter, March 25, 2019.

————. "SBJ Media: A Direct-to-Consumer Future for ESPN." *Street & Smith's SBJ Media with John Ourand*. Newsletter, November 20, 2019.

————. "Adam Silver Skeptical of Pay TV System." *Street & Smith's SBK Media with John Ourand*. Newsletter, December 4, 2019.

Ourand, John, and Ben Fischer. "NFL Takes a Long View on 'Sunday Ticket'." *Sports Business Journal*, June 12, 2019.

Pelzman, J.P. "How the CAA's Streaming Deal With FloSports Could Be a Blueprint for other College Conference." *Forbes*, August 29, 2019.

Pricewaterhouse Coopers. "Consumer Intelligence Series: I Stream, You Stream." (2017).

Retransmission consent. 47 C.F.R. § 76.64.

Sinclair Broadcast Group, Inc. "Form 10-K." February 26, 2016.

Smythe, Dallas W. "Communications: Blindspot of Western Marxism." *Canadian Journal of Political and Social Theory* 1, no. 3 (1977): 1–27.

Stephenson, Randall L. "Q2 2019 AT&T Inc. Earnings Call." July 24, 2019.

Tygart, Travis T. "Statement from USADA CEO Travis T. Tygart Regarding the US Postal Service Pro Cycling Team Doping Conspiracy." October 10, 2012. cyclinginvestication.usada.org.

Walley, Wayne. "Malone: Stations Must Give Extras to Get Fees." *Electronic Media*, February 22, 1993, 22.

Wojnarowski, Adrian, and Zach Lowe. "Source: NBA Considering Reseeding Conference Finalists, Postseason Play-in." *ESPN.com*, November 23, 2019.

Zubair, Atif. "Economics of Broadcast TV Retransmission Revenue 2019." S&P Global Market Intelligence, September 10, 2019. Accessed November 17, 2019.

INDEX